THE INFINITE CREATION

THE INFINITE CREATION

UNIFYING SCIENCE AND LATTER-DAY SAINT THEOLOGY

TRENT DEE STEPHENS, PhD

CFI
An imprint of Cedar Fort, Inc.
Springville, Utah

ISBN 13: 978-1-4621-3785-5

Published by CFI, an imprint of Cedar Fort, Inc.
2373 W. 700 S., Springville, UT, 84663
Distributed by Cedar Fort, Inc., www.cedarfort.com

Library of Congress Control Number: 2020938118

Cover design by Shawnda T. Craig

Printed in the United States of America

10 9 8 7 6 5 4 3 2 1

Printed on acid-free paper

TO MY INFINITE AND ETERNAL FAMILY

ACKNOWLEDGMENTS

I especially want to thank my darling wife, Kathleen, who is my greatest and most helpful critic. I am also grateful to Hal and Christy Smith, Steve Robison, Clip Holverson, Joseph Elison, Terri White, and Randy Taylor for reading portions of the manuscript and providing helpful feedback, comments, and corrections.

I also want to thank Shawnda T. Craig and Kimiko Hammari for their excellent design and editing skills, along with everyone else at Cedar Fort who helped make my book a success.

CONTENTS

INTRODUCTION

The title of this book is *The Infinite Creation*, not just *The Creation*, because the Creation is one of the three greatest events in all of eternity, one of the three pillars of God's infinite plan for us. The term "the three pillars of eternity" was first coined by Bruce R. McConkie of the Quorum of the Twelve Apostles in a speech given at Brigham University in 1981. He stated:

> I pray that we may receive a mighty outpouring of that Spirit as we consider the three pillars of eternity—the three great eternal verities upon which salvation rests.
>
> My purpose is to take the three greatest events that have ever occurred in all eternity and show how they are interwoven to form one grand plan of salvation.
>
> If we can gain an understanding of them, then the whole eternal scheme of things will fall into place, and we will be in a position to work out our salvation. If we do not build our house of salvation on a true foundation, we will never make the spiritual progress that will prepare us to enter the Eternal Presence.
>
> The three pillars of eternity, the three events, preeminent and transcendent above all others, are the creation, the fall, and the atonement. These three are the foundations upon which all things rest. Without any one of them all things would lose their purpose and meaning, and the plans and designs of Deity would come to naught.[1]

In a 1991 *Ensign* article, Russell M. Nelson stated:

> In a very real way, the atonement of Jesus Christ affects each of our lives and the life of every human being who ever lived. Understanding the significance of His atonement is fundamental to choices we make in all facets of our lives. The atonement of the Lord is central to our faith.

> We are scripturally bound to study it and to teach it. . . . But before one can comprehend the *atonement* of Christ, one must first understand the *fall* of Adam. And before one can comprehend the fall of Adam, one must first understand the *Creation*. These three pillars of eternity relate to one another.[2]

Concerning the eternal nature of the Atonement, Amulek stated in the Book of Mormon, "It must be an infinite and eternal sacrifice" (Alma 34:10). We also read in the Doctrine and Covenants, "By these things we know that there is a God in heaven, who is infinite and eternal, from everlasting to everlasting the same unchangeable God, the framer of heaven and earth, and all things which are in them" (D&C 20:17). These scriptures imply that the terms "eternal" and "infinite" are more-or-less equivalent. Both Jacob and Nephi (two Book of Mormon prophets) referred to the "infinite atonement" (2 Nephi 9:7; 2 Nephi 25:16). Thus, the "three pillars of eternity" may also be described as the "three pillars of infinity." The first pillar, then, can be called the *infinite Creation*, the second the *infinite Fall*, and the third the *infinite Atonement*.

In his book *The Infinite Atonement*, Tad Callister described the infinite nature of the Atonement by stating, "The phrase 'infinite atonement' or 'infinite sacrifice' may refer to an atonement or sacrifice by a God, a being who is infinite in knowledge, power, and glory. . . . Accordingly, the Atonement is 'infinite' because its source is 'infinate.'"[3]

Likewise, it may be said that the phrase "infinite Creation" refers to a creation orchestrated by God, a being who is infinite in knowledge, power, and glory. Accordingly, the Creation, the Fall, and the Atonement are all "infinite" because they all have their source in the "infinite." Furthermore, we are told in the book of Abraham (in the Pearl of Great Price) that the Creation has eternal, infinite implications because the earth was created as a place where we may be proven, and if we pass this earthly test we will "have glory added upon . . . [our] heads for ever and ever" (Abraham 3:24–26).

Concerning this first pillar of Creation, Elder Weatherford T. Clayton of the Seventy, said, "The journey our Father prepared for us is called the plan of salvation or the plan of happiness. (Alma 42:8) In a grand premortal council, our Father told us about His plan. (Abraham 3:24–28) When we understood it, we were so happy that we shouted for joy, and 'the morning stars sang together.' (Job 38:7) That plan is built upon three grand pillars: the pillars of eternity. The first pillar is the Creation of the earth, the setting for our mortal journey. (3 Nephi 9:15)"[4]

Callister stated the following in his book: "An attempt to master this doctrine requires an immersion of all our senses, all our feelings, and all our intellect. . . . The Atonement is not a doctrine that lends itself to some singular approach."[3] Intellectually, the *infinite* is not a simple concept. It requires every ounce of effort and intellectual energy we can muster. Our understanding of the infinite Creation must, of necessity, involve both what has been revealed to ancient and modern prophets and what has been revealed to modern science—much of which is intellectually challenging in the extreme. Nonetheless, we have been admonished by our current prophet to take up this weighty challenge, because understanding these infinite pillars "is fundamental to choices we make in all facets of our lives."[2]

Young people are constantly making fundamental choices. Some of those choices are made by pitting information they are learning from religion against information they are learning from science. Many Church leaders have admonished the youth that making such distinction is not necessary. I fully and heartily agree, but young people are often left without a clear path to reconciliation. One of the main reasons for this deficiency is that the path to scientific and religious reconciliation is not simple. It requires considerable intellectual rigor and integrity. As a young person, I spent years facing this seemingly irreconcilable dilemma, and I have spent my entire lifetime trying to solve it.

I am a scientist. I have bachelor of science degrees in both microbiology and zoology from Brigham Young University, as well as a master of science degree from BYU. I have a PhD in anatomy from the University of Pennsylvania. I completed a four-year postdoctoral study program at the University of Washington, Department of Pediatrics, before accepting a thirty–year position in the Department of Biological Sciences at Idaho State University. I teach biology from a straight-forward, evolutionary perspective. I have been actively involved in conducting research, writing, and teaching in the biological sciences, especially anatomy and developmental biology, for nearly fifty years. I have been deeply interested in the sciences for even longer—perhaps sixty years or more.

I am also deeply religious. I am a Christian in the most complete sense of the word. I have been a member of The Church of Jesus Christ of Latter-day Saints since I was baptized at the age of eight. In addition to my research and writing in mainstream science, I have spent most of my life pondering ways in which true science and true religion are compatible. I believe that truth does not contradict truth, no matter the source. I firmly believe that neither science nor religion has complete access to ultimate truth, and I believe that ultimate truth does actually exist. As a Christian, I believe that this universe was created by the great "I am," even Jesus Christ, the Savior of the World, under the direction of God the Eternal Father (see John 1:1–5; John 7:28–29; John 8:58). As a scientist, I believe that we can discover at least some of the secrets by which that creation was accomplished.

James E. Talmage, who was also a very religious scientist, a member of the Quorum of the Twelve Apostles, and a geologist, wrote, "We cannot sweep aside all the accumulated knowledge in geology, archeology, or any other branch of science simply because our interpretation of some isolated passage of scripture may seem to be opposed thereto."[5]

In order for us to understand the infinite Creation, infinity itself must be pondered, analyzed, and internalized. It is, by its very nature, the most supernal, mind-expanding, passionate concept the universe will ever know. Maybe we are not ready to comprehend the *infinite* in the opening years of the twenty-first century. Maybe we should wait patiently for the Second Coming of the Savior to obtain such knowledge. But as President Brigham Young admonished the Saints in Ogden, Utah, in 1860, God's people must prepare themselves before Christ's Second Coming:

> This earth must become a paradise—must be purged of the sin that has been upon it for many generations, for all sin and iniquity must be swept from it, and a people be prepared for the coming of the Son of Man. He will prepare a people long before the earth is celestialized and prepared for the presence of God. The Saints will increase, the Spirit of wisdom and knowledge will increase, and every grace of the Spirit of the Lord Jesus Christ must increase upon the earth, until a people and place are so prepared that the Savior can come and finish the work given him to do, when he will present the kingdom to the Father.
>
> There is a great work for the Saints to do. Progress, and improve upon, and make beautiful everything around you. Cultivate the earth and cultivate your minds . . . continually seek to adorn your minds with all the graces of the Spirit of Christ.[6]

Perhaps one of the factors that is delaying the Second Coming is the fact that we have not yet deeply enough pondered the infinite. Many mathematicians and physicists have even given up on the prospect that the infinite is real. Those who do accept that infinity might be real invoke quantum physics to even begin to understand it. Concepts of infinity are not for the weak of mind or spirit, but they are supremely rewarding, mind-expanding, and spiritually liberating.

We could delay discussing the infinite Creation for another fifty or one hundred years, when we know more about infinity or when everyone has a degree in quantum physics. I don't think that will ever happen. Not everyone who buys an automobile, a television, or a smart phone understands how it works, but they still buy them and rely upon them. Do we really want to wait another fifty years for "the Spirit of wisdom and knowledge" to increase? Do we really want to wait another one hundred years, "until a people and place are so prepared that the Savior can come and finish the work given him to do, when he will present the kingdom to the Father"?[4] I, for one, believe that, although we do not as yet fully comprehend the infinite, we can at least open a discussion that will, in turn, open our minds to the wisdom and knowledge we need to prepare for the Second Coming.

In the April 2018 general conference, President Russell M. Nelson stated, "Oh, there is so much more that your Father in Heaven wants you to know. . . . Our Savior and Redeemer, Jesus Christ, will perform some of His mightiest works between now and when He comes again."[7]

We may still say that we "see through a glass darkly" (1 Corinthians 13:12). Nonetheless, glass has changed considerably since Paul coined that line in the mid-first century AD. His glass was small, expensive, rare, and not at all transparent. Today, we can create entire buildings of perfectly smooth, perfectly transparent, and relatively inexpensive plate glass. Paul said that he could not even prophesy fully of our day (see 1 Corinthians 13:9). It is, therefore, possible that Paul saw our day dimly but did not have words to describe what he was seeing. Today, we live way beyond Paul's wildest imagination. Our knowledge of science and the scriptures is vastly greater than Paul's. Paul did not know of the microscopic world, made possible by highly polished lenses, that we now take for granted. He knew nothing of the physiology of respiration or digestion. Quantum physics was unheard of in his day. He did not have the New Testament, the Book of Mormon, the Pearl of Great Price, or the Doctrine and Covenants to enlighten his mind with modern revealed truth.

Paul recognized that he had only a very small part of a much larger picture. He stated, "But when that which is perfect is come, then that which is in part shall be done away. When I was a child, I spake as a child, I understood as a child, I thought as a child: but when I became a man, I put away childish things" (1 Corinthians 13:10–11). Those of Paul's era were certainly as children in their understanding of the world around them compared to what we know today of the earth and its wonders. Speaking for myself, however, even though I see creation more clearly than Paul could have ever seen, I still have not lost my sense of child-like wonder at its beauty and grandeur.

The Infinite Creation employs not just the scriptures and the words of modern prophets, but it also includes knowledge revealed by modern science. The scientific background of this book may be skimmed over by some readers. For those readers, it is there primarily to demonstrate its contribution to our knowledge of the Creation. For others, with more of a scientific foundation, the purpose of this book is to build upon that foundation, however imperfect, upon which further discussion, discovery, and revelation may enhance our comprehension of the infinite Creation in all its glory.

For me, personally, I do not distinguish where the truth revealed through God's spoken word ends and the truth revealed through science begins. To me, truth is glorious no matter the source, and it all fits together to provide a more complete and beautiful picture of God's creations. Having spent a lifetime digging deeply into both fields and always searching for the harmony there, I find the absolute truth that emerges to be sublime.

In a talk entitled "Seeing beyond the Leaf" given at the BYU Church History Symposium in March 2014, President Dieter F. Uchtdorf quoted Michael Crichton as stating, "You are a leaf that doesn't know it is part of a tree." President Uchtdorf then stated:

> One of the weaknesses we have as mortals is to assume that our 'leaf' is all there is—that our truth is complete and universal. . . . I want to emphasize that the truth embraced by The Church of Jesus Christ of Latter-day Saints extends beyond leaves. . . It extends beyond time and space and encompasses all truth.
>
> Isn't it a remarkable feeling to belong to a Church that embraces truth—no matter the source—and teaches that there is much more to come. . . . We understand our knowledge is a work in progress, that the leaf we have before us is simply one microscopic snapshot—part of an infinitely vast forest of fascinating knowledge.[8]

M. Russell Ballard, of the Quorum of the Twelve Apostles, taught the following to the Church Educational System religious educators in 2016:

> Gone are the days when a student asked an honest question and a teacher responded, "Don't worry about it!" Gone are the days when a student raised a sincere concern and a teacher bore his or her testimony as a response intended to avoid the issue. Gone are the days when students were protected from people who attacked the Church.
>
> Fortunately, the Lord has provided this timely and timeless counsel to teachers: "And as all have not faith, seek ye diligently and teach one another words of wisdom; yea, seek ye out of the best books words of wisdom; seek learning, even by study and also by faith." (D&C 88:118)[9]

Ballard then cited a statement by President Harold B. Lee:

> "We would remind you that the acquiring of knowledge by faith is no easy road to learning. It demands strenuous effort and a continual striving by faith. . . .
>
> "Learning by faith is no task for a lazy man [or woman]. Someone has said, in effect, that such a process requires the bending of the whole soul, the calling up from the depths of the human mind and linking it with God—the right connection must be formed. Then only comes 'knowledge by faith.'"[10]

In a BYU–Idaho devotional on March 13, 2018, Forest Gahn, a member of the BYU–Idaho geology faculty, stated, "Truth—absolute truth—defines and governs the cosmos. It exists independently of our perceptions or even our capacity to comprehend reality. Truth is not subject to our thoughts, biases, or desires; it is what it is regardless of how well we may or may not understand it. It is what it is whether we accept, reject, or ignore it."[11]

Richard G. Scott, of the Quorum of the Twelve Apostles, stated in an October 2007 general conference address,

> There are two ways to find truth—both useful, provided we follow the laws upon which they are predicated. The first is the scientific method. . . . [The second is] to go to the origin of all truth and ask or respond to inspiration. . . . Try as I might, I am not able, even in the smallest degree, to comprehend the extent, depth, and stunning grandeur of what our holy Heavenly Father, Elohim, has permitted to be

> revealed by the scientific method. . . . We can see the scientific method has brought about an extraordinary expansion of our understanding as the Lord has inspired gifted men who may not [even] understand who created these things nor for what purpose.[12]

In an 1874 discourse Brigham Young stated, referring to the youth of the Church:

> When they are old enough, place within their reach the advantages and benefits of a scientific education. Let them study the formation of the earth, the organization of the human system, and other sciences . . . form a class in geology, in chemistry or mineralogy; and do not confine their studies to theory only, but let them put in practice what they learn from books, by defining the nature of the soil, the composition or decomposition of a rock, how the earth was formed, its probable age, and so forth. . . . It is the duty of the Latter-day Saints, according to the revelations, to give their children the best education that can be procured, both from the books of the world and the revelations of the Lord.[13]

The Infinite Creation is not intended to be a science book, but some science is included so that I don't have to just say to the reader, "Trust me, I'm a scientist." Furthermore, some discussion of science is necessary to even begin to wrestle with the concepts of infinity and creation. For the scientists and future scientists reading this book, I hope that it may inspire future, even more expansive research into the infinite.

As with the dark glass of Paul's day compared to the perfectly clear plate glass and microscopic objectives of our day, the purpose of *The Infinite Creation* is to address the Creation, not as the simple, often fanciful story told by our ancestors, but as the expansive, beautiful story revealed by the scriptures in conjunction with modern scientific discoveries. The purpose of this book is not to pit science against scripture, but to meld the knowledge obtained from both realms of revealed truth. We certainly do not know everything about the infinite Creation, and we certainly expect more knowledge to be poured out upon the heads of the Latter-day Saints, but it is my hope and prayer that this work will take us down a path of mutual enlightenment that may someday lead us toward a more perfect knowledge of the infinite truth.

This book is written primarily to my fellow Latter-day Saints—not people who have been canonized by an ecumenical council, but everyday members of The Church of Jesus Christ of Latter-day Saints. However, it is my hope and prayer that anyone reading this book, whether a member of The Church of Jesus Christ or not, may be enlightened by its content. The language and jargon employed in this book are those of an older adult who has spent his entire life immersed in the Church.

ENDNOTES

1. Bruce R. McConkie, BYU Speeches, Feb. 17, 1981.
2. Russell M. Nelson, "Standards of the Lord's Standard-Bearers," *Ensign,* Aug. 1991, 5–6; italics in original.
3. Tad R. Callister, *The Infinite Atonement.* (Salt Lake City: Deseret Book, Salt Lake City, 2000); see also Doctrine and Covenants 19:10–12.
4. Clayton T. Weatherford T., "Our Father's Glorious Plan," April 2017 general conference.
5. James E., Talmage, letter to F. C. Williamson, Apr. 22, 1933. Signature Books Library, signaturebookslibrary.org
6. Brigham Young, "Religion, Progress, and Privileges of the Saints," *Journal of Discourses*, 8:83, 1860.
7. Russell M. Nelson, "Revelation for the Church, Revelation for Our Lives," April 2018 general conference.
8. Dieter F., Uchtdorf, "The Gospel Encompasses All Truth," *Ensign*, Feb. 2018.
9. M. Russell Ballard, "By Study and by Faith," *Ensign*, Dec. 2016.
10. Harold B. Lee, in Clyde J. Williams, ed., *The Teachings of Harold B. Lee*, (Deseret Book, 2009), 331.
11. Forest Gahn, *Truth and Other Treasures*, BYU—Idaho devotional, March 13, 2018.
12. Richard G. Scott, "Truth: The Foundation of Correct Decisions," October 2007 general conference.
13. Brigham Young, *Journal of Discourses*, 17:45, 1874.

CHAPTER 1

THE INFINITE CHRIST

Those who read this book and are members of The Church of Jesus Christ of Latter-day Saints should understand most of the background concepts presented herein. For them, this chapter may be largely unnecessary. However, for those who read this book and are not members of The Church of Jesus Christ of Latter-day Saints, an explanation of our beliefs—my beliefs—are probably necessary in order for much of the remaining material in the book to be rendered comprehensible. Of necessity, this chapter will be succinct. If the reader wishes additional information, he or she may visit the website ChurchofJesusChrist.org.

First of all, I "believe in God, the Eternal Father, and in His Son, Jesus Christ, and in the Holy Ghost" (Articles of Faith 1:1). I also believe that "the Father has a body of flesh and bones as tangible as man's; the Son also; but the Holy Ghost has not a body of flesh and bones, but is a personage of Spirit" (D&C 130:22). I believe that Jesus Christ was literally resurrected and that He invited His disciples to "Behold my hands and my feet, that it is I myself: handle me, and see; for a spirit hath not flesh and bones, as ye see me have" (Luke 24:39). "And while they yet believed not for joy, and wondered, he said unto them, Have ye here any meat? And they gave him a piece of a broiled fish, and of an honeycomb. And he took it, and did eat before them" (Luke 24:41–43). These latter verses suggest that Christ ate the fish and honeycomb as a demonstration that he *could* eat, because we may assume that God commanded

Jesus to demonstrate His ability to consume food, for Jesus said, "I do nothing of myself; but as my Father hath taught me . . . for I do always those things that please him" (John 8:28–29).

The proposition that the resurrected Jesus Christ could consume food insinuates that His resurrected body could also digest food. The digestion of food by the resurrected Christ suggests that His resurrected body could metabolize that food and, therefore, His body was a cellular body. Christ demonstrated to His disciples that His body was the *same* body that had been crucified. He invited them to behold and touch the nailprints in his hands and thrust their hands into His side (see John 20:25–27; see also 3 Nephi 11:14–15). Jesus's body was missing from the tomb and, reunited with His Spirit, He exhibited that same resurrected body to His disciples. Apparently, His resurrected body could do everything that the mortal body had done—right down to consuming food. The only apparent difference was that Jesus no longer required an open door to enter a room (see John 20:19).

Earlier in His mission, Christ told His disciples, "He that hath seen me hath seen the Father" (John 14:9). This scripture has often been misinterpreted down through the centuries to suggest that God the Father and Jesus Christ are physically the same being. They are not. Christ is the "spitting image" of His Father, but they are two separate individuals. God and Jesus are one in purpose, not one in body or substance. However, if Christ said that He looked like the Father—and Christ had a physical, cellular body—it is logical to assume that God the Father also has a physical, cellular body.

I believe that Stephen, the first Christian martyr, did indeed "see the heavens opened, and the Son of man standing on the right hand of God" (Acts 7:56). I also believe that revelation, miracles, and divine visitation did not end with the death of the Apostles. There was, for whatever reason, a significant hiatus for some eighteen hundred years during which time God and Christ did not personally visit the earth. Nonetheless, miracles did continue—see for example the life of Francis of Assize. Then, in the early spring of 1820, God and Jesus Christ, as two separate beings, just as Stephen saw them, appeared to a fourteen-year-old boy named Joseph Smith Jr. Later in his life, Joseph Smith would state, "I have always declared God to be a distinct personage, Jesus Christ a separate and distinct personage from God the Father, and that the Holy Ghost was a distinct personage and a Spirit; and these three constitute three distinct personages and three Gods."[1]

I believe that heavenly messengers continued to visit Joseph Smith during his life, first revealing an ancient record that outlined, as a second witness to Christ's resurrection, the visit by the resurrected Christ to the American continent (see 3 Nephi chapters 8–30).[2] The resulting book, entitled the Book of Mormon, was published in 1830, just before Christ's original Church was restored in the form of The Church of Jesus Christ of Latter-day Saints. During the process of this restoration, and during many subsequent years, modern revelation was also received by Joseph Smith and other modern prophets, some of which was published in two other books, the Doctrine and Covenants and the Pearl of Great Price. These additional scriptures provide further information about God and Jesus Christ, as well as about the Creation and the Fall. I consider these three books, hand in hand with the Bible, to constitute a library of sacred scripture (see Ezekiel 37:16–17).

As revealed in this more complete set of scriptures, I believe that Jesus Christ existed for all eternity before the foundations of the earth. "In the beginning was the Word, and the Word was with God, and the Word was God" (John 1:1). I do not believe, as apparently others interpret, this verse as saying that God and Jesus are one and the same physical being. I do believe that this verse is confirming that Jesus, "the Word," was, in the beginning, with God, and that Jesus Himself was also a God. Why, if Jesus was the only God in that verse, would we be told that Jesus was "with" God? During the Creation, "God said, Let us make man in our image, after our likeness" (Genesis 1:26). Furthermore, during the Fall, God said of Adam, "Behold, the man is become as one of us, to know good and evil" (Genesis 3:22). The terms "us" and "our" in those verses suggest that more than one God was involved in the Creation and Fall.

I believe that God the Father placed Jesus Christ in charge of the creation of this earth. We are told by the Apostle Paul in Ephesians, for example, that "God . . . created all things by Jesus Christ" (Ephesians 3:9). John tells us concerning "the Word," Christ, "All things were made by him; and without him was not any thing made that was made" (John 1:3). And, further, "He was in the world, and the world was made by him, and the world knew him not" (John 1:10). Then, Paul told the Hebrews,

> God, who at sundry times and in divers manners spake in time past unto the fathers by the prophets, Hath in these last days spoken unto us by his Son, whom he hath appointed heir of all things, by whom also he made the worlds; Who being the brightness of his glory,

> and the express image of his person, and upholding all things by the word of his power, when he had by himself purged our sins, sat down on the right hand of the Majesty on high; Being made so much better than the angels, as he hath by inheritance obtained a more excellent name than they. (Hebrews 1:1–4)

I believe that God and Jesus are infinite and eternal in existence, power, and knowledge. The Psalmist said, "Great is our Lord, and of great power: his understanding is infinite" (Psalm 147:5). Paul explained to the Romans, "For the invisible things of him from the creation of the world are clearly seen, being understood by the things that are made, even his eternal power and Godhead; so that they are without excuse" (Romans 1:20).

I also believe that through Jesus Christ we may be inheritors of eternal salvation. "Though he were a Son, yet learned he obedience by the things which he suffered; And being made perfect, he became the author of eternal salvation unto all them that obey him; Called of God an high priest after the order of Melchisedec" (Hebrews 5:9–10). "And for this cause he is the mediator of the new testament, that by means of death, for the redemption of the transgressions that were under the first testament, they which are called might receive the promise of eternal inheritance" (Hebrews 9:15).

Furthermore, I believe that not only can we have eternal salvation, but we are also inherently infinite beings ourselves. We existed before the foundation of the earth as the spirit children of God the Father. Paul said to the men of Athens, as they stood on Mars Hill, "For in him [God] we live, and move, and have our being; as certain also of your own poets have said, For we are also his offspring. Forasmuch then as we are the offspring of God, we ought not to think that the Godhead is like unto gold, or silver, or stone, graven by art and man's device" (Acts 17:28–29). Paul also wrote to the Hebrews, "Furthermore we have had fathers of our flesh which corrected us, and we gave them reverence: shall we not much rather be in subjection unto the Father of spirits, and live?" (Hebrews 12:9). God told Jeremiah, "Before I formed thee in the belly I knew thee; and before thou camest forth out of the womb I sanctified thee, and I ordained thee a prophet unto the nations" (Jeremiah 1:5).

I believe that the "intelligences" from which our spirits were made are immortal and eternal. They—we—have always existed and always will exist. "Man was also in the beginning with God. Intelligence, or the light of truth, was not created or made, neither indeed can be. All truth is independent in that sphere in which God has placed it, to act for itself, as all intelligence also; otherwise there is no existence" (D&C 93:29–30). I believe, therefore, that our intelligences, our spirit beings, while living within this created, temporary universe, are not confined to this universe but exist in the realms beyond its confines.

The belief system outlined above allows me to have faith in the verities of both science and religion. As a friend of mine once quipped, "The universe may have been made by a bunch of old men in funny hats and bow ties." I don't know about the bow ties, but my belief in real, tangible humanoid Gods and Creators is the foundation of my beliefs.

Another friend and colleague of mine once said to me, "I didn't know a scientist could be religious." For me, only belief in a real, physical, tangible God and separate, tangible Jesus Christ, as opposed to some mystical fusion between God and Jesus[3] allows science and religion to come together in any meaningful way. We are no longer the highly intelligent but extremely naïve church scholars of the first through fourth century, and we should employ our greater understanding of the human body toward a greater understanding of sacred concepts and not throw out the baby of true religion with the bathwater of human fables.

I pointed out to my friend who didn't know that scientists could be religious that the visible universe only accounts for 4.7 percent of the total universe and that, therefore, there is a huge portion of reality (95.3 percent) that we are currently unable even to detect—except indirectly and hypothetically. I believe that many of the interfaces between the "natural world" and the "supernatural world" can only be understood by applying concepts such as those from the enigmatic fields of quantum physics, entanglement, and the study of dark matter—and probably other, yet undiscovered, scientific specialties.

In a speech delivered at Caltech in April 2013, Stephen Hawking stated, "The missing link in cosmology is the nature of dark matter and dark energy." He further noted that "normal matter is only 5 percent of the energy density of the known universe; 27 percent is dark matter, 68 percent is dark energy."[4]

Estimates of the ratios between normal matter, dark matter, and dark energy tend to vary from year to year, and person to person. Kevin Pimbblet presented a pie chart in a November 2017 review showing that normal matter accounts for less than 4 percent of the total, dark matter 23 percent, and dark energy 73 percent.[5] Furthermore, Pimbblet broke down normal matter into free hydrogen and helium (3 percent), stars (0.5 percent), neutrinos (0.3 percent), and everything else in the universe, including our earth and everything on it (0.03 percent). Therefore, what we can actually *see* of the universe, including the stars and planets, accounts for only 0.53 percent of the total universe.

During the last few years of his life, Stephen Hawking was one of the most vocal scientists arguing that God had no place in the creation of the universe. He stated, for example, "The role played by time at the beginning of the universe is, I believe, the final key to removing the need for a grand designer and revealing how the universe created itself."[6] In a number of similar statements, Hawking made it quite clear that in his mind, time trumps everything, even God. So was Hawking right? Was he the official spokesperson for all scientists?

Hawking,[6] in my opinion correctly, pointed out that time and space began at the Big Bang and did not exist before that event. However, physics tells us that what was created at the Big Bang was what Hawking called "normal matter."[4] We cannot, however, say the same for dark matter or dark energy—the other 95-plus percent of the universe. Hawking would have us believe that God is limited by $E=mc^2$, but that equation only describes "normal matter," which is defined by what we can *see* or detect because of light (the electromagnetic spectrum; time, space and light are expressed as c in Einstein's famous equation).

If we now recognize, as Hawking acknowledged, that there apparently are distinct components of the universe (at least dark matter and dark energy) that we, at present, cannot detect, no matter how hard we've tried, then how can we be so arrogantly confident that there are not yet other parts of the universe we can't detect? In the face of such overwhelming numbers for the known unknown, how can we be so arrogantly confident that God is confined to the, at most, 5 percent of the universe that we can detect?

In his 2017 review, Pimbblet asked, as have others, is there an alternative to proposing dark matter and dark energy? After all, "scientists only proposed dark matter to explain how galaxies and galaxy clusters move due to a gravitational pull." Pimbblet speculated, "Suppose for a moment that both dark energy and dark matter are too strange a pill to swallow. What would the alternatives be? One way out would be to suppose that our understanding of the universe is at fault. Perhaps gravity and general relativity do not work in quite the way that we think they do." Pimbblet stated that André Maeder, has proposed a concept called "scale invariance," which suggests that the scaled invariance of the universe itself may account for galactic motion, without the need to invoke dark matter. Some preliminary tests appear to agree with this proposal. Pimbblet cautions, "However, there are many more tests that need to be run, Maeder has only investigated two galaxy clusters. And let's not forget the huge body of work suggesting that dark matter and dark energy do exist."[5]

In this book, I have attempted to explain how the creation of the universe, as sketched out in the scriptures, may be compatible with the more complete story that is unfolding through scientific investigation. This is not a book about intelligent design. I find the arguments for intelligent design to be interesting but unconvincing, lacking as they are, almost entirely, in relevant data. This book, rather, is an attempt to understand scriptural accounts that are often brief, possibly misinterpreted during translation, and usually quite vague and lacking in details in light of modern scientific data.

Paul stated, very accurately, for glass made when the last ancient scriptures were being written in the first century AD, "For now we see through a glass, darkly; but then face to face: now I know in part; but then shall I know even as also I am known" (1 Corinthians 13:12). Today, we see through glass almost perfectly, with little or no color or prismatic aberrations. Likewise, science was a complete mystery to first-century scholars and for nearly two millennia thereafter—during the critical time when the ancient scriptures were being translated and compiled. Physicians didn't even know what human beings looked like on the inside—as anatomy was a taboo practice. They had no idea concerning the function of the brain. Instead, they possessed a vague notion that the mind, or the soul, somehow, was associated with the heart, liver, and spleen. They had absolutely no concept of human reproduction, involving two microscopic cells: a sperm and an egg. They had no idea that artificial insemination was possible. Furthermore, they and other scientists of the time had no concept of the more than thirty trillion cells comprising each human body, the forty-six chromosomes in nearly every human cell, the twenty thousand or so genes associated with those chromosomes, or the billions of atoms forming the stuff of each cell.

Origen described the lack of knowledge in his day (c. AD 185–254), "of the whole number of miracles and marvels attributed to [Christ], there is one which . . . the weakness of mortal understanding can find no way to grasp or to compass. I mean the fact that . . . the very Logos [Word] of the Father . . . in whom all things visible and invisible were created . . . must be believed to have entered a woman's womb, to have been born as a small child, and to have squalled in the manner of crying children."[7]

However, despite all the knowledge deficiencies and the complications of bringing sacred writ to light in the early Christian era, it is my belief that much ancient scriptural content, especially when enhanced by modern scripture, conveys true religion vital to our eternal lives—even if that religious truth is only a tiny fraction of the full extent of a complete religion.

ENDNOTES

1. Joseph Smith, *Teachings of the Presidents of the Church: Joseph Smith* (Salt Lake City: The Church of Jesus Christ of Latter-day Saints, 2007), 41–42.
2. These chapters are in the Book of Mormon; this book and all other citations referencing to additional scriptures, as well as books written and talks given by leaders and other scholars in The Church of Jesus Christ of Latter-day Saints can be found at lds.org/scriptures or lds.org in general.
3. Wikipedia, Reference to *The Family Bible Encyclopedia* (Curtis Books, Inc., 1972), 3790.
4. Brett Smith, "Dark Matter at Caltech Speech," redOrbit.com, April 18, 2013.
5. Kevin Pimbblet, "Study finds dark matter and dark energy may not exist, here's what to make of it," theconversation.com, 30 November 2017.
6. Stephen Hawking, *Brief Answers to the Big Questions* (New York, Bantam, 2018).
7. Origen, *On First Principles*, 2.6.2; as quoted in Grant Underwood, "Condescension and Fullness, LDS Christology in Conversation with Historic Christianity." In Eric D. Huntsman, Lincoln H. Blumell and Tyler J. Griffin, eds, *Thou Art the Christ, the Son of the Living God, The Person and Work of Jesus in the New Testament*; The 47th Annual Brigham Young University Sidney B. Sperry Symposium (Salt Lake City: Deseret Book).

CHAPTER 2

LIFE BEFORE THE GRAND COUNCIL

It's not at all clear what we did before the Grand Council was convened. None of us seem to have any memory going that far back into the eons of infinity, and we're not told much about that time in the scriptures. We do know that we were intelligences. Joseph Smith taught, "Man was also in the beginning with God. Intelligence, or the light of truth, was not created or made, neither indeed can be" (D&C 93:29). In the April 1844 general conference, the Prophet Joseph Smith taught the following:

> The mind or the intelligence which man possesses is co-equal with God himself. . . . The intelligence of spirits had no beginning, neither will it have an end. . . . There never was a time when there were not spirits; for they are co-equal [co-eternal] with our Father in heaven. . . . The first principles of man are self-existent with God. . . . Intelligence is eternal and exists upon a self-existent principle. It is a spirit from age to age, and there is no creation about it.[1]

Of this eternal nature of intelligences, B. H. Roberts stated:

> Joseph Smith taught not only the eternal existence of intelligence, but of intelligences. These may be manifested as "spirits," "men," "angels," "Deities," according to the state of progress to which they have attained; and they may be of infinitely varying degrees of intelligence, moral quality, and soul greatness; yet all are equal in their eternity. Regarded as intelligences, whatever estates or changes they may have passed through, whatever their present status or whatever

> progressive estates may await them in future, there is a something in them not only uncreated, but from the nature of it uncreatable, and indestructible—without beginning and without end.[2]

From the book of Abraham we learn: "Now the Lord had shown unto me, Abraham, the intelligences that were organized before the world was; and among all these there were many of the noble and great ones; And God saw these souls that they were good, and he stood in the midst of them, and he said: These I will make my rulers; for he stood among those that were spirits, and he saw that they were good; and he said unto me: Abraham, thou art one of them; thou wast chosen before thou wast born" (Abraham 3:22–23).

Even during that infinity before the Grand Council, we were not all the same: "Howbeit that he made the greater star; as, also, if there be two spirits, and one shall be more intelligent than the other, yet these two spirits, notwithstanding one is more intelligent than the other, have no beginning; they existed before, they shall have no end, they shall exist after, for they are . . . eternal. And the Lord said unto me: These two facts do exist, that there are two spirits, one being more intelligent than the other; there shall be another more intelligent than they; I am the Lord thy God, I am more intelligent than they all" (Abraham 3:18–19).

We are told in Psalm 147:6, "Great is our Lord, and of great power: his understanding is infinite". In reference to God, Giordano Bruno, a sixteenth century Italian Dominican friar, stated, "God is infinite, so His universe must be too. Thus is the excellence of God magnified and the greatness of His kingdom made manifest; He is glorified not in one, but in countless suns; not in a single earth, a single world, but in a thousand, I say in an infinity of worlds."[3]

Unquestionably, one of the world's greatest thinkers, Isaac Newton, the seventeenth century English theologian and mathematician, said of God, "And from true lordship it follows that the true God is living, intelligent, and powerful; from the other perfections, that he is supreme, or supremely perfect. He is eternal and infinite, omnipotent and omniscient; that is, he endures from eternity to eternity; and he is present from infinity to infinity; he rules all things, and he knows all things that happen or can happen."[4]

It was revealed in 1829 to the Prophet Joseph Smith, "By these things we know that there is a God in heaven, who is infinite and eternal, from everlasting to everlasting the same unchangeable God, the framer of heaven and earth, and all things which are in them" (D&C 20:17).

Perhaps the greatest problem we have now, as humans trying to comprehend and describe infinity, is that we are surrounded by a finite world. Classical mathematics and physics, which serve us so well in many fields of science and human understanding, fall short when it comes to describing the eternal, the infinite. What we need is almost a new language to help finite mortals comprehend and describe our place in the infinite scheme of life and beyond—perhaps quantum physics is beginning to provide that language.

If time is viewed mathematically as an infinitely long line, any division of that line, such as one's lifetime, is meaningless (x/∞ is undefined). But with God, time is not an eternally long line; it doesn't exist at all. We are told in the scriptures that "time only is measured unto men" (Alma 40:8). That sounds a lot like what Albert Einstein, one of the founders of quantum physics, said: "Time is simply a human construct."[5] Furthermore, we are told in Abraham that there was a "beginning of time" (Abraham 1:3) and in Daniel that there is a "time of the end" (Daniel 12:9). Therefore, there is a beginning and an end to earth's existence and our sojourn here, which are measured by time. But before the beginning of time and after the end of time, there is no time in that infinity. Our individual time on earth is not an undefined portion of an infinite time line, but rather a key period during a defined time of earth, with a beginning and an end, in which we can obey commandments and receive ordinances that are critical to our eternal progression.

At some point in the past infinity, our intelligences were born as spirit children of heavenly parents, although we don't really know what either the terms "point" and "born" actually means. As we currently understand, with our very limited understanding of the infinite, there is no actual "point" in infinity. Did we have "birthdays" to celebrate? Joseph Smith spoke of the infinite nature of spirits.[2] Paul told the Hebrews, "Furthermore we have had fathers of our flesh which corrected us, and we gave them reverence: shall we not much rather be in subjection unto the Father of spirits, and live?" (Hebrews 12:9). The Psalmist said, "Ye are gods; and all of you are children of the most High" (Psalm 82:6) Paul stated in his first epistle to the Thessalonians: "Ye are all the children of light. . . . Therefore let us not sleep, as do others" (1 Thessalonians 5:5–6). What a thrilling declaration! We are immortal, infinite, eternal children of light; we are gods and the offspring of God. Some part of our spirit selves, referred to as intelligence, has existed throughout infinity. Then, at some point in our premortal existence, our intelligence was organized into a spirit, and we were born as the literal offspring of God (see Acts 17:29).

In her beautiful poem, later set to music to become the beloved hymn *O My Father*, Eliza R. Snow stated:

> I had learned to call thee Father,
> Thru thy Spirit from on high,
> But, until the key of knowledge
> Was restored, I knew not why.
> In the heav'ns are parents single?
> No, the thought makes reason stare!
> Truth is reason; truth eternal
> Tells me I've a mother there.[6]

Because we were all different as intelligences and as spirit children, we probably had different gifts of the spirit. Some of us were given the gift of faith, some of prophecy, some of languages, and others of great charity. Some of us were given the gift of seeking and teaching knowledge and wisdom (see Moroni 10:8–20). Some of us were content to know that we were intelligences, while others of us were curious to know what our intelligences are made of. If our intelligences have always existed, they must not be made of regular, observable matter, which we now understand through the discoveries of science to be finite. Given the enormous advancements of modern science into the realms of fundamental particles and the universe, is it possible that we, at last, are on the verge of discovering what this intelligence might be made of?

The Prophet Joseph Smith gave the following instructions at Ramus, Illinois, on May 17, 1843: "There is no such thing as immaterial matter. All spirit is matter, but is more fine or pure, and can only be discerned by purer eyes. We cannot see it, but when our bodies are purified, we shall see that it is all matter" (D&C 131:7–8).

It appears from this scripture that "intelligence" is some sort of matter, which is infinite, "fine and pure," and not "visible" like normal matter. Modern science teaches that all visible matter was created at the time of the Big Bang, or later. Is intelligence, from which spirits are made, some sort of matter that exists outside the confines of finite space and time—unaffected by the Big Bang? Is it some sort of infinite matter?

Visible matter is that which either emits light or reflects it. What we see in the blackness of space is either sources emitting light, such as the sun and stars, or objects reflecting light, such as the moon and planets. The "empty" space across which light travels is black because there is no visible matter in that space to reflect the light. What's more, we can only see a tiny fraction of the light given off by stars even in our own small neighborhood of the universe. If you gaze into the night sky in a remote area, where there is no light pollution and where the sky is full of stars, and count the number of stars you can actually see, the number turns out to be somewhat less than 10,000. That number is only about 0.000003 percent of the stars in the Milky Way Galaxy alone (about 250 billion ± 150 billion).[7] No wonder God told Abraham that the stars were numberless (see Genesis 15:5).

For thousands of years, humans connected the stars to the four primal elements: earth, air, fire, and water—with the sun, stars, planets, and moon being nearby celestial fires. Throughout that time, people found no need to add any additional elements to the list because those four elements and their interactions explained the entire known universe. I have given a number of firesides and other talks about the history of these four elements. In those talks, I begin with the following demonstration: I set out a glass of water, a small stone, a straw, and a match. I then ask the audience to make a series of predictions—hypotheses that can be tested right there at the podium. If I place this stone into the water, what will happen? I place the stone into the water and it sinks to the bottom of the glass, as predicted. What will happen if I blow air through the straw into the water? I blow through the straw into the water and, as predicted, bubbles form, which escape from the surface of the water into the air. What will happen if I light a match above the water? When a match is lighted, the fire ascends above the glass.

By this simple demonstration, I have proven that a rock (earth) is heavier than water, that air is lighter than water, and that fire is lighter than air. Likewise, we see this same relationship in nature: we stand on the earth, water tends to be found on the surface, the air is above the earth and water, and fire—the stars, moon, and sun—are in the sky above the air. For thousands of years, nothing more was needed to explain the universe.

Although many elements such as lead and gold, which we now understand to be basic elements, were discovered years ago, the Greeks—and their intellectual descendants—believed them to be only manifestations of the four basic elements. The first "modern" element discovered was phosphorus in 1669 by Hennig Brand. It would be another sixty-six years before the next element, cobalt, was discovered by Georg Brandt.[8] By 1789, thirty-three elements were recognized, and Antoine Lavoisier had organized them into groups based on their chemical characteristics.[9] In 1864, William Odling arranged the then fifty-seven elements by atomic weight.[10]

We now recognize 118 elements, all of which are atoms and made of the same basic building blocks: protons, neutrons, electrons, and neutrinos (plus many other subatomic particles)—in different amounts. It has taken us nearly four hundred years to arrive at this point—starting with the four original indivisible elements. Today, we also realize that those 118 elements are only a small portion of a much greater picture. We now realize that there is a lot more "stuff" in space than just light-emitting and light-reflecting bodies—composed of elements—which account for only 4.9 percent of the currently known universe. As it turns out, we have learned in the past half century that there is a vast amount of very unusual matter and energy out there in the universe, about which we know little or nothing. That additional matter, called dark matter, is apparently not comprised of elements, as is "regular" matter, but is made of something else—something we don't as yet know anything about. Is it possible that dark matter is not a single entity but could be comprised of some sort of "elements" that may be organized into a periodic table of its own? If visible matter accounts for only a tiny fraction of the matter proposed by science, is it possible that there may be even more matter in the universe than just visible matter and dark matter?

In 1901, at a meeting of the British Science Association in Glasgow, William Thomson (Lord Kelvin) described the rotation of stars within the Milky Way Galaxy. He proposed that the velocity of their rotation required a much greater mass to the galaxy than could be accounted for by the stars we can see in the galaxy.[11] Thomson thought those "dark bodies" were "extinct," burnt out stars, as did Henri Poincaré, who in 1906 coined the term "dark matter," or "matière obscure" in the original French, to describe them.[11]

The idea that there were more burned out stars in the universe than visible ones remained barely a footnote in physics textbooks over the next seventy years. Then, in 1976, the whole scientific world was turned upside down when the American astronomer Vera Rubin published a paper that shattered the existing comfortable view of the universe. Because most of the stars in spiral galaxies are clustered near the center, astrophysicists assumed that most of the mass—gravity and dark stars—would be clustered near the center as well. With the mass of the galaxy focused in the center, the speed of stars near the center should be greater than that of stars farther away—similar to Mercury's speed around the sun being much greater than that of Neptune's. However, Rubin found that stars in the outer reaches of spiral galaxies were moving just as fast as stars near the center. The implications of this discovery were staggering. Rubin calculated that there was ten times more dark matter associated with each galaxy than visible matter—not *inside* the galaxy, as was assumed, but *surrounding* the galaxy like some great halo.[12]

Although most of the world was oblivious to this new discovery of a universe filled with something other than common matter, the implications of Rubin's discovery stretched into infinity itself. Her discovery would be like Columbus discovering not just the New World but discovering that the New World then was more ten times larger than the previously known world, and was made not of rocks and soil but of some sort of invisible force-field-stuff.

The New York Times obituary for Vera Rubin, published in December 2016, stated that she "transformed modern physics and astronomy with her observations showing that galaxies and stars are immersed in the gravitational grip of vast clouds of dark matter. Her work helped usher in a Copernican-scale change in cosmic consciousness, namely the realization that what astronomers always saw and thought was the universe 'is just the visible tip of a lumbering iceberg of mystery.'"[13]

If dark matter isn't burned out stars, then what is it? What is this stuff that makes up the vast majority of the universe, this dark matter? By the end of the 1980s, the concept that dark matter might be made up of some not-as-yet-discovered subatomic particle was gaining momentum. Many possible solutions have been proposed, but none have yet won out.[11]

We now know that *at least* 95.1 percent of the matter and energy in the universe is made of unknown material. It is almost certain that someday some scientist will crack the secret of what dark matter is made of. Someday we may also discover that visible matter and dark matter *combined* are only a small fraction of some even larger, as yet completely unimagined and unidentified matter of which the universe is comprised.

Dark matter is only called "dark matter" because we can't see it and because Henri Poincaré thought it was a bunch of burned-out stars (I actually prefer Poincaré's original term "matière obscure"—obscure matter). Today we know it's not burned-out stars, but we don't know what it is. Why not call it invisible light? Because that's an oxymoron. We call something light because we *can* see it, but what our eyes can detect is only a tiny fraction of the electromagnetic spectrum—most of which we can only detect with instruments. So far, no one has constructed an instrument that can detect any hint of that "obscure matter."

Scientists have been constructing and testing instruments in an attempt to, if not "see" dark matter, at least observe its interaction with known matter. For example, the Large Underground Xenon (LUX) facility was constructed beginning in 2009, 1500 meters underground at the Sanford Underground Laboratory in the old Homestake Mine, Lead, South Dakota, at a cost of $10 million.[14]

The results of the experiment to detect dark matter were described by Lee Billings in the October 2016 issue of *Scientific American*. The bottom line is that after seven years and $10 million searching for the nature of dark matter, they found nothing. This announcement of the non-discovery came on July 21, 2016, and the non-discovery discovery was followed two weeks later (August 5) by an announcement from the Large Hadron Collider Center (LHC) near Geneva that they couldn't detect any part of dark matter either. Billings concluded, "These elusive particles . . . may simply be better at hiding than physicists thought. Alternatively, they may not exist, which would mean that something is woefully amiss in the underpinnings of how we try to make sense of the universe."[15]

Billings pointed out that Johnathan Feng and Jason Kumar, at UC Irvine, have shown that there may be "a hypothetical class of particles . . . [part of] a hidden realm of the universe filled with varieties of dark particles interacting with one another through a suite of dark forces, perhaps exchanging dark charges through bursts of dark light."[15] This proposal sounds a lot like the beginnings of a periodic table of "dark particles." It also sounds a lot like what Joseph Smith described for spirit matter back in 1843 (see D&C 131:7–8).

Billings quoted David Spergel of Princeton University: "'With the dark sector, you're free to invent almost whatever you want . . . the space of available models is huge. It's a playground where we don't know what the right choices are—we now need more hints from nature about where to go next.'"[15]

Lisa Randall, who is the Frank B. Baird, Jr., Professor of Science at Harvard University, and member of the *Scientific American* advisory board, has stated:

> Perhaps the most significant sign of the existence of dark matter . . . is our very existence. Despite its invisibility, dark matter has been critical to the evolution of our universe and to the emergence of stars, planets and even life . . . [it was] critical to the creation of structures such as galaxies—within the (relatively short) time span we know to be a typical galaxy lifetime . . . Without dark matter, radiation would have prevented clumping of the galactic structure for too long, in essence wiping it out and keeping the universe smooth and homogeneous. The galaxy essential to our solar system and our life was formed in the time since the big bang only because of the existence of dark matter.[16]

If I were in junior high, high school, or a college freshman interested in physics, the above quotes would be music to my ears; an open playground where one could "invent almost whatever you want." This is what having fun with science is all about! At the time of this writing, one of my granddaughters, just starting high school, is interested in theoretical astrophysics, particle physics, and quantum physics. To that fifteen-year-old generation of my granddaughter lies the future of discovering the secrets of obscure, invisible matter.

Even though I'm neither a teenager (except in my mind) nor a physics major, I'm going to invent what *I* want for this "dark" universe. Right now dark matter is just that. As a result, we are starting from a more primitive position than our remote ancestors who described the entire universe as being made of earth, air, fire, and water with our earth at the center. Today 95.1 percent of the "universe" is dark matter/energy with the "known" universe at the center—sounds a bit familiar.

Maybe you're not a teenage physics geek (I use the term as a compliment). Maybe you're a budding science fiction writer. I have a good friend and former student who is a science fiction writer and illustrator (he invented the animals and many of the plants on the planet Pandora for the movie *Avatar*). He once told me that these are tough times for science fiction writers. Hard science is moving so fast that it's difficult for science fiction writers to stay ahead of the curve. I think it's safe to say that there is a lot of fertile ground ahead of the dark matter curve for many years to come. I'm not talking about just parallel universes, which have been the fodder of science fiction for many years. I'm talking about a whole new periodic table of the dark elements. If I were a budding scifi writer, I'd start with the history of how that *new* periodic table was discovered. The very thought sends chills down my spine and conjures the image of Joseph Wright's painting *The Alchymist, In Search of the Philosopher's Stone*, depicting Hening Brand kneeling before his chemical distillation apparatus in 1669, the bright light of discovery reflecting in his face.

Another compelling question is, does dark matter predate the known, visible universe? Most cosmologists would say that it was created in the Big Bang, at the same time as the visible universe. However, if we don't have any idea what dark matter is, how does that lack of information fit into the Big Bang model? And what about dark energy? Stephen Hawking would also say "no" to anything existing before the Big Bang because before the space-time singularity there was no time, and with no time there was nothing.[17] How do we know that dark matter or dark energy even cares about time? If we know next to nothing about them, do we know that they're influenced by time at all? As we have no idea what dark matter is, except that it has mass, and we know even less about dark energy, how do we know if they even fit into the Penrose-Hawking singularity at all? Lee Billings proposed that because our search for dark matter has turned up empty, sitting our current models on their ears, there is "the possibility that Einstein's theory of gravity is wrong in some way."[15]

Is the next Einstein or Hening Brand sitting right now in some junior high, high school, or college physics or chemistry class? I have no doubt you are out there. If not you, who? If not now, when?

Joseph Smith was told, "Intelligence, or the light of truth, was not created or made, neither indeed can be" (D&C 93:29). All the matter we can understand at present was created at the time of the Big Bang, or later. But intelligence is some form of matter that is eternal and infinite, which was never created, and therefore can never be destroyed. With this profound knowledge of infinite matter, we can, at last, begin a scientific quest for the infinite.

ENDNOTES

1. Joseph Smith, *Teachings of the Prophet Joseph Smith*. Selected by Joseph Fielding Smith, (Salt Lake City: Deseret Book, 1938), 353–54. The bracketed insertion was in the original footnote. It says, "Undoubtedly the proper word here would be 'co-eternal,' not 'co-equal.' This illustrates the imperfection of the report made of the sermon." There are four original accounts of the King Follett Sermon: Willard Richards used the term "co-equal" in his account; Wilford Woodruff used the term "coequal" in his account; Thomas Bullock said, "Man is as immortal as God himself" in his account; William Clayton used the term "coequal" in his account. See josephsmithpapers.org/paper-summary/discourse-7–april-1844. Clearly Joseph said co-equal in the sermon.
2. B.H. Roberts, *A Comprehensive History of the Church of Jesus Christ of Latter-day Saints, Century I*, vol. 1. (Provo, Utah: Brigham Young University Press, 1965), 391–92.
3. Giordano Bruno, *On the Infinite Universe and Worlds,* 1584; see also Steven Soter, "The cosmos of Giordano Bruno," *Discover,* March 13, 2014.
4. Isaac Newton, *The Principia: Mathematical Principles of Natural Philosophy* (1687), 3rd edition (1726), trans. I. Bernard Cohen and Anne Whitman, General Scholium, 1999, 941.
5. The New Quotable Einstein, Alice Calaprice, ed. (Princeton Univ. Press, 2005).
6. Eliza R. Snow, "O My Father," *Hymns,* no. 292.
7. NASA and World Book, *nasa.gov,* November 29, 2007
8. Mary Elvira Weeks, "Discovery of the Elements," *Journal of Chemical Education*, 1956, books.google.com.
9. R. Siegfried, *From elements to atoms a history of chemical composition, American Philosophical Society*, vol. 92 (Philadelphia, Pennsylvania, 2002), 4–6.
10. W. Odling, "On the proportional numbers of the elements," *Quarterly Journal of Science,* 1:642–648, 1864; Eric R. Scerri, *The Periodic Table: Its Story and Its Significance (*Oxford University Press, 2006).
11. Stephanie M. Bucklin, "A history of dark matter," Ars Technica, arstechnica.com/science/2017/02/a-history-of-dark-matter, 2017
12. Lisa Randall, "Why Vera Rubin Deserved a Nobel," *The New York Times*, Jan. 4, 2017.
13. Dennis Overbye, "Vera Rubin, 88, Dies; Opened Doors in Astronomy, and for Women," *The New York Times*, Dec. 27, 2016.
14. D. Akerib, et al., "The Large Underground Xenon (LUX) experiment," *Nuclear Instruments and Methods in Physics Research A*, 704: 111–126, 2013.

15. Lee Billings, "In the Dark about Dark Matter," *Scientific American*, Oct. 2016, 14–16.
16. Lisa Randall, "What is dark matter?", *Scientific American*, June 2018, 58–59.
17. hawking.org.uk/the-beginning-of-time.html

CHAPTER 3

THE GRAND COUNCIL

Each of us is a child of God. In the book of Acts we are told, "For in him we live, and move, and have our being; as certain also of your own poets have said, For we are also his offspring" (Acts 17:28). Paul also wrote to the Hebrews, "Furthermore we have had fathers of our flesh which corrected us, and we gave them reverence: shall we not much rather be in subjection unto the Father of spirits, and live?" (Hebrews 12:9). We lived with God in a premortal world where we learned and progressed. "Even before they were born, they, with many others, received their first lessons in the world of spirits and were prepared to come forth in the due time of the Lord to labor in his vineyard for the salvation of the souls of men" (D&C 138:56).

The concept of a premortal life was taught to the first Christian converts in England as shown by the beautiful allegory given in 627 AD by Coifi, the chief priest of King Edwin of Northumbria:

> Your Majesty, let us give careful consideration to this new teaching; for I frankly admit that, in my experience, the religion that we have hitherto professed seems valueless and powerless, . . . Your Majesty, when we compare the present life of man on earth with that time of which we have no knowledge, it seems to me like the swift flight of a single sparrow through the banqueting-hall where you are sitting at dinner on a winter's day with your thegns and counsellors. In the midst there is a comforting fire to warm the hall; outside, the storms of winter rain or snow are raging. This sparrow flies swiftly in through

> one door of the hall, and out through another. While he is inside, he is safe from the winter storms; but after a few moments of comfort, he vanishes from sight into the wintry world from which he came. Even so, man appears on earth for a little while; but of what went before this life or of what follows, we know nothing. Therefore, if this new teaching has brought any more certain knowledge, it seems only right that we should follow it.[1]

We are told in the book of Moses, "For I, the Lord God, created all things, of which I have spoken, spiritually, before they were naturally upon the face of the earth. . . . And I, the Lord God, had created all the children of men; and not yet a man to till the ground; for in heaven created I them" (Moses 3:5) Furthermore, we read in the Doctrine and Covenants, "Thus saith the Lord your God, even Jesus Christ, the Great I Am, Alpha and Omega, the beginning and the end, the same which looked upon the wide expanse of eternity, and all the seraphic hosts of heaven, before the world was made" (D&C 38:1–2). Again from the Doctrine and Covenants we read, "And that it [the earth] might be filled with the measure of man, according to his creation before the world was made" (D&C 49:17).

In the Saturday morning session of the April 2016 general conference, Donald L. Hallstrom, of the Presidency of the Seventy, stated, "Our most fundamental doctrine includes the knowledge that we are children of a living God. That is why one of his most sacred names is father, Heavenly Father . . . it is among the most extraordinary knowledge we can obtain. A correct understanding of our heavenly heritage is essential to exaltation. It is foundational to comprehending the glorious plan of salvation and to nurturing faith in the firstborn of the Father, Jesus the Christ, and in his merciful atonement."[2]

In the priesthood session of that conference, Henry B. Eyring, of the First Presidency, stated: "Before we were born we lived in a family with our exalted and eternal Heavenly Father. He ordained a plan that enables us to advance and progress to become like him . . . The purpose of the plan was to allow us the privilege of living forever as our Heavenly Father lives. This gospel plan offered us a life of mortality in which we would be tested. A promise was given, that through the atonement of Jesus Christ, if we obey the laws and priesthood ordinances of the Gospel, we would have eternal life, the greatest of all His gifts."[3]

The earth was created in order for us to have "a life of mortality in which we would be tested."[3] Its creation was one of the key three pillars of eternity. Imagine the thrill we felt when the long-awaited Grand Council was announced. However, in addition to the council being a thrilling time, it was also a frightening time. We were told that not all of us would pass the test and return to our heavenly home. The task ahead was so daunting that one-third of our brothers and sisters chose to follow Satan and give up their agency rather than risk not coming through earth life safely. They even chose to follow Satan in being cast out of heaven in the belief, being convinced by Satan's rhetoric, that with him they could thwart God's plan and be the ones to return to heaven to reign under Lucifer's ultimate triumph.

We are told that we attended that Grand Council in heaven before the foundation of the world, and at least two-thirds of us marveled at the great plan of our God (see 2 Nephi 9:13) and shouted for joy at its prospect (see Job 38:7). Satan "came before . . . [God], saying—Behold, here am I, send me, I will be thy son, and I will redeem all mankind, that one soul shall not be lost, and surely I will do it; wherefore give me thine honor" (Moses 4:1). One can imagine that those evil but alluring words sent a chill down the backs of most of us listening. It would have been hard to comprehend that a brother or sister standing right next to you might have found those words so convincing as to follow his unsettling plan. Then God's "Beloved, which was my Beloved and Chosen from the beginning, said unto me—Father, thy will be done, and the glory be thine forever" (Moses 4:2). That plan felt good. It felt right. It was the plan we wanted to follow.

Abraham gave a slightly different, more poetic account of that Grand Council:

> And there stood one among them that was like unto God, and he said unto those who were with him: We will go down, for there is space there, and we will take of these materials, and we will make an earth whereon these may dwell; And we will prove them herewith, to see if they will do all things whatsoever the Lord their God shall command them; And they who keep their first estate shall be added upon; and they who keep not their first estate shall not have glory in the same kingdom with those who keep their first estate; and they who keep their second estate shall have glory added upon their heads for ever and ever. And the Lord said: Whom shall I send? And one answered like unto the Son of Man: Here am I, send me. And another answered and said: Here am I, send me. And the Lord said: I will send the first. And the second was angry, and kept not his first estate; and, at that day, many followed after him. (Abraham 3:24–28)

After Satan's plan was rejected by the council, he initiated a war and drew away one-third of heaven's host after him. The casting out of Satan and his host is described most poetically in Revelation: "And there was war in heaven: Michael and his angels fought against the dragon; and the dragon fought and his angels . . . And his tail drew the third part of the stars of heaven, and did cast them to the earth" (Revelation 12:7–4). This number of Satan's followers is confirmed in modern revelation: "The devil . . . rebelled against me, saying, Give me thine honor, which is my power; and also a third part of the hosts of heaven turned he away from me because of their agency" (D&C 29:36).

Apparently, not all the details of the plan were revealed in that first Grand Council. We are told in the book of Moses that "Satan . . . had drawn away many after him . . . [and that] . . . he knew not the mind of God, wherefore he sought to destroy the world" (Moses 4:6–19). This scripture suggests that there may have been other meetings of the council following the war in heaven and Satan's expulsion to which he and his minions were not privy.

One such portion of the great plan must have been details of Adam's role. The scripture just quoted is associated with Satan's tempting Adam and Eve in the garden—thus Satan may not have been fully aware of Adam and Eve's key roles in the great plan. In order for Christ's Atonement to make any sense, Adam's Fall must also have been discussed in those premortal councils. We must have all agreed to the Fall just as we agreed to the Atonement. Because those councils and those votes were inherently immortal, it would make no difference at all exactly *when* Adam and Eve were on the earth. There was no "when" in the plan, as that term is strictly a temporal one. The terms "first man" and "first lady" may be applied to Adam and Eve not as temporal statements but as majestic titles. This concept will be discussed in more detail later.

Those of us who followed the Savior's plan were all foreordained before we came to earth to accept Jesus Christ as our Savior, even those who would live and die before the Savior's lifetime.

Paul wrote to the Romans and Ephesians:

"And we know that all things work together for good to them that love God, to them who are the called according to his purpose. For whom he did foreknow, he also did predestinate to be conformed to the image of his Son, that he might be the firstborn among many brethren. Moreover whom he did predestinate, them he also called: and whom he called, them he also justified: and whom he justified, them he also glorified" (Romans 8:28–30).

"According as he hath chosen us in him before the foundation of the world, that we should be holy and without blame before him in love" (Ephesians 1:4).

All of us who hold the priesthood or hold specific callings in the Church also were foreordained to those callings before we came to earth, as explained by the following scriptures:

> And those priests were ordained after the order of his Son . . . being called and prepared from the foundation of the world according to the foreknowledge of God, on account of their exceeding faith and good works. (Alma 13:3)

> Before I formed thee in the belly I knew thee; and before thou camest forth out of the womb I sanctified thee, and I ordained thee a prophet unto the nations. (Jeremiah 1:5)

> And God saw these souls that they were good, and he stood in the midst of them, and he said: These I will make my rulers; for he stood among those that were spirits, and he saw that they were good; and he said unto me: Abraham, thou art one of them; thou wast chosen before thou wast born. (Abraham 3:22)

We then watched this grand creation unfold and even participated in its fruition (see Abraham 3:22–24). Even though we were there as witnesses and participants, we forgot those grand experiences when we came to earth as mortal beings. Some of what we had previously known has been revealed from time to time to prophets. We read in Abraham, "But the records of the fathers, even the patriarchs, concerning the right of Priesthood, the Lord my God preserved in mine own hands; therefore a knowledge of the beginning of the creation, and also of the planets, and of the stars, as they were made known unto the fathers, have I kept even unto this day, and I shall endeavor to write some of these things upon this record, for the benefit of my posterity that shall come after me" (Abraham 3:22–24).

But God did not reveal most of the details of the earth's creation through His prophets. That revelation has come from the hard work of numerous scientists over many years. In the April 1989 general conference, Dallin H. Oaks sated, "I believe that many of the great discoveries and achievements in science and the arts have resulted from a God-given revelation. Seekers who have paid the price in perspiration have been magnified by inspiration."[4]

One such revelation is that the creation of the earth has proceeded over a very long time. Our ancestors, going back only a couple of hundred years, were naïve when it came to extremely large numbers. They were only aware that the stars in the sky were innumerable. They were not aware that the Milky Way Galaxy alone has as many as 400 million stars[5] and that there are that many other galaxies. They were unaware that the human body is made up of as many as 37 trillion cells.[6] Most believed that the earth was created only several thousand years ago. They were not aware that the earth began to form around 4.567 billion years ago.[7]

As we come to grasp these very large numbers, we can better appreciate God, for whom time is irrelevant, meaningless, and the infinite nature of the creation—going all the way back into the timeless premortal life when we existed as intelligences. I worship a God for whom time is irrelevant, "for all things are present before mine eyes" (D&C 38:1–3). It appears that Nephi worshiped the same God: "For he is the same yesterday, today, and forever; and the way is prepared for all men from the foundation of the world, if it so be that they repent and come unto him. For he that diligently seeketh shall find; and the mysteries of God shall be unfolded unto them, by the power of the Holy Ghost, as well in these times as in times of old, and as well in times of old as in times to come; wherefore, the course of the Lord is one eternal round" (1 Nephi 10:18–19).

ENDNOTES

1. Bede, *Ecclesiastical History of the English People*, 731 AD; translated by Leo Sherley-Price, Penguin, 1955, 1990, 130.
2. Donald L. Hallstrom, April 2016 general conference.
3. Henry B. Eyring, April 2016 general conference.
4. Dallin H. Oaks, "Alternate Voices," April 1989 general conference.
5. NASA and World Book. *nasa.gov*. Nov. 29, 2007.
6. smithsonianmag.com/smart-news/there-are-372–trillion-cells-in-your-body-4941473
7. FM Gradstein, JG Ogg, Mark Schmitz, and Gabi Ogg, eds. The International Commission on Stratigraphy, ICS's *Geologic Time Scale 2012*, 118407th edition, Elsevier, 2012.

CHAPTER 4

WHO WERE THE GODS OF CREATION?

We read about God or the Gods who created the earth in Genesis, Moses, and Abraham:

> In the beginning God created the heaven and the earth . . . And God said, Let us make man in our image, after our likeness:" (Genesis 1:1, 26)

> By mine Only Begotten I created these things; yea, in the beginning I created the heaven, and the earth upon which thou standest. (Moses 2:1)

> We will go down . . . and we will take of these materials, and we will make an earth whereon these may dwell. (Abraham 3:24)

> And then the Lord said: Let us go down. And they went down at the beginning, and they, that is the Gods, organized and formed the heavens and the earth. . . . And they (the Gods) said: Let there be light; and there was light. (Abraham 4:1, 3)

> And by the word of my power, have I created them, which is mine Only Begotten Son, who is full of grace and truth. And worlds without number have I created; and I also created them for mine own purpose; and by the Son I created them, which is mine Only Begotten. (Moses 1:32–33)

Who were those "Gods" who created the earth? In addition to the Savior being the *power* by which the earth and other worlds were formed, other spirits were called and set apart to assist the Lord in the formation of the earth. They were the "us" and "our" spoken of in Genesis 1:26 and throughout the Abrahamic account. They were the "noble and great ones" spoken of in Abraham 3:22. The prophet Joseph Fielding Smith said, "It is true that Adam helped to form this earth. He labored with our Savior Jesus Christ. I have a strong view or conviction that there were others also who assisted them. Perhaps Noah and Enoch; and why not Joseph Smith, and those who were appointed to be rulers before the earth was formed?"[1]

Were there other noble and great ones involved in the creation? On October 3, 1918, one day before the opening of the 89th Semiannual General Conference of the Church, President Joseph F. Smith received a vision in Salt Lake City, Utah, "concerning the Savior's visit to the spirits of the dead while his body was in the tomb" (introduction to Doctrine and Covenants 138). President Smith saw that "from among the righteous, he [Christ] organized his forces and appointed messengers, clothed with power and authority, and commissioned them to go forth and carry the light of the gospel to them that were in darkness, even to all the spirits of men; and thus was the gospel preached to the dead" (D&C 138:30). "And [those so organized] continue thenceforth their labor as had been promised by the Lord, and be partakers of all blessings which were held in reserve for them that love him" (D&C 138:52). Those who continued the preaching to the dead were those who had lived on earth, "including [those involved in] the building of the temples and the performance of ordinances therein for the redemption of the dead, were also in the spirit world. I observed that they were also among the noble and great ones who were chosen in the beginning to be rulers in the Church of God" (D&C 138:54–55).

Thus, as recorded by the prophet Joseph F. Smith, those who were "among the noble and great ones" included those involved in "the building of the temples and the performance of ordinances therein for the redemption of the dead." Thus, those of us who have labored in God's temples for the redemption of the dead are counted "among the noble and great ones." Therefore, when Christ said, "We will go down . . . and we will take of these materials, and we will make an earth whereon these may dwell" (Abraham 3:24), He was speaking to "many of the noble and great ones" (Abraham 3:22)—those of us who have labored in the temples.

Therefore, at least some of us, if not all of us, ordinary people were helping do some very extraordinary things during the creation of the earth. Why shouldn't we have been doing extraordinary things? We are, after all, children of God.

Alma taught: "I would cite your minds forward to the time when the Lord God gave these commandments unto his children; and I would that ye should remember that the Lord God ordained priests, after his holy order, which was after the order of his Son, to teach these things unto the people . . . being called and prepared from the foundation of the world according to the foreknowledge of God, on account of their exceeding faith and good works" (Alma 13:1, 3–11).

In reference to this scripture in Alma, Bruce R. McConkie, of the Quorum of the Twelve Apostles, taught in the April 1974 general conference, "All those who receive the Melchizedek Priesthood in this life were, as Alma teaches, 'called and prepared from the foundation of the world according to the foreknowledge of God,' because they were among the noble and great in that premortal sphere."[2]

According to the revelation received by President Joseph F. Smith, the noble and great ones include *all* those who work in the temples, not just the Melchizedek Priesthood holders. Women also work in the temples, performing their own sacred ordinances through the power of the Melchizedek Priesthood.

Bruce R. McConkie stated that the noble and great ones in the premortal world included faithful women:

> This we know: Christ, under the Father, is the Creator; Michael, His companion and associate, presided over much of the creative work; and with them, as Abraham saw, were many of the noble and great ones. Can we do other than conclude that Mary and Eve and Sarah and myriads of our faithful sisters were numbered among them? Certainly these sisters labored as diligently then, and fought as valiantly in the war in heaven, as did the brethren, even as they in like manner stand firm today, in mortality, in the cause of truth and righteousness[3]

Speaking at the 1998 general women's conference, Carol B. Thomas, first counselor in the Young Women General Presidency, stated:

> It was my father who taught me about the premortal life. He explained that long ago you and I were born as daughters in our Heavenly Father's family. We made sacred decisions there that have

> influenced what we are doing now. When I was younger, my grandfather gave me a blessing. He blessed me that I would "continue my ministry here that I had so nobly performed there." Now, if I had a ministry in the premortal existence, then so did you. It is not by chance that you were born now, in this season of the world's history. Each one of you was a valiant and noble woman in your premortal life.
>
> Abraham said, "Now the Lord had shown unto me, Abraham, the intelligences that were organized before the world was; and among all these . . . were many of the noble and great ones." Do you know that he was talking about you? You are each noble and great, born to live at this time on the earth.[4]

Speaking to the youth of the Church, in the 1976 *New Era*, LeGrand Richards of the Quorum of the Twelve Apostles said, "If the veil could be parted and you could see who you were then, then have a recollection and vision of what awaits you—what the Lord had in mind for you noble and great ones who have come forth in this day and time—I do not think any of you would want to wile away your time. You would want to make sure that you are using those gifts and talents that God has endowed you with for the honor and glory of his name and the blessing of his children."[5]

In his 1998 book *Perfection Pending*, then Elder Russell M. Nelson stated, "If my fondest wish could be granted, it would be that we could know who we really are, and that we know we come from premortal realms where we were numbered 'among the noble and great ones who were chosen in the beginning to be rulers in the Church of God.'"[6]

We know, then, that as noble and great premortal spirits, we were called by our elder brother Jesus Christ to assist Him and Adam in creating the world. What were we doing when they were making the earth and all things on the face thereof? What was our role in the Creation? We are not told, either in the scriptures or by science. In ensuing chapters I will propose some possible activities in which we may have been involved as part of the Creation.

Alma suggested that *all* premortal male spirits who kept their first estate and were not cast out of God's presence for rebellion were foreordained to the Melchizedek Priesthood. It was subsequently the "hardness of their hearts and blindness of their minds" that kept them from being so ordained during their earth life. We should not forget, however, that this second estate includes the postmortal spirit world and that we can perform vicarious ordinations in the temples for our deceased brethren—including ordination to the Melchizedek Priesthood. Alma said, "And thus they have been called to this holy calling on account of their faith, while others would reject the Spirit of God on account of the hardness of their hearts and blindness of their minds, while, if it had not been for this they might have had as great privilege as their brethren. Or in fine, in the first place they were on the same standing with their brethren; thus this holy calling being prepared from the foundation of the world for such as would not harden their hearts, being in and through the atonement of the Only Begotten Son" (Alma 13:4–5).

The Psalmist stated, "I have said, Ye are gods; and all of you are children of the most High" (Psalm 82:6). This statement suggests that *all* the children of God are gods. During His life, the Savior made reference to this scripture in a discussion with the Jews who were bent on stoning Him:

> Then the Jews took up stones again to stone him. Jesus answered them, Many good works have I shewed you from my Father; for which of those works do ye stone me? The Jews answered him, saying, For a good work we stone thee not; but for blasphemy; and because that thou, being a man, makest thyself God. Jesus answered them, Is it not written in your law, I said, Ye are gods? If he called them gods, unto whom the word of God came, and the scripture cannot be broken; Say ye of him, whom the Father hath sanctified, and sent into the world, Thou blasphemest; because I said, I am the Son of God? (John 10:31–36).

Christ is stating here that all those "unto whom the word of God" has come "are gods." Because He was speaking to the Jews, He was telling them that they were *all* gods. By extension, we might conclude, with the Psalmist, that *all* the children of God are gods.

I will proceed with my discussion of the infinite Creation under the assumption that "in the first place . . . [we] were [all] on the same standing" (Alma 13:5) and, therefore, we all, every premortal spirit who would come to earth, had a part in creating the earth and all things thereon. We, as the children of God, were all the gods of creation. Of course, we were not all equal even as intelligences and we each had our own talents and abilities, but perhaps we were all equal in one aspect of the Creation—the creation, or organization, of our own mortal bodies.

ENDNOTES

1. *Doctrines of Salvation: Sermons and Writings of Joseph Fielding Smith*, edited by Bruce R. McConkie, 3 vols. (Salt Lake City: Deseret Book, 1954), 1:74–75.
2. Bruce R. McConkie, "God Foreordains His Prophets and His People," April 1974 general conference.
3. Spencer W. Kimball, *Woman* (Salt Lake City: Deseret Book, 1979), 59.
4. Carol B. Thomas, "Understanding Our True Identity," *Ensign*, May 1998.
5. LeGrand Richards, "A Constructive Life," *New Era*, June 1976.
6. Russell M. Nelson, *Perfection Pending* (Salt Lake City: Deseret Book, 1998).

CHAPTER 5

THE INFINITE CREATION

The poetic beauty of the opening lines of creation are breathtaking. Genesis 1:1–2 states, "In the beginning God created the heaven and the earth. And the earth was without form, and void; and darkness was upon the face of the deep. And the Spirit of God moved upon the face of the waters."

The comparable verses in Moses 2:1–2 state, "I am the Beginning and the End, the Almighty God; by mine Only Begotten I created these things; yea, in the beginning I created the heaven, and the earth upon which thou standest. And the earth was without form, and void; and I caused darkness to come up upon the face of the deep; and my Spirit moved upon the face of the water; for I am God."

Then in Abraham 4:1–2 we read, "And then the Lord said: Let us go down. And they went down at the beginning, and they, that is the Gods, organized and formed the heavens and the earth. And the earth, after it was formed, was empty and desolate, because they had not formed anything but the earth; and darkness reigned upon the face of the deep, and the Spirit of the Gods was brooding upon the face of the waters."

Then the three accounts describe the six creative days, or periods, in much the same way. I will not go into the detail of the first five days here, but will discuss some general issues of the Creation later in this chapter. Suffice it to say that we read in Abraham 4:18, "And the Gods watched those things which they had ordered until they obeyed."

In all three accounts, two separate creations are described. Genesis 2:5 says, "And every plant of the field before it was in the earth, and every herb of the field before it grew: for the Lord God had not caused it to rain upon the earth, and there was not a man to till the ground."

Moses 3:5 says, "And every plant of the field before it was in the earth, and every herb of the field before it grew. For I, the Lord God, created all things, of which I have spoken, spiritually, before they were naturally upon the face of the earth. For I, the Lord God, had not caused it to rain upon the face of the earth. And I, the Lord God, had created all the children of men; and not yet a man to till the ground; for in heaven created I them; and there was not yet flesh upon the earth, neither in the water, neither in the air; But I, the Lord God, spake, and there went up a mist from the earth, and watered the whole face of the ground."

Abraham 5:3–6 says,

> And the Gods concluded upon the seventh time, because that on the seventh time they would rest from all their works which they (the Gods) counseled among themselves to form; and sanctified it. And thus were their decisions at the time that they counseled among themselves to form the heavens and the earth. And the Gods came down and formed these the generations of the heavens and of the earth, when they were formed in the day that the Gods formed the earth and the heavens, According to all that which they had said concerning every plant of the field before it was in the earth, and every herb of the field before it grew; for the Gods had not caused it to rain upon the earth when they counseled to do them, and had not formed a man to till the ground. But there went up a mist from the earth, and watered the whole face of the ground.

In the description of Adam's creation, all three accounts state that the Gods created man in their image, after their likeness (even in Genesis, where God is singular, the following pronoun is plural). We are told in Genesis 1:26, "And God said, Let us make man in our image, after our likeness." In Moses 2:26 we read, "And I, God, said unto mine Only Begotten, which was with me from the beginning: Let us make man in our image, after our likeness." And Abraham 4:26 states, "And the Gods took counsel among themselves and said: Let us go down and form man in our image, after our likeness."

We are also told in all three accounts that Adam was made of the "dust of the ground." "And the Lord God formed man of the dust of the ground" (Genesis 2:7). "And I, the Lord God, formed man from the dust of the ground" (Moses 3:7). "And the Gods formed man from the dust of the ground" (Abraham 5:7). Brigham Young and Orson Pratt apparently had a disagreement over this issue.

In a talk delivered in the Tabernacle in Salt Lake City, 29 August 1852, Orson Pratt stated:

> The "Mormons" have a peculiar doctrine in regard to our pre-existence, different from the views of the Christian world, so called, who do not believe that man had a pre-existence. It is believed, by the religious world, that man, both body and spirit, begins to live about the time that he is born into this world, or a little before; that then is the beginning of life. They believe, that the Lord, by a direct act of creation, formed, in the first place, man out of the dust of the ground; and they believe that man is possessed of both body and spirit, by the union of which he became a living creature. Suppose we admit this doctrine concerning the formation of the body from the dust; then how was the spirit formed? Why, says one, we suppose it was made by a direct act of creation, by the Almighty Himself; that He molded the spirit of man, formed and finished it in a proper likeness to inhabit the tabernacle He had made out of the dust.[1]

One year later, President Brigham Young responded, "Supposing that Adam was formed actually out of clay, out of the same kind of material from which bricks are formed; that with this matter God made the pattern of a man, and breathed into it the breath of life, and left it there, in that state of supposed perfection, he would have been an adobie to this day. He would not have known anything . . . You believe Adam was made of the dust of this earth. This I do not believe, though it is supposed it is so written in the Bible; but it is not, to my understanding."[2]

In 1853, President Young did not understand modern concepts of physiology, biochemistry, and molecular biology. The only way he could understand humans being made of dust or clay was to mold the clay into a ceramic man, like a brick, and breathe into him the breath of life. This he would not accept. Whether Pratt had any sort of understanding of biochemistry is not clear. Maybe he was just staying with the conservative Bible account. Pratt initially referred to the concept of man being made from the dust as a Christian belief. Then he said, "Suppose we admit this doctrine concerning the formation of the body from the dust."[1] This sounds to me that he was keeping an open mind about the whole issue.

Thanks to modern scientific research, we now understand that we are literally made of the dust of the ground. Plants take up inorganic molecules from the earth, literally the dust, and breath in carbon dioxide. Then, by using the energy of the sun, they produce complex organic molecules, including carbohydrates, lipids, proteins, and nucleic acids, such as DNA. Herbivores eat the plants and take up the building blocks of these molecules from which they build their own carbohydrates, lipids, proteins, and nucleic acids; employing the energy obtained from breaking carbon bonds through glycolysis. Carnivores then eat the herbivores. Of course, none of this modern knowledge was available to anyone in the mid-nineteenth century. With the knowledge we have today of organic chemistry, biochemistry, molecular biology, physiology, and developmental biology, it is difficult to fully appreciate the mindset of a nineteenth-century thinker.

All three accounts of the Creation include the statement that the Gods gave Adam his "breath of life" through his nostrils. Genesis 2:7 states, "And the Lord God . . . breathed into his nostrils the breath of life; and man became a living soul." Moses 3:7 says, "And I, the Lord God . . . breathed into his nostrils the breath of life." Abraham 5:7 states, "And the Gods . . . took his spirit (that is, the man's spirit), and put it into him; and breathed into his nostrils the breath of life, and man became a living soul." Only in Abraham are we told about the spirit, but that is in addition to the breath of life. The issue of the breath of life will be discussed in much more detail in later chapters, but suffice it to say here that humans have known for hundreds of millennia that air, the "breath of life," is critical to survival. But only within the past one hundred fifty years have we understood why it is important.

After his creation, Adam was told by God, "I have set thee to be at the head; a multitude of nations shall come of thee, and thou art a prince over them forever" (D&C 107:55). Adam was "called and prepared from the foundation of the world" (Alma 13:3). Adam was not just a name but also a title. "Male and female created he them; and blessed them, and called their name Adam, in the day when they were created" (Genesis 5:2; see also Moses 6:9). Adam had the right of the high priesthood, "the right of the firstborn, or the first man, who is Adam, or first father" from before the foundation of the earth (Abraham 1:3). Adam presided over the first patriarchal generation "in the days of the first patriarchal reign, even in the reign of Adam" (Abraham 1:26). Eve was also a title as well as a name:

"And Adam called his wife's name Eve, because she was the mother of all living; for thus have I, the Lord God, called the first of all women, which are many" (Moses 4:26).

The earth's condition after the Creation and before the Fall has generated much heated debate over the past one hundred fifty years or so, as the discoveries of modern science have seemingly come more and more into conflict with religious beliefs. This question of what the earth was like immediately after the Creation is, perhaps more than any other issue, responsible for the perceived gulf between science and religion.

I will begin by stating the extremely conservative position, as expressed within the creationist movement. Connie Hunt stated on the Institute for Creation Research website:

> God saw that His creation was "good" six times throughout the creation week (Genesis 1:4, 10, 12, 18, 21, 25), but at the end of the sixth day (Genesis 1:31), He pronounced it *very* good. If we could take all of the above adjectives and put them into one incredibly descriptive word and then add *exceedingly* to all of that, we might begin to have an idea of what God's creation was like. It is deliberate ignorance to believe that God could have made such a statement at the end of some ghastly evolutionary struggle that had left multitudes of contorted fossil remains in petrified testimony to their final battle with death. But this is precisely what theistic evolutionism demands of its proponents. If the fossil record is historically placed at any point before the creation of man and God's "very good" pronouncement, then one is faced with the irreconcilable theological problem of a God who would make such a statement about sin's corruptive effects.[3]

I agree with the first one-third of her statement, and I believe that her perspective was probably the mainstream, unchallenged perspective before 1859. Indeed, the view of most Christians before the middle of the nineteenth century was that the earth may not have been all that violent up until just before the flood. We are told in Genesis 6:1–17, "And the Lord said, I will destroy man whom I have created from the face of the earth; both man, and beast, and the creeping thing, and the fowls of the air; for it repenteth me that I have made them . . . And God looked upon the earth, and, behold, it was corrupt; for all flesh had corrupted his way upon the earth. And God said unto Noah, The end of all flesh is come before me; for the earth is filled with violence through them; and, behold, I will destroy them with the earth. . . . And, behold, I, even I, do bring a flood of waters upon the earth, to destroy all flesh, wherein is the breath of life, from under heaven; and every thing that is in the earth shall die."

Orson Pratt expressed a similar opinion to that of Ms. Hunt in an 1853 article in his periodical *The Seer*: "If any living creature, had been subject to death, or any manner of pain, it would not have been perfect in its organization; it could not have been pronounced good; neither would it have been consistent, as the work of an all-wise and supremely good Being. Perfection characterizes all the works of God, therefore, all the tabernacles which he made from the dust, must have been capable of eternal endurance."[4]

The problem with pronouncements such as those made by Elder Pratt and Ms. Hunt is that they presume to know the mind of God. Is it possible for a human to know what is good or perfect to God? Isaiah tells us, "For my thoughts are not your thoughts, neither are your ways my ways, saith the Lord. For as the heavens are higher than the earth, so are my ways higher than your ways, and my thoughts than your thoughts" (Isaiah 55:8–9). An omniscient God knew perfectly well that the animals He created and pronounced that "all these things were good" (Moses 2:25) would behave according to their creation: herbivores eat grass and carnivores eat herbivores. To believe that carnivores only existed after the Fall, as the result of sin, is to give Satan the power of their creation. Satan is not the author of creation. God created the carnivores, knowing full well their nature. He was not surprised at all by their behavior.

Terryl and Fiona Givens pointed out the following:[5] "Many have concluded, along with the novelist Norman Mailer, that the specter of colossal human pain requires no God, a perverse God, or a God self-limited by human freedom. Mailer said, 'If God is good, then He is not all powerful. If God is all powerful, then He is not all good.'"[6]

The wolves my family and I have visited at the Grizzly and Wolf Discovery Center in West Yellowstone are gorgeous, majestic animals. They are truly among God's amazing, wonderful creations. Their teeth were perfectly created for eating meat. Their digestive tracts were created for digesting meat. Fed a diet of grass, wolves would die of starvation. They eat meat, not to be violent but to survive. Only humans hunt game that we don't even eat only to make trophies of them. Oh, but imagine a cute little bunny nibbling on grass, when along comes a big bad wolf and gobbles it up. What a tragic story—no, "big bad wolves" are the stuff of fairy tales. But isn't the eating of a cute little bunny tragic? It probably is to children, when told to them by adults in the context of a cute little bunny being eaten by a big bad wolf. But this is not a tragic story from the perspective of the grass that the rabbit is eating or from the perspective of a biologist who knows from years of data collection and many published papers that if wolves, coyotes, and other predators are eliminated, rabbits breed out of control and can destroy hundreds of acres of plant-life. I do not mean to say that bunnies and rabbits are not a beautiful part of God's creation (the are), but the *real* beauty of God's creation is the system of checks and balances that He created to keep a given species from overrunning part of the world. Believe me, I grew up on a dairy farm in southern Idaho, and I know what a plague of jackrabbits looks like—it is not a pretty sight.

My wife and I live on three acres of juniper-covered foothill. In our yard we have billions of microorganisms and countless worms and arthropods. We have fish in our ponds and many varieties of birds in our trees. We have chickens and cats. We are visited by salamanders, snakes, voles, deer mice, squirrels, rabbits, hares, skunks, porcupines, coyotes, and deer. We love nature and spend many hours in our gardens, but we can't raise tulips, some of our favorite flowers. In the early spring, the deer come into our yard and eat any tulips we have planted. They don't bother our daffodils or crocuses, so we have to rely on these flowers for our Easter colors. The deer don't just eat the stems of the tulips, but they violently pull up the bulbs and eat them, thus murdering the plants. They also violently rip the bark and buds from our fruit trees, killing them as well. I can state with the confidence of experience that they are the most violent animals that visit our yards. I must assume, based on religious tradition, that before the Fall, or perhaps before the flood, before the deer became violent, that they only ate the tulip stems and not the bulbs. But if they ate the stems, wouldn't they have also eaten the flowers? And where's the beauty in that?

I love the beauty of a ripe pear or apple, some of God's most perfect creations. But after enjoying the beauty, I take a great big bite of the fruit and consume it. That's the reason trees make fruit—so that animals will eat the fruit, including the seeds, which resist digestion to be distributed by the animal as waste, thus dispersing the seeds to grow more trees. The apricot tree in our backyard grew because our children planted apricot pits there after devouring the fruit. I know that eating fruit did not begin after the Fall or with the "introduction of violence" just before the Flood because Adam and Eve were commanded to eat the fruit of the trees in the Garden of

Eden. To a biologist, there is no difference between the "lifeness" of a plant and that of an animal. Before the advent of the microscope and advancement of the cell theory, people did not fully appreciate that *all* living things are made of cells and that eukaryotic organisms, plants and animals alike, are made of cells that contain nuclei with DNA. To a biologist, all life is equally living and all life is beautiful. There is no difference between the death of a rabbit so that a wolf may live and the death of a tulip that a deer may live. Everything is beautiful in its own way.

What about Pratt's concept that "any manner of pain . . . would not have been perfect in its organization"?[4] From a medical perspective, pain is *good*. Pain is the body's way of telling us that something is not right or to warn us against injury. Congenital insensitivity to pain (CIP), or congenital analgesia, is a very rare disorder in which a person is born with no sense of pain. That sounds like a great idea, but people with congenital analgesia are constantly injuring themselves because they have no pain to teach them to avoid injurious situations. In other words, pain is an important part of a perfect organization.

Furthermore, to view death as a tragedy brought on by the sinful curse of the Fall is to assume we know the mind of God in His great eternal plan. Viewed from our puny, earthly perspective, we think what a tragedy for a cute little bunny to be murdered in the spring of its life, what a tragedy for a tulip to be murdered before it even presents its first bloom, what a tragedy that a beautiful little adult mayfly's entire lifespan is less than twenty-four hours, what a tragedy that my son was murdered on the killing fields of Iraq before his twenty-fifth birthday. We simply don't see the picture from God's perspective. We should have learned something of life from the beautiful, poetic story told by Coifi, chief priest of King Edwin of Northumbria, in 627 AD, to the king's court explaining why the people of the British Isles should turn from their pagan beliefs toward the light of Christianity (as recounted in the previous chapter; repeated in part here), "when we compare the present life of man on earth with that time of which we have no knowledge, it seems to me like the swift flight of a single sparrow through the banqueting-hall where you are sitting at dinner on a winter's day with your thegns and counsellors . . . Even so, man [or bunnies, or tulips, or mayflies] appears on earth for a little while; but of what went before this life or of what follows, we know nothing."[7]

Oh that we were as wise today as was Coifi in 627 AD. How quickly we forget the words of the Great Creator Himself: "Are not five sparrows sold for two farthings, and not one of them is forgotten before God?" (Luke 12:6). With little more knowledge of what comes before or after our hour on the stage than Coifi possessed, how can we possibly presume to know what is "good" in God's eyes? We see the mayfly for one brief day, but we seldom see the lifetime it spent as a nymph before emerging into the sunlight for that one brief day. But what is a day to God before whom there is no time? What is a human lifetime, but one short day to God? God created us all—the mayfly, the tulip, the bunny, the deer, the wolf, and the human—to live in harmony and balance in this beautifully spectacular world.

When thru the woods and forest glades I wander,
And hear the birds sing sweetly in the trees,
When I look down from lofty mountain grandeur
And hear the brook and feel the gentle breeze,
Then sings my soul, my Savior God, to thee,
How great thou art! How great thou art![8]

In my opinion, Billy Graham put science and creation into beautiful perspective:

> I don't think that there's any conflict at all between science today and the Scriptures. I think we have misinterpreted the Scriptures many times and we've tried to make the Scriptures say things that they weren't meant to say, and I think we have made a mistake by thinking the Bible is a scientific book. The Bible is not a book of science. The Bible is a book of Redemption, and of course, I accept the Creation story. I believe that God created man, and whether it came by an evolutionary process and at a certain point He took this person or being and made him a living soul or not, does not change the fact that God did create man . . . whichever way God did it makes no difference as to what man is and man's relationship to God.[9]

ENDNOTES

1. Orson Pratt, *Journal of Discourses*, 1:54, 1952.
2. Brigham Young, *Journal of Discourses*, 2:6, Oct. 23, 1853.
3. Connie J. Horn, *God's "Very Good" Creation*, Institute for Creation Research, icr.org, no date listed.
4. Orson Pratt, *The Seer* 1:70, May 1853.

5. Terryl and Fiona Givens, *The Crucible of Doubt* (Salt Lake City: Deseret Book, 2014), 111.
6. Norman Mailer, *The Gospel According to the Son* (Random House, 1999).
7. Bede, *Ecclesiastical History of the English People*, 731 AD; translated by Leo Sherley-Price (Penguin, 1955, 1990), 130.
8. Stuart Hine, *How Great Thou Art*, Stuart Hine Trust, 1953.
9. Billy Graham, *Doubt and Certainties*, Interview with David Frost, BBC Two, 1964.

CHAPTER 6

THE BIG BANG

We are told in Abraham 4:1–4, "And then the Lord said: Let us go down. And they went down at the beginning, and they, that is the Gods, organized and formed the heavens and the earth. And the earth, after it was formed, was empty and desolate, because they had not formed anything but the earth; and darkness reigned upon the face of the deep, and the Spirit of the Gods was brooding upon the face of the waters. And they (the Gods) said: Let there be light; and there was light. And they (the Gods) comprehended the light, for it was bright."

Verse 1 tells us that the Gods "organized the heavens and the earth." Verse 2, then, appears to have been inserted as a parenthetical statement: "the earth, after it was formed." That phrase appears to be describing a condition of the earth that had not at this point been realized. Some scholars in the past have taken the part in verse 2, "because they had not formed anything but the earth," literally in the context of the temporal sequence, which seems to imply that the earth was formed before any other part of the solar system or even the universe. However, there are no scientific data suggesting that the earth was in any way created separately either temporally or physically from the rest of the universe and solar system. Why throw out all we have learned in cosmology because of one verse, which may have been inserted out of sequence? If all of verse 2 is placed into parentheses, then the whole story follows a very different pattern—a pattern much more consistent with what is unfolding from science. The Genesis and Moses accounts of the opening verses of the Creation are similar to that in Abraham, but the pause in Abraham 4:2 is a bit more dramatic and obvious.

If we read verses 1 and 3–4 together, setting aside verse 2, as reference to some later state of the earth during its creation, then we read as follows: "And then the Lord said: Let us go down. And they went down at the beginning, and they, that is the Gods, organized and formed the heavens and the earth . . . And they (the Gods) said: Let there be light; and there was light. And they (the Gods) comprehended the light, for it was bright."

During the first milliseconds of the universe, according to our current understanding of cosmology, there was apparently such an enormous explosion of energy that mortal beings struggle to comprehend the event. We, as premortal, infinite beings witnessing that explosion—the greatest fireworks exhibit ever—must have burst into exuberant, enthusiastic cheering, with high-fives all around. Maybe it went something like this: And the Gods said, "10, 9, 8, . . . 4, 3, 2, 1, Let there be light!" And, holy cow, was there ever light! Eventually.

Technically, there was actually about a one-second delay before any light burst forth, because photons (light) were not formed until the universe was about one second old. Another technicality, it may have been another 380,000 years before the initial flash of light could be seen because the early photons were trapped in the early opaque plasma soup that filled the universe and dissipated the light like fog. It may have been only the future science geeks who were thrilled by the first release of photons. Maybe everyone else went home or just hung out, waiting for the really big burst of light later in the day—380,000 years later by today's calculations. Of course, for the infinite beings we are, the concepts we understand today of "waiting" and "day" probably had no meaning for us then. It is hard to imagine that anyone was disappointed in that final burst of light. After all, we are still picking up background radiation from that flash 13.8 billion years later. That radiation was first discovered in 1964 by Arno Penzias and Robert Wilson, earning them the 1978 Nobel Prize in physics. That cosmic microwave background is the oldest observed phenomenon we have ever discovered in the universe.[1]

Science has a name for that gigantic explosion of energy at the beginning of the universe: the Big Bang. The Big Bang theory is the current best model of the origin of the universe and explains a number of observed phenomena: the cosmic microwave background, the distribution of galaxies, the abundance of hydrogen and helium in the universe, and the observation that distant galaxies are moving away from us at an ever-increasing rate.[2]

From the time of Aristotle, into the 1930s, scientists had believed that the universe was constant—referred to as the eternal steady-state universe—and thus matter is eternal and the universe did not have a beginning of time. For more than 2200 years after Aristotle, scientists considered Genesis 1:1 to be a myth, because there was no beginning and there was no creation; matter and the universe had always existed. This scientific belief was in direct opposition to most Jewish, Christian, and Islamic beliefs that God created the earth ex nihilo—out of nothing. Ex nihilo, in turn, was opposed to the early Greek creation myths that the gods created the earth from already existing primordial matter, called chaos. In 1215 at the Lateran Council, the Catholic Church formalized this belief in ex nihilo into what is now the 296th Catechism. This belief was consistent with Hebrews 11:3, which teaches that "through faith we understand that the worlds were framed by the word of God, so that things which are seen were not made of things which do appear." We now recognize that, as often happens, the truth lies somewhere between the Greek concept of chaos and the Catholic view of ex nihilo. As it turns out, there was *something* there at the beginning of the universe. Modern science simply does not know what that *something* was.

The steady-state universe hypothesis is pretty much the way matters stood until the early twentieth century, with science and theology at odds over the issue of a "beginning." Then, in 1912, Vesto Slipher, working at the Lowell Observatory in Flagstaff, Arizona, discovered that spiral nebulae did not appear to be stationary, as the steady-state universe hypothesis would predict; but they appeared to be moving—away from his vantage point.[3]

Seven years later, the world's largest, 100–inch Hooker Telescope was built in 1919 at the Mount Wilson Observatory in Los Angeles, California. That same year, the twenty-nine-year-old Edwin Hubble was hired to run the telescope. At the time, the prevailing scientific view was that the Milky Way Galaxy comprised the entire steady-state universe. Using this giant new telescope, in 1922–23, Hubble calculated that several spiral nebulae, including the Andromeda Nebula (now known as the Andromeda Galaxy), were too far away to be part of the Milky Way Galaxy and were, in fact, entire galaxies themselves. The problem had been that previous telescopes could not resolve the individual stars of the galaxy out of what appeared to be a cloud in space (thus the term nebula—"cloud"). Also in 1922, Alexander Friedmann concluded, based on formulas derived from Einstein's general theory of relativity, that the universe might not be static but may be expanding.[4]

In 1924, Hubble also found that these newly discovered galaxies were moving at great speed away from us, in agreement with Slipher's earlier observations.[4] This new observation challenged the notion of a steady-state universe.

Then, in 1927, the Belgian Roman Catholic priest Georges Lemaître, astronomer and professor of physics at the Catholic University in Leuven, Belgium, applied Einstein's theory of general relativity to Hubble's observations and concluded that the universe is expanding away from some primordial place in space, which he called the "primeval atom" or the "Cosmic Egg."[5]

Partly because Lemaître's hypothesis smacked of bringing religion into cosmology and supporting Genesis 1:1—Lemaître was, after all, a Catholic priest—most physicists and cosmologists of the time rejected the notion of an expanding universe from a single starting point. But two years later, in 1929, Hubble published his own paper on the expanding universe, confirming Lemaître's model.[6] Today, numerous calculations from different perspectives place the Cosmic Egg—that uniform, dense, hot state from which the universe evolved—at approximately 13.8 billion years ago.[7]

The original Cosmic Egg, which, hypothetically, appeared about one millionth (10^{-6}) of a second after the Big Bang, was about the size of a golf ball.[1] All we know about the universe is what happened after that one-millionth of a second following the Big Bang. We don't know what actually occurred during that first fraction of a second. We can only speculate because all science is capable of describing is the visible universe, which did not exist during that fraction of original time, as we know it; and we know nothing of what might have transpired before the Big Bang. Indeed, many scientists argue that "before the Big Bang" is a misnomer, as "before" suggests time, and there was no time, as we calculate it, before the Big Bang.

Probably the most famous statements concerning God's role in the Big Bang, and Creation in general, were made by the British cosmologist and theoretical physicist Stephen Hawking. In his book *A Brief History of Time: From the Big Bang to Black Holes*, Hawking stated:

> Hubble's observations suggested that there was a time, called the big bang, when the universe was infinitesimally small and infinitely dense. Under such conditions all the laws of science, and therefore all ability to predict the future, would break down. If there were events earlier than this time, then they could not affect what happens at the present time. Their existence can be ignored because it would have no observable consequences. One may say that time had a beginning at the big bang, in the sense that earlier times simply would not be defined. . . . One can imagine that God created the universe at literally any time in the past. On the other hand, if the universe is expanding, there may be physical reasons why there had to be a beginning. One could still imagine that God created the universe at the instant of the big bang, or even afterwards in just such a way as to make it look as though there had been a big bang, but it would be meaningless to suppose that it was created *before* the big bang. An expanding universe does not preclude a creator, but it does place limits on when he might have carried out his job![8]

I have great respect for Stephen Hawking's work and career. He has made major contributions to our understanding of the universe. However, the fact that he was a genius and a brilliant scientist does not make him immune to error.

The problem with Hawking's conclusion that, "If there were events earlier than this time, then they could not affect what happens at the present time," is that his paradigm presumes that everything both inside and outside the *entire universe* began at the time of the Big Bang. All of the known laws of physics, including quantum physics, deal only with events occurring *inside* the *visible* universe. For example, the universe itself is expanding at a rate faster than the speed of light. That can only be true because that expansion is not confined *within* the universe. Furthermore, neither Hawking nor anyone else knows anything about dark matter other than it apparently has gravity. It is certainly, at least at present, not part of the visible universe (thus the term "dark") and, therefore, cannot be assumed to either have begun at the time of the Big Bang or to be controlled by the laws that originated at the Big Bang and govern the visible universe.

The Big Bang theory does not actually describe the origin of the universe; it describes only the origin of the visible universe. We take the existence of energy, time, and space as axiomatic, but the Big Bang theory does not discuss from whence they came. The theory also does not explain why the Cosmic Egg was so dense and hot.[9]

The visible universe is only a fraction of the total universe. It has been calculated many times over that dark energy accounts for about 68 percent of all the matter/energy in the universe. Dark matter comprises approximately 27 percent of the universe, and the so-called visible matter makes up roughly the remaining 5 percent.[10] Of that 5 percent, however, around 80 percent (around 4 percent of the total universal matter/energy) is free hydrogen and helium—out in space. The entire universe with which we deal on a regular basis, therefore, comprises only around 1 percent of the total universe. Of that tiny slice of the pie, 30 percent is made up of neutrinos and 50 percent is tied up in stars. That leaves only 20 percent of the 1 percent, or somewhere around 0.2 percent of the entire universe with which we interact—aside from looking up at the stars at night.[11]

The universe did not expand into space—it was creating space and time as it exploded. During the infinitesimally small fraction of a second of initial inflation (10^{-34} second of the universe's life), space itself expanded much more rapidly than the speed of light[1]—but we have always been taught that nothing can travel faster than the speed of light. Einstein's theory of relativity, however, which describes the speed of light as a limit, is only true *within* space and time. It does not apply to anything *outside* space and time or to the expanding space-time continuum itself. We might say of this early universe that it was expanding into infinity itself.

Is the infinite territory outside the universe a void, or is it filled with something? Because we know next to nothing about dark matter, it is possible that that infinity contains dark matter or some other undiscovered "matter." It is possible that the space/time continuum is expanding into the dark matter surrounding it.

What was the force pushing this early expansion of space/time? We don't know. It was some peculiar form of energy about which we know next to nothing. It may have been the same as or similar to the dark energy that showed up later in the universe to cause its renewed rapid expansion, or it may have been some entirely different form of dark energy. After all, we only call dark energy "dark" because we know nothing about it.

During the first picosecond (10^{-12}) the currently understood laws of physics did not apply. The initial, runaway inflation of space/time only slowed down when (10^{-6} seconds after the beginning) the initial energy was transformed into the type of energy and matter we can begin to understand through "regular" physics.[12]

At that point, the universe began to cool to the point where first gravity began to appear; and then the strong force, which holds the nuclei of atoms together, began to appear. Before 10^{-6} seconds the temperature was so extreme that, hypothetically, those basic forces of the universe did not yet exist. Then, with slightly more cooling, the weak force and the electromagnetic force appeared. These are the four forces we recognize today as holding the fabric of the universe together. One second after the beginning, the temperature of the universe cooled to about one trillion degrees and huge numbers of the first fundamental and subatomic particles appeared: photons, electrons, quarks, neutrinos, and so on. Quarks, in turn, collided to form protons and neutrons.[1]

Within the next two minutes, temperatures cooled from 100 nonillion (10^{32}) degrees Kelvin to one billion (10^{9}) degrees Kelvin, and the first elements, hydrogen and helium, appeared.[1, 12] These are still today the primary elements in the universe (80 percent of the "known," non-dark matter in the universe).

Around 380,000 years after the Big Bang, the universe cooled enough for more atoms to form. The foggy plasma soup dissipated, resulting in transparent space, setting loose a huge flash of light, detectable today as cosmic microwave background. This was probably the real flash of light we premortals were waiting for. "Let there be light" indeed! (Abraham 4:3). After this initial flash of light, however, the universe went dark for the next 400 million years or so, because no stars had yet formed to illuminate the sky.[1,12]

Then, for the next 500 million years, foam-like strands of dark matter were drawn together throughout the universe. John Wheeler proposed such foam of quantum gravitational fluctuation in 1955, which he called "quantum foam."[13] Clouds of the early elements were attracted to this dark matter foam and coalesced by the force of gravity, within halos of dark matter, to form stars and galaxies. The first stars were probably made almost entirely of hydrogen and may have been very short-lived, lasting only a few million years, before exploding into supernovae. Those early explosions produced the rest of the elements we see today—scattering them across space and seeding the universe.

When I was young, I marveled at the facsimiles in the book of Abraham. I was especially intrigued by Facsimile 2 and Joseph Smith's translations, wherein were described the interconnection between heavenly bodies, "said by the Egyptians to be the Sun, and to borrow its light from

Kolob through the medium of Kae-e-vanrash, which is the grand Key, or, in other words, the governing power" (possibly ke-'eban-raš; a keystone)[14] I wondered, how could the sun borrow light from some other celestial body, whereas it was, in itself, a source of light? Perhaps the "light" described in Facsimile 2 is not the ordinary light we perceive emanating from the sun. Is it possible that this Kae-e-vanrash, or ke-'eban-raš, this grand keystone as revealed to Abraham and taught by him to the Egyptians, is another name for "dark matter," which interconnects and governs all the heavenly bodies? We are told in Doctrine and Covenants that God "ascended up on high, as also he descended below all things, in that he comprehended all things, that he might be in all and through all things, the light of truth. . . . Which light proceedeth forth from the presence of God to fill the immensity of space—The light which is in all things, which giveth life to all things, which is the law by which all things are governed, even the power of God" (D&C 88:6, 12–13).

Some of the oldest stars in our Milky Way Galaxy formed shortly after the origin of the universe, around 13.8 to 12.5 billion years ago.[15] Our galaxy flattened into the disc-shaped Milky Way roughly 8.8 billion years ago (around five billion years after the Big Bang);[16] its shape being molded by the halo of dark matter surrounding it. Around 9.2 billion years after the Big Bang (around 4.6 billion years ago), our sun and solar system began to form[17]—our future home was at last under construction.

ENDNOTES

1. Charles Q. Choi, space.com/52–the-expanding-universe-from-the-big-bang-to-today.html, June 16, 2017.
2. Simon Singh, *Big Bang: The Origin of the Universe* (New York: Harper Perennial, 2005).
3. Harry Nussbaumer, "Slipher's redshifts as support for de Sitter's model and the discovery of the dynamic universe." In Way, M.J.; D. Hunter, eds., *Origins of the Expanding Universe:* 1912–1932, 25–38, San Francisco: ASP Conference Series 471, Astronomical Society of the Pacific, 2013; O'Raifeartaigh, Cormac, The Contribution of V.M. Slipher to the discovery of the expanding universe, *In*, Way, M.J.; D. Hunter, eds., *Origins of the Expanding Universe: 1912–1932,* 49–62, San Francisco: ASP Conference Series 471, Astronomical Society of the Pacific, 2013
4. Aleksandr Sergeevich Sharov and Igor Dmitrievich Novikov, *Edwin Hubble, the Discoverer of the Big Bang Universe* (Cambridge University Press, 1993).

5. G. Lemaître, "Un univers homogène de masse constante et de rayon croissant rendant compte de la vitesse radiale des nébuleuses extragalactiques," *Annals of the Scientific Society of Brussels, 47A:41, 1927;* Translated in: Lemaître, G., A Homogeneous Universe of Constant Mass and Growing Radius Accounting for the Radial Velocity of Extragalactic Nebulae, *Monthly Notices of the Royal Astronomical Society,* 91:483–490, 1931; If one extrapolates the known laws of physics back to a high density state, where gravity becomes infinite, a singularity results (described by Roger Penrose and Stephen Hawking). Within a singularity, the normal laws of space/time do not exist. One such singularity is associated with the origin of the Big Bang. It is not clear whether the universe began as a singularity or if our current knowledge (either from general relativity or quantum mechanics) is not sufficient to describe the events of the first milliseconds of the Big Bang.
6. E. Hubble, "A Relation Between Distance and Radial Velocity Among Extra-Galactic Nebulae," *Proceedings of the National Academy of Sciences*, 15:168–173, 1929.
7. Planck Collaboration, Planck 2015 results. XIII. Cosmological parameters, *Astronomy and Astrophysics,* 594: A13, 2015.
8. Stephen Hawking, *A Brief History of Time: From the Big Bang to Black Holes* (New York: Bantam, 1988), 8–9.
9. Brief Answers to Cosmic Questions, cfa.harvard.edu
10. science.nasa.gov/astrophysics/focus-areas/what-is-dark-energy
11. Ben Finney, commons.wikimedia.org/wiki/File:Cosmological_Composition_–_Pie_Chart.svg
12. physicsoftheuniverse.com/topics_bigbang_timeline.html
13. J. A. Wheeler, Geons, *Physical Review,* 97: 511–536, 1955; see also Ng, Y. Jack, Quantum foam, gravitational thermodynamics, and the dark sector, *J. Phys.: Conf. Ser.*, 845: 012001
14. onoma.lib.byu.edu
15. J. J. Cowan, et al., "The Chemical Composition and Age of the Metal-poor Halo Star BD +17o3248," *Astrophysical Journal,* 572: 861–879, 2002; R. Cayrel, et al., "Measurement of stellar age from uranium decay," *Nature,* 409: 691–692, 2001.
16. E. F. del Peloso, "The age of the Galactic thin disk from Th/Eu nucleocosmochronology. III. Extended sample," *Astronomy and Astrophysics,* 440: 1153–1159, 2005.
17. A. Bouvier, A. and M. Wadhwa, "The age of the Solar System redefined by the oldest Pb–Pb age of a meteoritic inclusion," *Nature Geoscience*, 3, 637–641, 2010.

CHAPTER 7

CREATION OF THE STARS

We are told in the Genesis account of the creation, "And God made two great lights; the greater light to rule the day, and the lesser light to rule the night: he made the stars also" (Genesis 1:16). It is most interesting that this part of creation transpired on the fourth day, three days after God said, "Let there be light" (Genesis 1:3) and one day *after* the plants were created on day three (see Genesis 1:11–13).

The account in Moses states,

> And I, God, said: Let there be lights in the firmament of the heaven, to divide the day from the night, and let them be for signs, and for seasons, and for days, and for years; And let them be for lights in the firmament of the heaven to give light upon the earth; and it was so. And I, God, made two great lights; the greater light to rule the day, and the lesser light to rule the night, and the greater light was the sun, and the lesser light was the moon; and the stars also were made even according to my word. And I, God, set them in the firmament of the heaven to give light upon the earth, And the sun to rule over the day, and the moon to rule over the night, and to divide the light from the darkness; and I, God, saw that all things which I had made were good; And the evening and the morning were the fourth day. (Moses 2:14–19)

The Abrahamic account says,

> And the Gods organized the lights in the expanse of the heaven, and caused them to divide the day from the night; and organized them

> to be for signs and for seasons, and for days and for years; And organized them to be for lights in the expanse of the heaven to give light upon the earth; and it was so. And the Gods organized the two great lights, the greater light to rule the day, and the lesser light to rule the night; with the lesser light they set the stars also; And the Gods set them in the expanse of the heavens, to give light upon the earth, and to rule over the day and over the night, and to cause to divide the light from the darkness. And the Gods watched those things which they had ordered until they obeyed. And it came to pass that it was from evening until morning that it was night; and it came to pass that it was from morning until evening that it was day; and it was the fourth time. (Abraham 4:14–19)

In all three accounts, we are told that these were spiritual creations. Again, we read in the Genesis account: "Thus the heavens and the earth were finished, and all the host of them . . . These are the generations of the heavens and of the earth when they were created, in the day that the Lord God made the earth and the heavens, And every plant of the field before it was in the earth, and every herb of the field before it grew: for the Lord God had not caused it to rain upon the earth, and there was not a man to till the ground. But there went up a mist from the earth, and watered the whole face of the ground" (Genesis 1:1, 4–6).

The Mosaic account goes into more detail in this part of the story:

> Thus the heaven and the earth were finished, and all the host of them . . . And now, behold, I say unto you, that these are the generations of the heaven and of the earth, when they were created, in the day that I, the Lord God, made the heaven and the earth, And every plant of the field before it was in the earth, and every herb of the field before it grew. For I, the Lord God, created all things, of which I have spoken, spiritually, before they were naturally upon the face of the earth. For I, the Lord God, had not caused it to rain upon the face of the earth. And I, the Lord God, had created all the children of men; and not yet a man to till the ground; for in heaven created I them; and there was not yet flesh upon the earth, neither in the water, neither in the air; But I, the Lord God, spake, and there went up a mist from the earth, and watered the whole face of the ground. (Moses 3:1, 4–6)

The Abrahamic account states,

> And the Gods came down and formed these the generations of the heavens and of the earth, when they were formed in the day that the

> Gods formed the earth and the heavens, According to all that which they had said concerning every plant of the field before it was in the earth, and every herb of the field before it grew; for the Gods had not caused it to rain upon the earth when they counseled to do them, and had not formed a man to till the ground. But there went up a mist from the earth, and watered the whole face of the ground." (Abraham 5:4–6)

The Mosaic account has one phrase not included in either the Genesis or the Abrahamic accounts: "For I, the Lord God, created all things, of which I have spoken, spiritually, before they were naturally upon the face of the earth" (Moses 3:5). We often describe the Genesis 1 and the Moses 2 accounts as the spiritual creation, followed by the accounts in Genesis 2 and Moses 3 as the physical creation. However, if read carefully, one sees that this dichotomous description holds only for the biological (essentially botanical) portion of creation "upon the face of the earth" and may not apply to the extraterrestrial part of creation.

In any case, whether the spiritual versus temporal creations were confined to only the biological portion of creation upon the earth or included the spiritual and temporal creation of the entire universe, including the stars, the order of events seem a little odd. There are at least two possible explanations for why there was light on day one of creation but the lights apparently responsible for that light were not created until day four. One explanation is that, as discussed in the chapter on the Big Bang, light first appeared between one minute and 380,000 years after the Big Bang (depending on how dramatic one wants to be about its initial appearance), but stars did not appear for some 400 million years.[1] This explanation, however, does not address why the creation of the plants was mentioned in between. A second, more likely explanation, is that even though the sun, moon, and stars were created during the first day of creation, between 13.4 billion years ago for the stars and 4.51 billion years ago for the moon,[2] the entire early earth was likely completely enveloped in a thick layer of clouds. Thus, much like a cloudy day in our time, it was light on the earth during the day but the cloud cover obscured the sun, moon, and stars; and they could only be seen after the cloud cover dissipated.

The creation of the stars apparently proceeded in the following manner. After the Big Bang, the distribution of the earliest elements, hydrogen and helium, was not uniform; but those elements were distributed as cloud-like clusters by quantum gravitational fluctuations in the foam-like background of dark matter.[3] Those clouds of hydrogen and helium coalesced and condensed by the force of the gravity within halos of dark matter to form the early stars and galaxies. The earliest stars were giant but short-lived spheres of hydrogen, lasting a matter of only a few million years each before exploding into supernovae. Those early stellar explosions created the rest of the elements that exist today—scattering them across space and seeding the universe with the matter that would form the long-term stars and planets.

Our sun is one of those later stars, now composed of about 75 percent hydrogen, 25 percent helium, and trace amounts of various metals. Its energy derives from the fusion of hydrogen—producing helium as the by-product. It began burning about 4.6 billion years ago and has enough fuel left to burn for approximately another 5 billion years. As the hydrogen fuel is depleted, it will consume helium and other elements by fusion, until those are also depleted.[4] During this process, the helium will become compressed, speeding the rate of hydrogen combustion and expanding the outer regions of the sun into a red giant, which will consume the inner planets, including the earth. The compressed helium in the core will become hot enough to fuse into carbon. Some of the helium and carbon will fuse to form oxygen.[5]

In much larger stars, carbon and oxygen will fuse to form larger elements, but in stars the size of the sun, those two elements will collect at the center. After a few million years, the outer layers of the red giant will be shed into space as a planetary nebula, and the core will remain as a white dwarf star, composed mostly of carbon and oxygen. A white dwarf is only about the size of the earth but is incredibly dense and hot—about half the mass of the sun and 200,000 times as dense as the earth.[5] Over the next billion years or so, the white dwarf will begin to cool down. The carbon and oxygen will form a crystalline lattice resembling a diamond.[6] It is estimated that this diamond in the sky will last 10^{34}–10^{36} years or more—essentially for eternity.[7]

This eternal diamond is reminiscent of the "sea of glass" mentioned in Revelation: "And before the throne [of God] there was a sea of glass like unto crystal" (Revelation 4:6). John further stated, "And I saw as it were a sea of glass mingled with fire: and them that had gotten the victory over the beast, and over his image, and over his mark, and over the number of his name, stand on the sea of glass, having the harps of God" (Revelation 15:2). Joseph Smith asked God, "What is the sea of glass spoken of by John, 4th chapter, and 6th verse of the Revelation?" And God answered, "It is the earth, in its sanctified, immortal, and eternal state" (D&C 77:1). Joseph also taught the Saints living in Ramus, Illinois, in 1843, "The angels do not reside on a planet like this earth; But they reside in the presence of God, on a globe like a sea of glass and fire, where all things for their glory are manifest, past, present, and future, and are continually before the Lord" (D&C 130:6–7).

Thus, it appears that the final destiny of the earth is to be consumed by the sun, which, in turn, will become a diamond-like white dwarf resembling a sea of glass where exalted beings will dwell forever in the presence of God.

ENDNOTES

1. Charles Q. Choi, space.com/52–the-expanding-universe-from-the-big-bang-to-today.html, June 16, 2017; see also physicsoftheuniverse.com/topics_bigbang_timeline.html
2. Charles Q. Choi, space.com/52–the-expanding-universe-from-the-big-bang-to-today.html, June 16, 2017; see also physicsoftheuniverse.com/topics_bigbang_timeline.html; Barboni, Melanie, Boehnke, Patrick, Keller, Brenhin, Kohl, Issaku E., Schoene, Blair, Young, Edward D., and McKeegan, Kevin D., Early formation of the Moon 4.51 billion years ago, *Science Advances*, Jan 11;3(1):e1602365. doi: 10.1126/sciadv.1602365, 2017
3. J. A. Wheeler, "Geons," *Physical Review,* 97: 511–536, 1955; see also Y. Jack Ng, "Quantum foam, gravitational thermodynamics, and the dark sector," *J. Phys.: Conf. Ser.*, 845: 01200.
4. space.com/14745–sun-composition.html
5. windows2universe.org/sun/fate.html
6. imagine.gsfc.nasa.gov/science/objects/dwarfs2.html
7. Fred C. Adams and Gregory Laughlin, "A dying universe: The long-term fate and evolution of astrophysical objects," *Reviews of Modern Physics,* 69:337–372, 1997.

CHAPTER 8

THE CHAOS OF PLANET FORMATION

We are told in the book of Abraham that "we will take of these materials, and we will make an earth whereon these may dwell" (Abraham 3:24). When large stars (greater than 1.4 times the size of the sun) have burned up all their hydrogen fuel, the core collapses with a gigantic explosion called a supernova.[1] This cataclysmic explosion also instantly vaporizes any planets orbiting that spent sun. In this catastrophic event, existing elements in the star, as well as new elements formed during the collapse of the star, are released by the explosion of this supernova. This debris, along with that from perhaps other supernovae, coalesce to form a nebula. Our solar system is the product of several generations of supernova events. In other words, many solar systems have been formed and passed away before ours was created. The Lord taught us this principle long before it was discovered by scientific investigation. We read in Moses 1:38, "And as one earth shall pass away, and the heavens thereof even so shall another come; and there is no end to my works, neither to my words."

Our solar system was created about 4.5682 billion years ago when a solar nebula condensed from a molecular cloud in space.[2] That description sounds a lot like the earth being formed from "materials" (Abraham 3:24) that were "without form, and void" (Moses 2:2). The cloud, by gravitational collapse, began to spin and flatten into the sun and "circumstellar disc" from which the sun and planets formed. The sun accounts for more than 99 percent of the total mass of the solar system.[2]

The oldest rocks on the earth have been dated to about 3.9 billion years ago, suggesting that for the first half billion years or so of the earth's life, it was a ball of molten lava. Ninety nine percent of the earth is still molten, while we live on a very thin outer crust, which is only 5–10 kilometers (3–6 miles) thick under the oceans and 30–50 kilometers (20–30 miles) thick under the continents.[3] The early molten earth may have been about 6,000° C (nearly 11,000° F), about as hot as the sun. The boundary between the inner and outer core is still about that hot today.

The heat of the earth's core is apparently derived from two sources, about half from the original heat of the condensing solar system and half from radioactive decay. Within the core, radioactive uranium decays through several steps to eventually forming helium and lead as end products. As magma reaches the surface and cools to form rocks, the uranium, lead, and helium are trapped in the solid rock. The ratio of these elements gives a very precise date of when that rock was formed.[4]

Planetary evolution from that circumstellar disc was a violent process—but probably very exciting to watch from a distance, sort of like watching a demolition derby on a grand scale. I hope that our premortal spirit bodies were privileged to witness this spectacular celestial exhibition. Front row tickets may have gone for a premium.

Dust particles clumped together, initially forming asteroid-sized objects and eventually coalescing into planetesimals, each a few hundred kilometers in diameter—about the size of several of the mid-sized moons of Saturn (from Rhea down to Tethys). Within about 500,000 years, the cores of some of the larger planetesimals began to heat up and spin, creating electromagnetic fields. During this early period of planetary evolution, the solar system was crowded with perhaps thousands of planetesimals, which often slammed together, forming larger planetesimals. In other cases, collisions caused explosive splitting or even disintegration.

After numerous collisions and accretions, some planetesimals became large enough—thousands of kilometers in diameter—to be counted as planetary embryos, ranging from around the size of Callisto (Jupiter's moon), Mercury, Titan (Saturn's largest moon, which is larger than Mercury), and Ganymede (Jupiter's moon, the largest moon in the solar system) to as large as Mars. Some of the planet embryos accumulated ponds of water and pools or volcanoes of hot magnum on their surfaces.[5]

With additional accretion, including collisions of planetesimals and asteroids into planetary embryos, six of the planetary embryos grew large enough to attract other planetary material out of their own orbits, crashing into and adding to the mass of the planet. Those impacts released clouds of gas that formed early atmospheres. Two planets, Mars and Mercury, never grew beyond the planetary embryo stage and had too little gravity to retain much of an atmosphere. Two other planets, Saturn and Jupiter, accumulated such an immense atmosphere that they became gas giants—rivaling the size of small suns. Other planetesimals, approaching a growing planet at high speed, entered lunar orbits around the planet.[5] Other planetesimals and debris came into orbit around the sun, between the orbits of Mars and Jupiter, forming the asteroid belt.

One of the growing planets came into the Goldilocks Zone orbit around the sun, just the right distance from the sun where most water on the surface was neither so hot as to boil away nor too cold to permanently freeze solid.[6] The term "Goldilocks Zone" emerged in the 1970s to describe what Stephen Dole had termed the "habitable zone" in his 1964 book, *Habitable Planets for Man*.[7] In his book, Dole guesstimated that there may be as many as 600 million habitable planets in the Milky Way Galaxy alone. Then, in 2009, NASA launched a space observatory, called Kepler, designed to look for more habitable zones in our galaxy. In November 2013, it was announced, based on Kepler observations, that there may be as many as 40 billion habitable zones within the Milky Way and that 11 billion of those may be surrounding sun-like stars.[8]

Originally, the Goldilocks Zone didn't even include the entire earth because it was believed that there were places on earth that were either way too cold or way too hot for anything to live. However, over the past forty years or so, our knowledge of life in extreme environments has expanded exponentially. There is now a whole list of microorganisms, called extremophiles (lovers of the extreme), which not only live but even thrive under extreme environmental conditions. Microbes have been discovered that thrive in high salt concentrations, extremely low pH or extremely high pH, boiling water such as the hot pools at Yellowstone Park, and even inside nuclear reactors. Scientists have discovered entire ecosystems around deep sea vents where temperatures are hot enough to melt lead.[6]

Searching for life in the universe is one of NASA's top research priorities, and scientists here on earth are poking into every nook and cranny in an attempt to discover all of the possible environments where extremophiles might be living.[6] That search for extreme life on earth has lead researchers to suggest that extraterrestrial life may exist on planets and moons outside the Goldilocks Zone. For example, the presence of life around deep sea thermal vents suggests that if such thermal activity exists elsewhere in space, such as on one or more moons of Saturn, life may exist in such locations. Currently, the concept of where life might be found in space is expanding as more information becomes available.[9]

Of course the extremophiles on earth are all microorganisms. The expectation is that the search for extraterrestrial life is also a search for microorganisms. As exciting as these searches and their ultimate discoveries—especially in terms of DNA structure—may be (for example, Enceladus, one of Saturn's moons, is a leading candidate for nearby extraterrestrial life),[10] the ultimate goal of the Goldilocks Zone for God's purposes in the Creation was not just to prepare a habitation for microbial life but to prepare a place where humans may dwell and prove ourselves (Abraham 3:24–25).

Thanks to the earth being in just the right place for human habitation, we are told by the Lord, "For the earth is full, and there is enough and to spare; yea, I prepared all things, and have given unto the children of men to be agents unto themselves" (D&C 104:17). We are also told that not only was God in charge of the Creation, but that the "bounds set for the heavens or to the seas, or to the dry land, or to the sun, moon, or stars [including a place in the heavens just right for human habitation]—All the times of their revolutions, all the appointed days, months, and years, and . . . all their glories, laws, and set times, shall be revealed in the days of the dispensation of the fulness of times—According to that which was ordained in the midst of the Council of the Eternal God of all other gods before this world was, that should be reserved unto the finishing and the end thereof. . . . As well might man stretch forth his puny arm to stop the Missouri river in its decreed course, or to turn it up stream, as to hinder the Almighty from pouring down knowledge from heaven upon the heads of the Latter-day Saints" (D&C 121:30–33).

Oh what a glorious promise! We are to be the recipients in these latter days of knowledge, "which our forefathers have awaited with anxious expectation to be revealed in the last times" (D&C 121:27). We live in a time when "nothing shall be withheld" (D&C 121:28). We are promised that "God shall give unto you knowledge by his Holy Spirit, yea, by the unspeakable gift of the Holy Ghost, that has not been revealed since the world was until now" (D&C 121:26). We are told that the Spirit of God can rest upon those who are not full recipients of the Holy Ghost and direct them toward discovering truths that are of great worth to the Latter-day Saints (see 1 Nephi 13:12–13). We are the beneficiaries of all these great and marvelous revelations reserved until the last days. Whether those revelations come directly from the Spirit of revelation or through the revelations obtained by the hard work of myriad scientists, it matters not as long as it is truth. We are also promised that if we study all these things, ponder upon them, and pray earnestly for answers, "by the power of the Holy Ghost ye may know the truth of all things" (Moroni 10:5).

ENDNOTES

1. A. Heger, C. L. Fryer, S. E. Woosley, N. Langer, D. H. Hartmann, "How Massive Single Stars End Their Life," *Astrophysical Journal,* 591:288–300, 2003.
2. A. Bouvier and, M. Wadhwa, "The age of the Solar System redefined by the oldest Pb–Pb age of a meteoritic inclusion," *Nature Geoscience*, 3, 637–641, 2010.
3. G. Brent Dalrymple, Special Publications, *Geological Society of London* 190:205–221, 2001; Tera, F., *Carnegie Inst. of Wash Year Book,* 79:524–531, 1980; Alfè, D. et al., *Earth and Planetary Science Letters* 195:91–98, 2002.
4. T. Oberthür, DW Davis, TG Blenkinsop, A. Hoehndorf, "Precise U–Pb mineral ages, Rb–Sr and Sm–Nd systematics for the Great Dyke, Zimbabwe—constraints on late Archean events in the Zimbabwe craton and Limpopo belt," *Precambrian Research,* 113:293–306, 2002.
5. Linda T. Elkins-Tanton, "Solar System Smashup," *Scientific American*, December 2016.
6. science.nasa.gov/science-news/science-at-nasa/2003/02oct_goldilocks
7. Stephen H. Dole, *Habitable Planets for Man,* (Santa Monica, CA: Blaisdell Publishing Company, Rand Corp., 1964).
8. Eric A. Petigura, Andrew W. Howard, and Geoffrey W. Marcy, "Prevalence of Earth-size planets orbiting Sun-like stars," *Proceedings of the National Academy of Sciences of the United States of America,* 110:19273–19278, 2013).
9. James F. Kasting, Daniel P. Whitmire, and Ray T. Reynolds, "Habitable Zones around Main Sequence Stars," *Icarus,* 101:108–118, 1993; H. Lammer, J. H. Bredehöft, A. Coustenis, M. L. Khodachenko, "What makes a planet habitable?" *Astronomy and Astrophysics Review,* 17:181–249, 2009.
10. futurism.com/alien-life-saturn-moon.

CHAPTER 9

THE EARTH'S BAPTISM

In a sermon delivered to the Saints in Ogden, Utah, on June 12, 1860, President Brigham Young stated that the earth has been baptized: "This earth, in its present condition and situation, is not a fit habitation for the sanctified; but it abides the law of its creation, has been baptized with water, will be baptized by fire and the Holy Ghost, and by-and-by will be prepared for the faithful to dwell upon."[1]

Many Church scholars and general members have assumed for years that the baptism referred to by President Young was the flood of Noah. For example, Kent Nielson, at the time an assistant professor of the history of science at Brigham Young University, stated in a 1980 *Ensign* article: "Within this enlarged view of a celestial uniformity, the worldwide flood of Noah's time, so upsetting to a restricted secular view, fits easily into place. It is the earth's baptism. Brigham Young pointed out that the earth 'abides the law of its creation, has been baptized with water, will be baptized by fire and the Holy Ghost, and by-and-by will be prepared for the faithful to dwell upon' (in *Journal of Discourses,* 8:83)."[2]

But why would the earth need to be baptized twice with water?

We are told that the earth was covered with water, that is, it was baptized, during the early phases of its creation: "And God said, Let the waters under the heaven be gathered together unto one place, and let the dry land appear: and it was so. And God called the dry land Earth; and the gathering together of the waters called he Seas: and God saw that it was good" (Genesis 1:9–10; compare Moses 2:9–10; Abraham 4:9–10).

It is clear from these verses that if the waters were to be gathered together in one place, and the dry land was to appear, then 1) the waters must have been previously dispersed over the face of the earth, and 2) there was no dry land showing. In Abraham chapter 4, we are told, "And the Gods ordered, saying: Let the waters under the heaven be gathered together unto one place, and let the earth come up dry . . . And the Gods pronounced the dry land, Earth; and the gathering together of the waters, pronounced they, Great Waters" (Abraham 4:9–10).

Scientific data are in complete agreement with this scenario of the earth covered with water during its early creation, whereas, there is not a shred of scientific evidence that Noah's flood was universal. The story of Noah is one of obedience to God's commandments and warnings—not a scientific discourse proposing that everything on earth was covered with water and destroyed a mere 4364 years ago.[3] Noah's story is important to teach us obedience. The flood did not have to be universal for Noah's story to be relevant. If the earth only had to be baptized once to "abide the law of its creation," then I put my money on the baptism described in Genesis, Moses, and Abraham, which is solidly supported by scientific data.

As the molten earth began to cool, water vapor formed, and water accumulated on the surface of the earth. The early atmosphere was rich in carbon dioxide, and the resulting atmospheric pressure was very high; therefore, oceans of liquid water existed on the young earth's surface despite temperatures of nearly 450 degrees F.[4] Most of the earth's water originated from the earliest eons of its history. During the early solar smashup of planetesimals when the planets were forming, apparently many of those planetesimals contained water—captured from the parent nebula as part of their early formation. Around 4.6 billion years ago, as the earth was forming from such crashes, water with the same deuterium-to-hydrogen ratio (deuterium is a hydrogen isotope) as in today's oceans accumulated.[5]

Any given chemical element has a specific number of protons and neutrons in its nucleus, and the same number of electrons as protons located in various orbital clouds surrounding the nucleus. Changing the number of protons and electrons changes the chemical nature of the element. Changing the number of neutrons, however, does not change the chemical nature of the element, but can provide a specific signature for that element. Each unique neutron number for a given element is called an isotope. Hydrogen has three naturally occurring isotopes designated ^{1}H, ^{2}H, and ^{3}H. ^{1}H is considered the "normal" isotope of hydrogen (usually just called hydrogen but sometimes referred to as protium) with one proton and no neutron, whereas ^{2}H (deuterium) and ^{3}H (tritium) have one and two neutrons respectively, in addition to the proton.[8] Hydrogen (protium) is by far the most abundant of the isotopes, accounting for 99.985 percent of the hydrogen isotopes found in water, such as the earth's oceans. Deuterium accounts for almost the entire remaining portion (0.015 percent or 150 ppm).[6] This deuterium-to-hydrogen ratio (0.015 to 99.985) can be thought of as the "fingerprint" of the earth's ocean water and identical fingerprints found elsewhere on earth or in space are assumed to have the same origin.

Evidence for this early origin of earth's water was obtained in 2012 by Adam Sarafian and colleagues at the Woods Hole Oceanographic Institution (WHOI), who discovered water with the same deuterium-to-hydrogen ratio as earth's ocean water in meteorites originating from the asteroid Vesta.[7] Chunks of rock and even some planetesimals, like Vesta, hundreds of miles in diameter (Vesta is 326 miles in diameter),[7] left over from the planetesimal collisions of the early solar system are scattered in several orbits around the sun. Most of that rocky debris, called asteroids (star-like) or planetoids (planet-like) if they are large enough, are located in the Main Asteroid Belt.[6] Vesta is actually large enough to be seen with a telescope or even binoculars in the night sky. According to *National Geographic* author Andrew Fazekas, "It is visible low in the southwestern sky after dusk, about 6 degrees above the bright orange star Antares. . . . Although you can easily see the asteroid with binoculars, a telescope will allow you to watch it move in front of a background of stars."[7]

Sarafian and colleagues have discovered that the earth's water accrued very early on, about 4.6 billion years ago, while the inner planets of the solar system were forming. To accomplish their discovery, the WHOI group analyzed meteorites formed at different times during the evolution of the solar system.[5] The team first examined the oldest known meteorites ever found on earth. The oldest meteorites had been circulating around within the solar system since about the time the sun was forming, but before the planets were accruing. Eventually they were caught in earth's gravitational pull and fell to earth. Concerning meteorites in general, the Planetary Science Institute has stated, "It is estimated that probably

500 meteorites reach the surface of the Earth each year, but less than 10 are recovered. This is because most fall into the ocean, land in remote areas of the Earth, land in places that are not easily accessible, or are just not seen to fall (fall during the day). . . . Five to ten meters is probably the smallest object that would likely survive passage through the Earth's atmosphere."[10]

However, most of the bulk of those five to ten meter meteorites is burned up as they pass through earth's atmosphere, so the piece that strikes the earth surface and is found is much smaller. Those meteorites are of all different ages compared to the age of the solar system. The earliest ones originated as fragments broken off as parts of the solar system were forming and then glided through space until finally being caught up in earth's gravitational pull. So the meteorite discovered just last week could be one of the oldest ever discovered, such as a piece broken off from Vesta, whereas one discovered ten years ago may have been blown off from an impact of an asteroid with Mars relatively recently. Sune Nielsen, a member of the WHOI team, stated, "These primitive meteorites [from Vesta] resemble the bulk solar system composition. They have quite a lot of water in them, and have been thought of before as candidates for the origin of Earth's water." Whereas the WHOI team is not ruling out the fact that some of the earth's ocean water may have arrived later (as described below), the team's data suggest that the bulk of the earth's water was here much earlier than previously thought.[11]

Furthermore, volcanic moon rocks brought back to earth by Apollo 15 and 17 astronauts also exhibit the same deuterium-to-hydrogen ratio as terrestrial water. These data tell us at least three things: first, the moon apparently broke away from the earth as one large chunk; second, most of the water tied up in moon rock came from the earth; and third, the moon broke off the earth at a time when the earth already had water.[12]

In addition to the water originating in the earth, comets and meteors from the asteroid belt, described as "dirty snowballs," also pummeled both the earth and the moon, bringing water from outer space.[13] By 2.5 billion years ago, the entire earth was apparently covered in water. The snowball meteors hitting the earth were probably a mixture of silicate rock and ices—some but not all of which was water ice. That frozen mixture would make up the core of the meteor, which would be surrounded by a fragile, brittle crust of rock.[14]

Between the water inherently present in the primordial earth, which existed 4.6 billion years ago as the result of water-bearing planetesimal collisions, and additional water brought in to the earth by water-bearing meteorites over the next two billion years, there was enough water present to cover the entire surface of the earth around 2.5 billion years ago. This would be equivalent to a 15-year-old person being baptized at age 8, or an 80-year-old being baptized at age 43. That unitary ocean was more shallow than the oceans today. About one billion years ago, land appeared relatively quickly (from a geologic perspective) over about a 200 million-year period. The emergence of a large land mass caused changes in ocean currents, extreme weather conditions, and the emergence of seasons. Those changes, in turn probably contributed to the rise in atmospheric oxygen levels, which preceded the explosion of new life on earth about 500 million years ago.[15] Thus, following the earth's baptism, it was prepared for the emergence of plant and animal life on its dry land.

ENDNOTES

1. Brigham Young, "Religion, Progress, and Privileges of the Saints, &c," *Journal of Discourses*, 8:83, 1860.
2. F. Kent Nielson, "The Gospel and the Scientific View," *Ensign*, Sept., 1980.
3. James Barr, "Why the World Was Created in 4004 BC: Archbishop Ussher and Biblical Chronology," *Bulletin of the John Rylands University Library of Manchester*, 67:575–608, 1984.
4. N.H. Sleep, K. Zahnle, and P.S. Neuhoff, "Initiation of clement surface conditions on the earliest Earth," *Proceedings of the National Academy of Sciences,* 98:3666–3672, 2001.
5. Adam R. Sarafian, Sune G. Nielsen, Horst R. Marschall, Francis M. McCubbin, and Brian D. Monteleone, "Early accretion of water in the inner solar system from a carbonaceous chondrite–like source," *Science*, 346:623–626, 2014.
6. Zachary D. Sharp, *Principles of Stable Isotope Geochemistry* (Upper Saddle River, NJ: Prencie Hall, 2006).
7. C. T. Russell, et al., "Dawn at Vesta: Testing the Protoplanetary Paradigm," *Science*, 336: 684–686, 2012.
8. Nola Taylor Redd, "Asteroid Belt: Facts & Formation," space.com, May 4, 2017.
9. Andrew Fazekas, "Mystery of Earth"s Water Origin Solved," *National Geographic*, Oct. 30, 2014.
10. Planetary Science Institute, psi.edu/epo/faq/meteor.html, 2018.

11. Andrew Fazekas, "Mystery of Earth's Water Origin Solved," *National Geographic*, news.nationalgeographic.com, Oct. 30, 2014; also see the report of the actual study: Adam R. Sarafian, Sune G. Nielsen, Horst R. Marschall, Francis M. McCubbin, and Brian D. Monteleone, "Early accretion of water in the inner solar system from a carbonaceous chondrite–like source," *Science*, 346:623–626, 2014.
12. Alberto E. Saal, Erik H. Hauri, James A. Van Orman, and Malcolm J. Rutherford, "Hydrogen Isotopes in Lunar Volcanic Glasses and Melt Inclusions Reveal a Carbonaceous Chondrite Heritage," *Science*, 340:1317–1320, 2013.
13. James P. Greenwood, Shoichi Itoh, Naoyo Sakamoto, Paul Warren, Larence Taylor, and Hiyayoshi Yurimoto, "Hydrogen isotope ratios in lunar rocks indicate delivery of cometary water to the Moon," *Nature Geoscience*, 4:79–82, 2011.
14. M. M. Woolfson, *The Origin and Evolution of the Solar System*, The Graduate Series in Astronomy and Astrophysics, Book 6, Series Editors: M. Elvis and A. Natta (Bristol and Philadelphia, Institute of Physics Publishing, 2000).
15. Eldridge M. Moores, "Pre-1 Ga (pre-Rodinian) ophiolites: Their tectonic and environmental implications," *Geological Society of America Bulletin*, 114: 80–95, 2002.

CHAPTER 10

THE EARTH WAS PREPARED

We are told in the book of Abraham that the Gods planned for and then created the earth. We read initially that the early earth was empty and desolate: "And then the Lord said: Let us go down. And they went down at the beginning, and they, that is the Gods, organized and formed the heavens and the earth. And the earth, after it was formed, was empty and desolate, because they had not formed anything but the earth; and darkness reigned upon the face of the deep, and the Spirit of the Gods was brooding upon the face of the waters" (Abraham 4:1–2).

Then we are told that the earth was *prepared* to bring forth plants:

> And the Gods said: Let us prepare the earth to bring forth grass; the herb yielding seed; the fruit tree yielding fruit, after his kind, whose seed in itself yieldeth its own likeness upon the earth; and it was so, even as they ordered. And the Gods organized the earth to bring forth grass from its own seed, and the herb to bring forth herb from its own seed, yielding seed after his kind; and the earth to bring forth the tree from its own seed, yielding fruit, whose seed could only bring forth the same in itself, after his kind; and the Gods saw that they were obeyed. And it came to pass that they numbered the days; from the evening until the morning they called night; and it came to pass, from the morning until the evening they called day; and it was the third time. (Abraham 4:11–13; compare Moses 2:11–13 and Genesis 1:11–13)

I live on a ridge of loess—a silt-sized sediment formed by the accumulation of wind-blown dust[1]—blown into dunes along the Portneuf Valley about 10,000 years ago.[2] The native topsoil is only about an inch or two thick, and below that the soil is largely empty and desolate. Only the roots of our very hardy native juniper trees and sage brush have tapped into the loess for the precious little moisture contained there. In order for us to plant a garden, a shrub, or a tree, the soil must first be prepared. My wife and I love to garden. We prepare the ground for planting by digging deeply into the loess and then mixing in organic matter from compost.

In order to compost, we bring together organic matter such as leaves, grass clippings, and kitchen waste. Then we invite in local microorganisms to chew up those items. Bacteria are the most numerous and occupy the bottom of the microorganism food chain. Fungi, such as molds and yeast, help break down materials that bacteria cannot chew, such as woody material. Left to themselves, however, the bacteria and fungi can get out of control, so protozoans consume the bacteria and fungi—keeping them in check. But the protozoans can also get a bit out of control, so rotifers help control them and the bacteria. Last come the big guys. Earthworms not only help digest partly composted material, but they also dig tunnels in the compost, creating aeration and drainage systems. So where do we obtain all these little creatures? They're already there—right in the soil onto which we start the compost pile. Keep the pile watered and aerated, and the whole community is one big happy family—of course, we haven't personally interviewed the bacteria to see how they feel about being at the bottom of the food chain.[3]

It turns out that the Gods apparently *prepared* the earth to bring forth higher plants in almost exactly the same way, except that they started with much more difficult composting material—rocks. No problem, the Gods "created" bacteria and archaea (also single-celled organisms similar to bacteria but with unique properties) called lithotrophs—literally meaning "rock eaters"—that can chew up rocks and use the inorganic materials in them as sources of energy.[4] It takes time to make good compost, and it takes even longer to make compost from rocks—when there are no other living organisms except bacteria around. God had all of eternity to create the earth; He certainly did not have to rush the job and create the world in six days, or six thousand years. He created the laws of nature, those beautiful laws by which the miracle of life unfolded upon this earth—over millions of years—as the Gods declared every glorious step of that creation to be "good." By those laws, the Gods prepared the earth to bring forth the abundance of life. It feels so good to hold that well-prepared compost in my hands and use it to prepare loess to bring forth an abundance of plants. I can imagine shouting for joy as those early lithotrophs began to prepare the earth for more complex life-forms.

In 2016, Allen Nutman and his colleagues at the University of Wollongong, Australia, uncovered a 1–4-centimeter-thick layer of stromatolites in a recently exposed outcrop of 3.7 billion-year-old rocks in the Isua supracrustal belt (ISB) in southwest Greenland.[5] Stromatolites are structured calcium carbonate layers produced by bacteria. In this case, the microbial communities producing the stromatolite mats were living in a shallow marine environment, with evidence in the surrounding sediment of storm-generated waves, dating from the time when the earliest sediments were forming on Earth. These data provided evidence of the oldest life yet discovered on earth, and are consistent with genetic molecular clock data, placing the origin of microbial life on earth at approximately 4 billion years ago.[6] The presence of bacterial-produced stromatolites suggests shallow marine carbonate formation by bacteria from CO_2 available in the environment.[7] These single-celled bacteria remained the dominant life-forms on earth for about the next three billion years and were critical to breaking down the largely inorganic soil and providing an organic foundation for plants.

Not only were microorganisms breaking down the rocks to form soil, but the ocean itself was also at work. A while ago, my wife and I were strolling along the beautiful sandy beach of Diver's Cove at Laguna Beach, California. At one point along the beach, we stopped to ponder the inspiring beauty of smooth pebbles from the size of a marble to that of a baseball rolling up and down the beach with the surf. Those rolling stones, over millions of years, had been gradually worn down by the surf to form the sand of the beach. Each time the surf rolls in and the waves crash upon the shore, tiny fragments of stone are broken off and added to the sand. This beautiful natural process has been going on for billions of years all over the earth. Almost anyone who walks along the thousands of beaches around the world can thrill at the awesome splendor of the sand beneath their feet and the inspiring rhythm of waves rolling in and out along the coast.

We are told in the book of Abraham that the earth was *prepared* to bring forth plants (see Abraham 4:11). Modern research indicates that land plants first appeared 460–700 million years ago.[8] Those myriad plants filled the atmosphere with oxygen, the by-product of their respiration of

CO_2, with which the atmosphere was rich from the metabolism of huge amounts of bacteria and from geologic activity. Bacteria metabolize a wide range of substrates and many give off carbon dioxide and/or methane, among other molecules, as by-products. Volcanoes, which were very active in the young earth, also give off large amounts of gases, including CO_2. I find this correlation between the scriptures and modern science to be truly inspirational. The scriptures state that the Gods "prepared the earth" to bring forth plants, and modern science has shown us how that preparation was accomplished.

The O_2 produced by the plants prepared the oceans and the earth for the advancement of animal life on the planet.

> And the Gods said: Let us prepare the waters to bring forth abundantly the moving creatures that have life; and the fowl, that they may fly above the earth in the open expanse of heaven. And the Gods prepared the waters that they might bring forth great whales, and every living creature that moveth, which the waters were to bring forth abundantly after their kind; and every winged fowl after their kind. And the Gods saw that they would be obeyed, and that their plan was good. And the Gods said: We will bless them, and cause them to be fruitful and multiply, and fill the waters in the seas or great waters; and cause the fowl to multiply in the earth. . . . And the Gods prepared the earth to bring forth the living creature after his kind, cattle and creeping things, and beasts of the earth after their kind; and it was so, as they had said . . . and the Gods saw they would obey. (Abraham 4:20–22; 4:24–25)

The first fishes appeared about 500 million years ago.[9] Again, the correlation between the scriptures and science is inspiring, in that the Gods *prepared* the waters to bring forth the fishes. Just like land animals, fishes breathe in oxygen, but the oxygen they breathe is dissolved in the water. They were created with gills to efficiently extract that dissolved oxygen picked up from the atmosphere or produced by plant and microbial life in the water. Not all fish were created equally in terms of their oxygen needs, and fishes are extremely sensitive to water oxygen content in which they live. Among freshwater fishes, trout require about 14 mg/L dissolved oxygen and live in the upper reaches of the water column, whereas bass live in deeper water where the dissolved oxygen is 9–10 mg/L, perch live in water with an oxygen content of 7–8 mg/L, and pike live in very deep water, with an oxygen content of 3–4 mg/L. A similar story may be told of marine fishes; sea bass live in the water column where the oxygen content is 11–12 mg/L, whereas tuna live in much deeper water, where the oxygen content is 5–6 mg/L.[10]

The scriptures tell us that the waters brought forth "every living creature." That's the same story we're getting from modern science. Life on earth began in the oceans, and without a moon to cause tides, the transition from water to land would not have occurred. Not only do we live on a "Goldilocks" planet, just the right distance from the sun where everything is just right, but the moon also is part of that Goldilocks world.

The first vertebrate land animals appeared around 375 million years ago.[11] The first birds appeared on earth about 160 million years ago.[12] It may be debatable whether fishes are considered to be flesh—that's why for centuries, Catholics could eat fish on meatless Fridays. However, vertebrate land animals are certainly considered "flesh." There are literally billions of fossil fish and land animals, which attest to the beauty, splendor, and diversity of aquatic and terrestrial life millions of years ago.

Some members of the Church are concerned about taking the statement in Moses 3:7 literally as to the physical creation of humans: "And I, the Lord God, formed man from the dust of the ground, and breathed into his nostrils the breath of life; and man became a living soul, the first flesh upon the earth, the first man also; nevertheless, all things were before created; but spiritually were they created and made according to my word" (Moses 3:7).

In my opinion, it is important to ponder the last portion of that scripture, which reminds us that all things were created spiritually before they were created physically. In this context, it may be very likely that humans were the first *spiritual* creation of God but certainly not the first physical creation. It would not be wise for us to disregard the entire fossil record based on two words in the scriptures—and this is the only reference to "first flesh" in all the scriptures. The issue of Adam being the "first man" will be addressed elsewhere, as will the notion, advanced by some Church members that all the fossils we see came from some other planet.

I will also address the issue of "no death before the Fall" elsewhere. Suffice it to say here that if there was no death before the Fall, the earth would not have been *prepared* for our being here. Compost cannot be prepared without the death of the murid of plants put in to that compost. Without compost higher plants cannot survive. Without plants animals cannot survive. People who argue that there was no death before the Fall miss the fact that 98 percent of all species that have ever lived on the earth are now extinct—most long before humans came on the scene. Those billions of fossils that have been collected around the world—the vast majority of which were discovered in the past one hundred years or so—give enormous testimony to the splendor of the earth's infinite Creation.

ENDNOTES

1. M. Frechen, "Loess in Europe," *Quaternary Science Journal,* 60:3–5, 2011.
2. KL Pierce, MA Fosbergz, WE Scott, GC Lewis, and SM Colman, In, Bonnichsen, B and Breckenridge, RM, Cenozoic Geology of Idaho, *Idaho Bureau of Mines and Geology Bulletin*, 26:717–725, 1982.
3. Composting—Compost Microorganisms, Cornell University, compost.css.cornell.edu/microorg.html
4. Kenneth Chang, "Visions of Life on Mars in Earth's Depths," *The New York Times,* Sept. 12, 2016.
5. A.P. Nutman, V.C. Bennett, C.R.L. Friend, M.J. van Kranendonk, and A.R. Chivas, "Rapid emergence of life shown by discovery of 3,700–million-year-old microbial structures," *Nature*, 537:535–538, 2016.
6. S. B. Hedges, "The origin and evolution of model organisms," *Nat. Rev. Genet.* 3, 838–849, 2002.
7. A.P. Nutman, V. C. Bennett, C.R.L. Friend, M. J. van Kranendonk, M.J., and A.R. Chivas, "Rapid emergence of life shown by discovery of 3,700–million-year-old microbial structures," *Nature*, 537:535–538, 2016.
8. Daniel Heckman, DM Geiser, BR Eidell, RL Stauffer, NL Kardos, and SB Hedges, "Molecular evidence for the early colonization of land by fungi and plants," *Science* 293:1129–1133, 2001.
9. Simon Morris and Jean-Bernard Caron, "A Primitive Fish from the Cambrian of North America," *Nature* 512:419–422, 2014.
10. fondriest.com/environmental-measurements/parameters/water-quality/dissolved-oxygen
11. Edward Daeschler, NH Shubin, NH, and FA Jenkins Jr., "A Devonian Tetrapod-like Fish and the Evolution of the Tetrapod Body Plan," *Nature*, 440:757–76, 2006.
12. D.Y. Hu, L. Hou, L. Zhang, L., and X. Xu, "A pre-Archaeopteryx Troodontid Theropod from China with Long Feathers on the Metatarsals," *Nature*, 461:640–643, 2009.

CHAPTER 11

THE MICROSCOPIC CREATION

In his first epistle to the Corinthians, the Apostle Paul stated, "For now we see through a glass, darkly; but then face to face: now I know in part; but then shall I know even as also I am known" (1 Corinthians 13:12). The context of Paul's statement can be appreciated, at least in part, by what he had said a few verses earlier in that epistle: "For we know in part, and we prophesy in part. But when that which is perfect is come, then that which is in part shall be done away" (1 Corinthians 13:9–10). If we put Paul's statement into a more modern interpretation, what he was saying might be viewed as, "At present, our knowledge is imperfect, but someday our knowledge will be much more complete." (This interpretation is using one definition of perfect as complete.)

We still often quote Paul's statement to remind us that we are a very long way from knowing everything, from having a perfect knowledge, from knowing what God knows. Nonetheless, people have been polishing glass for nearly two thousand years since Paul made his famous statement, and we have learned a thing or two since then. Sometimes, in the twenty-first century, it is difficult for us to appreciate just how much people didn't know two thousand years ago.

Take, for example, the glass to which Paul referred. Paul's letters were written in Koine, or Hellenistic, Greek. The Greek word for glass is *hýalos*, meaning a transparent or see-through stone. So the closest the Greek language came to describing glass was as a clear stone—for example, quartz, which is usually translucent rather than transparent. Thus their vision through quartz was far from perfect. The Romans learned glass-making from the Greeks, but apparently didn't even have a name for glass (vitrum) until the first century AD. Early Roman glass was employed mainly for items such as drinking vessels and mosaic tiles, although some small amounts of window glass were produced. Most of this early glass was intensely colored, but during the first century AD, glass blowing and colorless or "aqua" glass were introduced. Most of this colorless glass, like the native quartz, was more translucent than transparent, and window glass was produced in very small pieces and provided a distorted image at best. Early glass was considered a luxury item, was very expensive, and was not readily available. It is certainly possible that the glass to which Paul referred was a colored glass vessel rather than a window. He would have been amazed at the modern *perfection* of the glass industry allowing for the construction of entire buildings facades of perfectly clear glass.[1]

Blown plate window glass was manufactured as early as the fourteenth century but still emerged as wavy glass in relatively small pieces and quantities. According to an anonymous 1899 *Scientific American* review, mirrors produced by this technique were "good for nothing but reflecting the shaggy faces of antiquarians." Modern, fully transparent glass produced by casting, or pouring plate glass, was invented in France in 1688 by Louis Lucas de Nehou and Abraham Thevart.[2]

About the same time that plate glass was being invented, Antonie Philips van Leeuwenhoek took the concept of seeing through glass to a whole new level, revealing a world unimagined by any previous generation. Leeuwenhoek was a Dutch draper who started making magnifying lenses to better visualize the weave in his draperies. By the 1670s, he had perfected lens polishing to the point where he could see what is now called microscopic life with his single-lens microscope. Leeuwenhoek called the tiny creatures that he discovered, moving about, seemingly everywhere, *animalcules*. Leeuwenhoek also was the first to discover bacteria, spermatozoa, muscle fibers, red blood cells, and blood flow through capillaries.[3]

Perhaps Leeuwenhoek's most famous statement came in 1674, after he had examined a drop of lake water:

> I now saw very plainly that these were little eels, or worms, lying all huddled up together and wriggling just as if you saw, with the naked eye, a whole tubful of little eels and water, with the eels squirming among one another; and the whole water seemed to be alive with these multifarious animalcules.

> This was for me, among all the marvels that I have discovered in nature, the most marvelous of all; and I must say, for my part, that no more pleasant sight has ever yet come before my eyes that these many thousand of living creatures seen all alive in a little drop of water, moving among one another, each several creature having its own proper motion.[4]

A seventeenth-century British contemporary of Leeuwenhoek, Robert Hooke, turned his single-lens microscope to this "unseen" world and published his meticulously illustrated book, *Micrographia*, in 1665, which became an overnight sensation. Hooke described this new microscopic world, including the tiny hairs of a stinging nettle, a flea, and the little honeycomb-shaped rooms of a section of cork, which he called cells.[4]

Two lens-makers, Zacharias Jansen and his father, Hans, put lenses into the ends of a tube in 1595 and invented the compound microscope.[5] But the compound microscope did not come into practical use until Joseph Lister solved the problem of spherical aberration (light bending at different angles depending on where it passes through the lens) in 1830 by placing lenses at precise distances from each other.[4] By Lister's advancement, the light microscope was becoming perfected—in a very real sense of Paul's seeing through a glass. Today, thanks to the work of inventors and manufacturers such as Ernst Leitz, Carl Zeiss, and others, the variety of modern light microscopes has reached a level of *perfection* previously unimagined.[4]

But, as it turns out, not even Paul, who could only "prophesy in part" (1 Corinthians 13:9), knew that glass and light have their limitations when it comes to seeing the microscopic world. Light is limited by its wavelength to magnify only objects of 0.2 microns or larger (500x to 1000x magnification; a human cell is around 7–20 microns across). In 1931, Max Knoll and Ernst Ruska invented the electron microscope, in which electrons, focused by magnets, are either passed through (transmission electron microscope, TEM) or bounced off the surface (scanning electron microscope, SEM) of specially prepared specimens. TEMs can magnify an object up to two million times its actual size.[6]

Modern microscopic research has revealed that each person has around 30–35 trillion (3×10^{13}) human cells in his or her body.[7] That means that there are more than 100 times as many cells in a single human being than there are stars in the Milky Way Galaxy (200 billion; 2×10^{11}).[8] You have more cells in your little finger than there are visible stars in the night sky

(10,000). Equally amazing, it turns out that we each carry around about as many bacterial cells as human cells.[7] Most of the bacterial cells we transport are not harmful; on the contrary, many are critical to normal health. To boggle the mind even further, each cell contains around 100 trillion atoms.[9] Taken all together, each individual person carries around over 10,000 times more atoms than there are stars in the known universe. The complexity of the unseen world is almost incomprehensible, yet it is very real.

The nucleus of each human cell is around six microns in diameter. The DNA (deoxyribonucleic acid) in each human cell nucleus is divided into forty-six pieces, which, during nuclear and cell division super coil to form forty six chromosomes (colored bodies) that can be seen under a microscope in a stained cell preparation. The basic building blocks of a DNA strand are called bases, and because DNA naturally forms a double helix, the bases are paired.[10] The DNA in each human cell is comprised of three billion base pairs, and the DNA strand from a single cell if stretched out completely is over six feet long. All the DNA in all the cells of a single human being, placed end to end, could encircle the entire solar system twice.[11] All of that DNA is supercoiled, along with proteins that regulate the coiling and uncoiling of the DNA as well as the transcription and translation of the message to synthesize new proteins, into the space of a six-micron nucleus.

I am aware that many people struggle to wrap their heads around the concept of DNA and chromosomes. Perhaps an analogy might help. We may think of the bases in DNA as letters in a sentence—the DNA. Each word in the sentence may be thought of as a gene within the DNA strand. Genes, just like the words in a sentence, tell us our characteristics. For example, "brown hair" are two genes that help make a person's hair brown. Sentences are woven together into chapters—the chromosomes—and forty-six chapters make the human book. Even the gaps between the words and the punctuation marks are coded into a DNA strand.

It turns out that there are only 171,476 words in the English language. Yet, from those 171,476 words, more than 130 million books have been written so far—and the rate is increasing. Each year, in our modern world, there are around one million new books being published in the US alone. Likewise, there are only around 20,000 genes in the human genome (the assemblage of all genes), and yet there are 8.7 million known species of eukaryotes (plants and animals with nuclei in their cells) on earth today. That number probably represents only 20 percent of the actual number living today (The other 80 percent hasn't even been identified. Nearly every time someone shakes a tree in the Amazon, new species of insects fall out that haven't as yet been named), and maybe only 1 percent of all the organisms (plants, animals, bacteria, and archaea) that have ever lived.

Most of the words in any two given books are the same—just appearing in different orders, but there are also a number of words that appear in one book but not the other. Likewise in living organisms. When the mouse genome is compared to that of humans, about 98 percent of the genes are the same, with only about 2 percent found in one species but not the other.[12] Most of the genes are not different but show up in different orders and on different chromosomes (in different chapters of the books).

DNA and RNA are the basis of all life no matter how small. In human cells, called eukaryotic cells, most of the DNA is contained in the nucleus. Bacterial cells, by comparison, have no nucleus and are called prokaryotic cells. Each bacterium is about ten times smaller than a human cell and has only around one thousandth the amount of DNA—contained in one single, circular chromosome.[13] As described in the previous chapter, the fossils of single-celled microorganisms in a shallow marine environment have been discovered in 3.7 billion-year-old rocks.[14] Those single-celled bacteria remained the dominant life-forms on earth for about three billion years.

But bacteria were not the first life on planet Earth. In 2017, Matthew Dodd and colleagues described possible fossilized traces of archaea microorganisms that are at least 3.770 billion years old and possibly even as old as 4.280 billion years. Those fossils were found in iron-containing sedimentary rocks, "interpreted as seafloor-hydrothermal vent-related precipitates, from the Nuvvuagittuq belt in Quebec, Canada."[15] Although some scientists are skeptical of the Dodd group's interpretation of their data,[16] such a source for the earliest life on Earth is very likely.

God created the laws (or, more probably from what we know about God, obeyed and applied the eternal laws of nature) that govern the characteristics of life. Once those criteria were met, life exploded all over the earth. The most basic, and one might argue, the first law of life, is that life is built upon the special chemistry of water and carbon. Perhaps the second law of life is that life is largely based upon four key families of chemicals: carbohydrates (sugars), lipids (fats), amino acids (the building blocks of protein), and nucleic acids (the building blocks of RNA and DNA). Any successful model of abiogenesis, or prebiogenesis, must encompass the origins and interactions of those four families of molecules. It should be kept in mind, however, that life was initially created on Earth under conditions that are strikingly different from those we see today.[17] The third law of life might be that life is encapsulated, surrounded by a semipermeable membrane.

Since the early 1950s, scientists have been trying to discover those laws and how life began on Earth. In 1953, Stanley Miller described a series of experiments in which he and his associate, Harold Urey, attempted to simulate conditions that they believed existed in the early earth, and synthesize molecules thought to be critical to life.[18] In the so-called Miller-Urey experiment, they started with methane, ammonia, and hydrogen in a sealed, sterile, five-liter spherical flask connected to a second five-hundred-milliliter flask half-filled with water. The water in the smaller flask was heated to boiling, and the released water vapor was piped to the larger flask. Therein, electrical sparks were shot between electrodes to simulate lightning in the water vapor-methane-ammonia-hydrogen atmosphere. The atmosphere was then cooled, and the condensed water was collected in a U-shaped trap below the larger flask. After one week of percolation, the mixture in the collecting trap was analyzed by paper chromatography—the best analytical equipment they had at the time. Miller identified five amino acids in the solution: solution: glycine, α-alanine, ß-alanine, aspartic acid, and α-aminobutyric acid.

In subsequent studies, Miller was able to synthesize eleven of the twenty amino acids essential to living cells.[19] Recent studies by Brooks and others have examined the amino acid coding regions in the "oldest" sections of ancient genes—those genes common to widely different extant species descended from an assumed "last universal ancestor." Those studies revealed that the amino acids coded for by the DNA in those regions were the very amino acids most commonly produced in the Miller-Urey experiments. These results suggest that the earliest genetic code was based on coding for a smaller number of amino acids than common in modern cells.[20]

Furthermore, after Miller's death in 2007, one of his former students, Jeffrey Bada, inherited sealed sample vials from the original study. Examination of the content of those vials employing more sophisticated, modern analyses, identified far more amino acids in those solutions than Miller had originally discovered. These new data demonstrated that although his experiments were successful, Miller was never able to discover, with the equipment available to him at the time, the full extent of his success. With the more sophisticated equipment, a total of twenty-five amino acids have been identified resulting from those original investigations.[21]

In addition to the original experiments, Miller conducted other studies. One designed to simulate conditions in deep-sea volcanic vents involved a nozzle that sprayed a jet of steam into the electrical spark. Eleven vials from that study were sealed and not examined until 2008, at which time modern techniques of high-performance liquid chromatography and mass spectrometry revealed more organic molecules than Miller had discovered. Those experiments demonstrated that the volcano-like environment produced more amino acids (twenty-two), in addition to five amines and many hydroxylated molecules. These results suggest that deep-sea volcanic vent regions became rich in organic molecules, and with carbonyl sulfide, peptides may have been produced.[22]

In a review of the origin-of-life conundrum, Robert Service stated,

> The origin of life on Earth is a set of paradoxes. In order for life to have gotten started, there must have been a genetic molecule—something like DNA or RNA—capable of passing along blueprints for making proteins [made from amino acids], the workhorse molecules of life. But modern cells can't copy DNA and RNA without the help of proteins themselves. To make matters more vexing, none of these molecules can do their jobs without fatty lipids, which provide the membranes that cells need to hold their contents inside. And in yet another chicken-and-egg complication, protein-based enzymes (encoded by genetic molecules) are needed to synthesize lipids.[23]

All of the hypothetical models for pre-biotic chemistry leading to life-giving molecules were based on either–or assumptions. The early world was either an RNA world or an amino acid world. But recently, a team of researchers led by John Sutherland set out to envisage a world where the three critical components—nucleic acids, amino acids, and lipids—could all be created from a common, simple starting point *at the same time*. They found that an environment of hydrogen cyanide (HCN) and hydrogen sulfide (H_2S), powered by ultraviolet (UV) light, could provide the key ingredients. The Sutherland team stated, "We show that precursors of ribonucleotides, amino acids and lipids can all be derived by the reductive homologation of hydrogen cyanide and some of its derivatives, and thus that all the cellular subsystems could have arisen simultaneously through common chemistry."[24]

Conditions on the early earth were favorable for the chemical reactions described by the Sutherland team. Hydrogen cyanide and hydrogen sulfide were both apparently common in the young earth, and there was apparently plenty of UV radiation—all the right ingredients in just the right amounts to start the prebiotic world on its course toward life.[26] Once more, the earth was in a Goldilocks state; everything was just right and prepared for the earth to bring forth life.

"And the Gods said: Let us prepare the waters to bring forth abundantly the moving creatures that have life; and the fowl, that they may fly above the earth in the open expanse of heaven. And the Gods prepared the waters that they might bring forth great whales, and every living creature that moveth, which the waters were to bring forth abundantly after their kind; and every winged fowl after their kind. And the Gods saw that they would be obeyed, and that their plan was good" (Abraham 4:20–21).

There were many other ingredients involved in preparing the earth to bring forth every living creature. One of the most important of these came from the very rocks of the earth itself—phosphorus. Phosphorus and the sugar ribose form the backbone of RNA (ribonucleic acid) and links all the nucleic acids together; likewise, phosphorus and deoxyribose form the backbone of DNA (deoxyribonucleic acid), so without phosphorus there would be no RNA or DNA. Furthermore, three phosphorus molecules linked to one nucleic acid, adenine, forms adenosine triphosphate (ATP), the energy currency of life itself. And more, phosphorus attached to lipids make them phospholipids, the key ingredients in cell membranes.[10]

In the modern world, glycolysis (the Embden-Meyerhof pathway), which is the pathway by which sugars are broken following digestion to produce ATP (the cell's energy currency), requires a number of enzyme-catalyzed steps.[10] In 2014, Keller and colleagues demonstrated that under conditions of the early earth, glycolysis and pentose phosphate synthesis (a key components of nucleic acids) can occur in the presence of iron—which is thought to be a major mineral component of the early ocean.[25]

A major step in the creation of life is the sequestering of life's chemical ingredients into a semiconfined package—the cell. In a 2018 paper, Elkin Lopez-Fontal and colleagues proposed that confinement of complex chemical reactions, such as those necessary for life "stabilizes complex self-assembled structures. . . . The confinement effect renders complex self-assembled species robust and persistent under conditions where they do not form in bulk solution. . . . Therefore, we believe that the confinement effect described here would have played an important role in shaping the increase of chemical complexity within protocells during the first stages of abiogenesis."[26]

Abiogenesis is the chemical processes necessary for life, which functioned for millions of years on earth to prepare the earth to produce life. The Gods commanded the earth to bring forth life and then waited to see "that they would be obeyed, and that their plan was good" (Abraham 4:20–21). Many scientists have dismissed God from the creative process because the abiogenic chemical reactions can bring about life spontaneously, given the proper conditions. But those scientists fail to appreciate who made the laws that we call "natural" and who put all the ingredients together in just the right combinations for life to evolve. Who made the laws that built the three bears' cabin into which Goldilocks wandered? Where is the law without the lawgiver? Furthermore, the transition from abiotic, or prebiotic, conditions on Earth to the creation of living organisms did not occur as a single event but, rather, was a gradual process of increasing complexity, as more and more complex laws of nature were enjoined—laws we have yet to discover.[27]

In addition to meteorites bringing water to the fledgling earth, some of the early molecular building blocks necessary for the prebiotic reactions leading to life also may have come to Earth from outer space. During the early phases of planet building, all of the matter on Earth came from interstellar gas and dust. We are literally made of star dust. Then as the earth began to cool, larger molecules, including complex organic molecules, reached the earth in the dirty snowballs of comets and meteorites—tied up in the icy cores—and contributed to the growing complexity of the prebiotic molecular mix.[28] Delivery of those extraterrestrial molecules may have made a significant contribution to the complex organic inventory critical to the origin of life. Complex organic molecules have been discovered via astronomical observations to be ubiquitous within the molecular clouds of interstellar space. Of these clouds, Pascale Ehrenfreund and Jan Cami have stated, "Interstellar molecular clouds and circumstellar envelopes are factories of complex molecular synthesis. A surprisingly large number of molecules that are used in contemporary biochemistry on Earth are found in the interstellar medium, planetary atmospheres and surfaces, comets, asteroids and meteorites, and interplanetary dust particles."[29]

It has been the objective of a number of scientists for many years to discover the laws necessary to create an artificial cell in the laboratory.

A major step in that direction was taken in 2001, when David Deamer and colleagues demonstrated that phospholipids could be produced in their laboratories starting from simple molecules such as likely existed on the early Earth and in icy comets striking the earth, and with UV light as an energy source. Those phospholipids, in turn, could self-assemble into spherical vesicles.[30] Other laboratory simulations by that group have demonstrated that phospholipid vesicles can not only spontaneously form, but can readily encapsulate functional life-promoting macromolecules, such as nucleic acids and polymerases (protein enzymes involved in assembling nucleic acids into RNA or DNA).[31] Then in 2004, Reza Mozafari and colleagues demonstrated in their laboratory that phospholipids can also self-assemble into vesicles even at high temperatures that simulate the conditions of the deep sea hydrothermal systems—a likely candidate where life may have begun on Earth.[32]

In order for a phospholipid vesicle to begin functioning like a cell, not only do reactions have to be contained within the vesicle, but there must also be selective communication with the vesicle's (cell's) immediate environment. This communication involves selective permeability of the vesicular membrane. In 2007, David Deamer's group demonstrated that they could construct an artificial phospholipid membrane sufficiently permeable to allow certain molecules—some as large as nucleoside triphosphates (NTPs, such as ATP, which is not only the energy currency of the cell but the building blocks for RNA and DNA) to enter the vesicle.[33]

Perhaps the leading model of life's origin on Earth is the so-called RNA world model, which proposes that, early on in Earth's history, RNA was the molecule controlling both the self-replication and organizational template for prebiotic biochemistry.[34] It has been proposed that the abundant inorganic clay available in the early Earth may have provided the first templates for nucleotide assembly into RNA chains. In 2011, Anand Subramaniam and colleagues reported that stable, inorganic, semi-permeable vesicles can be easily created from a natural plate-like clay mineral that is common and widely available on Earth. Such clay vesicles can function as inorganic catalysts for the creation of lipid membranes and RNA polymerization—joining nucleotides to form longer chains.[35]

In 2017, Martin Van Kranendonk, David Deamer, and Tara Djokic teamed up to propose that life may have started in hot pools on land, like those at Yellowstone Park, where the edges go through repeated wet-dry cycles. The hot, wet periods mixed the early macromolecules around, creating all sorts of combinations, and the dry periods marooned the mixtures in tiny lipid-clay cavities where they could interact and concentrate. The team proposed that hydrothermal ponds were common on the early earth's surface. Deamer conducted a field experiment in a natural hot pool by dumping in a small amount of four specific amino acids, the four nucleotides that form nucleic acids, phosphate, glycerol, and lipid. Within minutes after the cocktail was poured into the hot pool, "white, frothy foam [of tiny vesicles] emerged around the spring's edges." In the laboratory, Deamer and colleagues mixed nucleotides and lipids in wet-dry cycles at high temperatures. "The result: longer polymers [of nucleic acids] ranging from 10 to more than 100 nucleotides in length." Thus, hot pools, with dry-wet cycles seem to be good candidates for where life on Earth may have started.[36] I'm betting that someday soon, Deamer's team, or some other group, will put all the puzzle pieces together to build the first true synthetic protocell.

I was five years old when the results of the first Miller–Urey experiments were published, and I was probably about thirteen or fourteen when I first read about them. I was incredibly excited by what I learned and wanted to repeat the experiments myself. My dad owned a dairy farm with the first bulk milk tank in the Raft River Valley. The milk from the cows ran through glass tubes into a one-foot diameter glass sphere before going on to the bulk tank for cold storage. That glass sphere was almost exactly like the one described in the Miller–Urey experiment, and on more than one occasion, I cast a felonious eye on that precious sphere. But I also knew it was vital to our dairy business. Alas, I never put together the equipment to repeat that famous study.

I never saw the Miller–Urey data as anything but exciting new information. I never saw those data as a challenge to my religious beliefs. I feel exactly the same about all the other exciting data I have discussed in this and other chapters in this book. I am well aware that several famous scientists cite these data as supporting their beliefs as atheists. I have great respect for those scientists, and have read their opinions with great interest. I do not have to agree with someone's opinion to read it, enjoy it, and respect it.

Atheism is not science, it is religion—or anti-religion. The opinions of scientists are not science but become philosophy when discussing opinions not directly related to the data being presented. Discovering laws says nothing about where or under what circumstances those laws originated.

Science, while having a foundation in philosophy, goes way beyond the limits of simple philosophy to generating data, which reveal the truths about the previously hidden mysteries of the universe. Science is impartial. It doesn't care about your beliefs. Truth is revealed through science if the right questions are asked.

It has always been my belief that God created the universe. Even more exciting, we apparently helped in that creation. My religion teaches me these truths. It is also my belief that science can teach us how the Gods created the universe. Science can reveal the methods by which the Gods enacted this marvelous creation. Through science we can learn the truths about the laws employed and through religion we can learn the truths about the lawgiver.

In the book of Alma we learn of a preacher named Korihor who "began to preach unto the people that there should be no Christ. And after this manner did he preach, saying: O ye that are bound down under a foolish and a vain hope, why do ye yoke yourselves with such foolish things? Why do ye look for a Christ? For no man can know of anything which is to come . . . How do ye know of their surety? Behold, ye cannot know of things which ye do not see; therefore ye cannot know that there shall be a Christ . . . it is the effect of a frenzied mind; and this derangement of your minds comes because of the traditions of your fathers, which lead you away into a belief of things which are not so" (Alma 30:12–16).

Further, we are told in Alma that Korihor taught the people that "there could be no atonement made for the sins of men, but every man fared in this life according to the management of the creature; therefore every man prospered according to his genius, and that every man conquered according to his strength; and whatsoever a man did was no crime. And thus he did preach unto them, leading away the hearts of many, causing them to lift up their heads in their wickedness, yea, leading away many women, and also men, to commit whoredoms—telling them that when a man was dead, that was the end thereof" (Alma 30:17–18).

In modern times, these teachings have been called Social Darwinism—a philosophy, not a science, although painted and presented in the guise of science. One of the early proponents of this concept was Charles Darwin's cousin, Francis Galton, who coined the term eugenics (good genetics), which prompted some of the worst "science" ever conducted and which ultimately promoted the idea in Nazi Germany that some people benefited society and deserved to live, while others, who did not benefit society, deserved to die.[37]

Today many people will, almost word for word, repeat the preaching of Korihor. From such turn away. Although a number of famous scientists teach atheism under the guise of science, do not be fooled by their philosophies. Remember that they have no idea where the laws they are discovering originated, and they dismiss God because of philosophy, not science. Remember the wise council of Jacob: "O that cunning plan of the evil one! O the vainness, and the frailties, and the foolishness of men! When they are learned they think they are wise, and they hearken not unto the counsel of God, for they set it aside, supposing they know of themselves, wherefore, their wisdom is foolishness and it profiteth them not. And they shall perish. But to be learned is good if they hearken unto the counsels of God" (2 Nephi 9:28–29).

ENDNOTES

1. E. M. Stern, "Roman Glassblowing in a Cultural Context," *American Journal of Archaeology*, 103: 441–484, 1999.
2. Anonymous, *Scientific American Supplement*, 1202: 19270–19272, Jan. 14, 1899.
3. Clifford Dobell, *Antony van Leewenhoek and His "Little Animals": being some account of the father of protozoology and bacteriology and his multifarious discoveries in these disciplines*, (New York: Dover, 1932; 1960).
4. microscope.com/education-center/microscopes-101/history-of-microscopes
5. history-of-the-microscope.org/hans-and-zacharias-jansen-microscope-history.php
6. Tim Palucka, "Overview of Electron Microscopy," caltech.edu/5456/1/hrst.mit.edu/hrs/materials/public/ElectronMicroscope/EM_HistOverview.ht
7. R. Sender, S. Fuchs, and R. Milo, "Revised Estimates for the Number of Human and Bacteria Cells in the Body," *PLoS Biol*, 19:14: e1002533, Aug. 19, 2016.
8. space.com
9. *thoughtco.com*, March 6, 2017.
10. R. R. Seeley, T. D. Stephens, and P. Tate, *Anatomy and Physiology*, 8th edition (Dubuque : McGraw-Hill, 2007).
11. sciencefocus.com Jul. 18, 2011.
12. RJ Mural RJ, et al. "A comparison of whole-genome shotgun-derived mouse chromosome 16 and the human genome," *Science*, 296:1661–1671, 2002.
13. lehigh.edu/~jas0/G16.html

14. A.P. Nutman, V.C. Bennett, C.R.L. Friend, M.J. van Kranendonk, and A.R. Chivas, "Rapid emergence of life shown by discovery of 3,700–million-year-old microbial structures," *Nature,* 537:535–538, 2016.
15. Matthew S. Dodd, et. al. "Evidence for early life in Earth's oldest hydrothermal vent precipitates," *Nature*, 543:60–64, 2017.
16. Carl Zimmer, "Scientists Say Canadian Bacteria Fossils May Be Earth's Oldest," *New York Times*, Mar. 1, 2017, nytimes.com/2017/03/01/science/earths-oldest-bacteria-fossils.html
17. Peter Ward and Joe Kirschvink, *A New History of Life: the Radical Discoveries About the Origins and Evolution of Life on Earth* (London: Bloomsbury Press, 2015).
18. Stanley L. Miller, "Production of Amino Acids Under Possible Primitive Earth Conditions," *Science,* 117:528–9, 1953.
19. Exobiology: An Interview with Stanley L. Miller, *Accessexcellence.org*
20. D. J. Brooks, J.R. Fresco, A. M. Lesk, and M. Singh, "Evolution of amino acid frequencies in proteins over deep time: inferred order of introduction of amino acids into the genetic code," *Molecular Biology and Evolution,* 19:1645–1655, 2002.
21. *he Spark of Life*, TV documentary, BBC 4, Aug. 26, 2009.
22. A. P. Johnson, H. J. Cleaves, J. P. Dworkin, D. P. Glavin, A. Lazcano, and J. L. Bada, "The Miller volcanic spark discharge experiment," *Science,* 322:404, 2008; "Lost Miller-Urey Experiment Created More of Life's Building Blocks," *Science Daily,* Oct. 17, 2008.
23. Robert F. Service, "Researchers may have solved origin-of-life conundrum," sciencemag.org/news/2015/03/researchers-may-have-solved-origin-life-conundrum, 2015.
24. B. H. Patel, C. Percivalle, D. J. Ritson, C. D. Duffy, and J. D. Sutherland, "Common origins of RNA, protein and lipid precursors in a cyanosulfidic protometabolism," *Nat. Chem.*, 7:301–307, 2015.
25. Markus A. Keller, Alexandra V. Turchyn, Alexandra V., and Markus Ralser, "Non-enzymatic glycolysis and pentose phosphate pathway-like reactions in a plausible Archean ocean," *Molecular Systems Biology,* 10:725, DOI 10.1002/msb.20145228, 2014.
26. Elkin Lopez-Fontal, Anna Grochmal, Tom Foran, Lilia, Milanesi, and Salvador Tomas, "Salvador, Ship in a bottle:confinement-promoted self-assembly," *Chem. Sci.*, 9:1760–1768, 2018.
27. Elizabeth Howell, "How Did Life Become Complex, and Could It Happen Beyond Earth?", *Astrobiology Magazine,* Dec. 8, 2014; astrobio.net/origin-and-evolution-of-life/life-become-complex-happen-beyond-earth
28. J. Oró, *Nature,* 190:389–390, 1961; A. H. Delsemme, *Origins Life,* 14:51–60, 1984; E. Anders, *Nature,* 342:255–257, 1989; C. F. Chyba, and C. Sagan, *Nature,* 355:125–131, 1992

29. Pascale Ehrenfreund and Jan Cami, "Cosmic Carbon Chemistry: From the Interstellar Medium to the Early Earth ,"*Cold Spring Harbor Perspectives in Biology* (Cold Spring Harbor, NY: Cold Spring Harbor Laboratory Press, 2010), 2:a002097.
30. J. P. Dworkin, D. W. Deamer, S. A. Sandford, and L. J. Allamandola, "Self-assembling amphiphilic molecules: synthesis in simulated interstellar/precometary ices," *Proc. Natl. Acad. Sci. USA*, 98:815– 819, 2001.
31. David Deamer, Jason P. Dworkin, Scott A. Sandford, Max P. Bernstein, and Louis J. Allamandola, "The First Cell Membranes," *Astrobiology*, 2:371–381, 2002.
32. M. Reza Mozafari, Celia Reed, and Christopher Rostroni, "Formation of the Initial Cell Membranes Under Primordial Earth Conditions," *Cell. Mol. Biol. Lett.*, 9:97–99, 2004.
33. Pierre-Alain Monnard, Andrej Luptak, David W. Deamer, "Models of primitive cellular life: polymerases and templates in liposomes," *Philos Trans R Soc Lond B Biol Sci*, 362:1741–1750, 2007.
34. Eric Smith and Harold J. Morowitz, *The Origin and Nature of Life on Earth: The Emergence of the Fourth Geosphere* (New York: Cambridge University Press, 2016).
35. Anand Bala Subramaniam, Jiandi Wan, Arvind Gopinath, and Howard A. Stone, "Semi-permeable vesicles composed of natural clay," *Soft Matter*, Issue 6, 2011, http://pubs.rsc.org/en/content/articlelanding/2011/sm/c0sm01354d#!divAbstract Issue 6, 2011
36. Martin J. Van Kranendonk, David W. Deamer, and Tara Djokic, "Life Springs," *Scientific American*, 28–35, Aug. 2017.
37. Diane Paul, "Darwin, social Darwinism and eugenics," In, Hodge, Jonathan, and Radick, Gregory, *The Cambridge Companion to Darwin,* Cambridge University Press, Cambridge, 2006.

CHAPTER 12

THE EONS OF EARTH

In the priesthood session of the October 2016 general conference, President Henry B. Eyring stated:

> My father . . . was a seasoned and wise holder of the Melchizedek Priesthood. Once he was asked by an Apostle to write a short note about the scientific evidence for the age of the earth. He wrote it carefully, knowing that some who might read it had strong feelings that the earth was much younger than the scientific evidence suggested.
>
> I still remember my father handing me what he had written and saying to me, "Hal, you have the spiritual wisdom to know if I should send this to the apostles and prophets." I can't remember much of what the paper said, but I will carry with me forever the gratitude I felt for a great Melchizedek Priesthood holder who saw in me spiritual wisdom that I could not see.[1]

The Apostle to whom President Eyring referred was Adam S. Bennion. President Eyring's father was Dr. Henry Eyring, an internationally renowned chemist. And the "short note" was dated December 16, 1954. The note is now in possession of the Henry Eyring family, and a photocopy was included in Steven H. Heath's M.A. thesis, "Henry Eyring, Mormon Scientist," at the University of Utah in 1980. The note stated,

> Here I will briefly sketch a few of the more or less familiar lines of evidence on the age of the earth. The world is filled with radioactive clocks which can be read with varying accuracy but usually within ten

> percent or so and often considerably better. The principle involved is essentially simple. The heaviest elements such as uranium are unstable and fly apart sending out particles which can be counted in a Geiger Counter. From the number of counts one can tell how much of the radio-active substance one has. As the substance continues to decompose, the counts decrease, always remaining proportional to the number of particles not yet decomposed. Now the particles that are shot out are helium so that if the decomposing uranium is enclosed in a rock this helium will also be entrapped. Thus by determining how much helium is entrapped and how much uranium is present in the rocks one can tell exactly how long it has been since the rocks were laid down in their present form, since it always takes exactly the same amount of time for a given fraction of the uranium to decompose. There is another check on this. Each time a uranium atom decomposes it leaves a lead atom behind as well as ejecting the helium atom. Thus the ratio of these residual lead atoms to uranium is another wonderful clock. Four and one half billion years must elapse in order that half of the uranium present will be gone. Half of what remains will decompose in another four and a half billion years and so on. Thosium, another radioactive clock, has a half-life of fourteen billion years and there are a variety of other long time clocks as well as some short time ones like carbon fourteen with a half-life of five and one half thousand years. The radioactive clocks, together with the orderly way many sediments containing fossils are laid down, prove that the earth is billions of years old. In my judgement anyone who denies this orderly decomposition of sediments with their built in radioactive clocks places himself in a scientifically untenable position.[2]

What has happened to radiometric dating since 1954? As with almost every field of science since that time: improvement, improvement, improvement. We now have well over a dozen different radiometric dating methods, many of which can be used to provide multiple testing methods on the same sample. For example, metamorphic rock (called gneiss) in western Greenland has been dated to 3.56 ± 0.10 million years ago by lead-lead dating and 3.6 ± 0.05 million years ago by uranium-lead dating.[3] Based on those figures, the internal error rate for lead-lead dating is 2.8 percent, and the internal error rate for uranium-lead dating is 1.4 percent (compared to the 10 percent stated by Dr. Eyring in 1954). The between method error rate, comparing the lead-lead to uranium-lead method, is 1.1 percent. To bring Dr. Eyring's statement more up to date, one can now state that anyone who denies the data obtained from these radioactive clocks places himself in a highly "scientifically untenable position," which is ten times more untenable than it was in 1954. Anyone who dismisses radiometric dating on the grounds that there is variation (at least all those that I have read) always fails to state the range of variation. Of course there is variation in radiometric dating, in the range of 1.1 percent to 2.8 percent.

Given what we know today about radiometric dating, I will proceed to discuss the eons of earth's history from a modern scientific perspective. If the reader wishes to check the accuracy of the individual dates, he or she is encouraged to read the original material cited in the footnotes.

In the April 1988 general conference, Boyd K. Packer, of the Quorum of the Twelve Apostles, said,

> We look up, and in the universe we see the handiwork of God and measure things by epochs, by eons, by dispensations, by eternities. The many things we do not know we take on faith.
>
> But this we know! It was all planned before the world was. Events from the Creation to the final, winding-up scene are not based on *chance;* they are based on *choice!* It was planned that way.
>
> This we know! This simple truth! Had there been no Creation, no Fall, there should have been no need for any Atonement, neither a Redeemer to mediate for us. Then Christ need not have been.[4]

The Merriam-Webster dictionary gives three definitions of eon: 1) "an immeasurably or indefinitely long period of time," 2) "a very large division of geologic time usually longer than an era," and 3) "a unit of geologic time equal to one [approximately] billion years."[5]

The word *eon* is not found in the scriptures. Of the eons involved in the earth's creation, Genesis says, "In the beginning God created the heaven and the earth. And the earth was without form, and void; and darkness was upon the face of the deep. And the Spirit of God moved upon the face of the waters (Genesis 1:1–2).

We read in Moses, "And the earth was without form, and void; and I caused darkness to come up upon the face of the deep; and my Spirit moved upon the face of the water; for I am God" (Moses 2:2).

We are given more information in the book of Abraham: "And then the Lord said: Let us go down. And they went down at the beginning, and they, that is the Gods, organized and formed the heavens and the earth. And the earth, after it was formed, was empty and desolate, because they had not formed anything but the earth; and darkness reigned upon the face of the deep, and the Spirit of the Gods was brooding upon the face of the waters" (Abraham 4:1–2). "And the Gods came down and formed these the generations of the heavens and of the earth, when they were formed in the day that the Gods formed the earth and the heavens" (Abraham 5:4) .

But even Abraham's account is brief. Apparently God has left to science the pleasure of filling in the details. Geologists divide these early ages of the earth into eons.

The earliest geologic eon is called the Hadean Eon, which lasted from about 4.60 to 4.031 billion years ago, and is known as the chaotic phase of planet formation and the time from when the oldest minerals are found on the earth.[6] It is estimated that the earth first formed approximately 4.567 billion years ago.[7] The early part of this eon was a time when the earth was bombarded by numerous planetoids and planetoid fragments. One such giant impact around 4.51 billion years ago created the moon,[8] which, by governing the tides, is so critical to the formation of higher lifeforms on the earth. Comets and asteroids began to bring massive amounts of water to the earth about 4.404 billion years ago. Plate tectonics, which today we associate with mountain building and earthquakes, apparently began round 4.280 billion years ago. Also about this time, unusually high amounts of light carbon isotopes began to appear, which is interpreted as evidence of life. There is evidence from about 3.4 billion years ago that primordial life was beginning to undergo photosynthesis.[9] The earth was again bombarded about this time by more massive asteroids and even planetoids.

Because it took only half a billion years for life to appear on earth after its initial creation, some scientists have speculated that the first life on earth arrived from outer space with the asteroids and planetoids that were bombarding the earth—a process called panspermia.[10] Francis Crick, who shared the 1962 Nobel Prize with James Watson and Maurice Wilkins for discovering the structure of DNA, along with the British chemist Leslie Orgel, who specialized in research into the origin of life, was one of the first proponents of what is called directed panspermia (the seeding of life on earth by some advanced extraterrestrial beings).[11] The RNA world hypothesis caused Crick and Orgel to change their minds in favor of RNA-based life origins on earth.[12] Personally, I see no reason to choose one hypothesis over the other. It is my opinion that life is abundant in space, just as on earth, and earth's early life could have come from both sources (minus the alien intervention). No matter the early sources of life on earth, whether some clay matrix, protein template, RNA, or DNA, DNA will always win out in the end because it is so efficient at storing and transferring biological information and it will entrain all other macromolecules to its bidding.

The next eon is called the Archean Eon, which lasted from about 4.031 to 2.420 billion years ago. During this eon, the earth's crust cooled enough for continent formation to begin. Simple single-celled life, archaea and early bacteria, began to appear early in this eon, around 4.0 billion years ago, producing bacterial mats called stromatolites, resulting in the earliest known microfossils. Some of these bacteria apparently began producing oxygen. Toward the end of this eon, about 2.5 billion years ago, the entire earth was apparently covered with water.[13]

The next eon is called the Proterozoic Eon, which lasted from 2.42 billion years ago to 541 million years ago.[14] This eon began with a band of iron oxide around the world, giving evidence of what is called the "oxygen catastrophe," when large enough amounts of oxygen accumulated in the atmosphere to cause significant oxidation and the extinction of many early life-forms that could not tolerate high oxygen levels—but which was critical for many other life-forms, including us, to appear. Because of plate tectonics and the subsequent crumpling of the earth's crust, orogeny—mountain building—began during this period. Toward the end of this eon, the first complex single-celled life-forms with nuclei (eukaryotes) appeared. Those cells, called protists, were neither animal, plant, nor fungal and may have derived through a number of separate paths from earlier prokaryotic (non-nucleated) cells. Then, about 1.0 billion years ago, simple multicellular eukaryotes begin to appear.

Even though it only required half a billion years for life to first appear on earth after its original creation, it apparently took nearly 3.5 billion years for life on earth to evolve from simple prokaryotes, the archaea and early bacteria, to eukaryotic multi-cell colonies—that's over 85 percent of the earth's entire history. Apparently it's a very big step to go from simple prokaryotic cells with no nucleus to eukaryotic cells with a nucleus and other internal cell organelles (1.3 billion years), and an even larger step from simple eukaryotes to multicellular eukaryotes (2 billion years). Science has yet to discover most of the rules governing the transition of life during this time period. Such discoveries will be the joy of future generations. Even though those of us watching earth's progress in the premortal world were oblivious to time, there may have been a lot of thumb twiddling during this eon, and it may have been a good time to go out for popcorn.

Around 720 million years ago the earth went through its first great freeze. This one was so severe and so extensive that this has been called the time of the "Snowball Earth."[15] Once the earth thawed out, about 570 million years ago, something extraordinary happened. Large multicellular organisms of all shapes and sizes began to appear. Some of the premortal spirits who had gone out for popcorn may have come back in, saying, "What did I miss?" From that point on the Creation story became fast-paced and exciting.

ENDNOTES

1. Henry B. Eyring, "That He May Become Strong Also," priesthood session of October 2016 general conference.
2. Steven H. Heath, "The Reconciliation of Faith and Science: Henry Eyring's Achievement," *Dialogue: A Journal of Mormon Thought*, vol. 15, Autumn 1982; Letter: Henry Eyring to Adam S. Bennion, Dec. 16, 1954, in possession of Henry Eyring family; photocopy in Steven H. Heath, "Henry Eyring, Mormon Scientist," M.A. thesis, University of Utah, 1980.
3. G. Brent Dalrymple, *The Age of the Earth* (Standford, CA: Stanford Univversity Press, 1994).
4. Boyd K. Packer, "Atonement, Agency, Accountability," April 1988 general conference.
5. merriam-webster.com
6. F. M. Gradstein, J. G. Ogg, Mark Schmitz, and Gabi Ogg, editors, The International Commission on Stratigraphy, ICS's *Geologic Time Scale 2012*, 118407th edition, Elsevier, 2012.
7. A. Bouvier and M. Wadhwa, *Nature Geoscience*, 3, 637–641, 2010; Jane Greaves, *Science,* 307:68–71, 2005.
8. Melanie Barboni, Patrick Boehnke, Brenhin Keller, Issaku E. Kohl, Blair Schoene, Edward D. Young, and Kevin D. McKeegan, "Early formation of the Moon 4.51 billion years ago," *Science Advances*, Jan 11;3(1):e1602365. doi: 10.1126/sciadv.1602365, 2017.
9. Nancy Y. Kiang, "The Color of Plants on Other Worlds," *Scientific American*, Apr. 2008.
10. F. Hoyle and N. C. Wickramasinghe, *Evolution from Space*, 35–49 (New York: Simon & Schuster Inc. and London: J.M. Dent and Son, London, 1981); see also Wickramasinghe, J., Wickramasinghe, C. and Napier, W., *Comets and the Origin of Life* (Singapore, World Scientific, 2010), 137–54.

11. F. H. Crick and L. E. Orgel, "Directed Panspermia," *Icarus,* 19: 341–348, 1973.
12. L. E. Orgel and F. H. Crick, "Anticipating an RNA world. Some past speculations on the origin of life: where are they today?", *FASEB J*, 7:238–239, 1993.
13. M. Woolfson, "The origin and evolution of the solar system," *Astronomy and Geophysics,* 41:12, 2000.
14. Brian Speer, "The Proterozoic Eon," *University of California Museum of Paleontology, ucmp.berkeley.edu/precambrian/proterozoic.php*
15. D. S. Abbot, and I. Halevy, "Dust aerosol important for snowball Earth deglaciation," *Journal of Climate*, 23:4121–4132, 2010.

CHAPTER 13

THE CREATION OF PLANTS

After eons of waiting in the premortal world for the earth to be created, I'm certain that we shouted for joy at the first signs of photosynthesis on our fledgling planet. The three accounts of the formation of plants are given in Genesis 1, Moses 2, and Abraham 4.

Here is the Genesis account: "And God said, Let the earth bring forth grass, the herb yielding seed, and the fruit tree yielding fruit after his kind, whose seed is in itself, upon the earth: and it was so. And the earth brought forth grass, and herb yielding seed after his kind, and the tree yielding fruit, whose seed was in itself, after his kind: and God saw that it was good. And the evening and the morning were the third day." (Genesis 1:11–13)

Here is the account in Moses: "And I, God, said: Let the earth bring forth grass, the herb yielding seed, the fruit tree yielding fruit, after his kind, and the tree yielding fruit, whose seed should be in itself upon the earth, and it was so even as I spake. And the earth brought forth grass, every herb yielding seed after his kind, and the tree yielding fruit, whose seed should be in itself, after his kind; and I, God, saw that all things which I had made were good; And the evening and the morning were the third day" (Moses 2:11–13).

And here is the Abrahamic account: "And the Gods said: Let us prepare the earth to bring forth grass; the herb yielding seed; the fruit tree yielding fruit, after his kind, whose seed in itself yieldeth its own likeness upon the earth; and it was so, even as they ordered. And the Gods organized the earth to bring forth grass from its own seed, and the herb to bring forth herb from its own seed, yielding seed after his kind; and the earth to bring forth the tree from its own seed, yielding fruit, whose seed could only bring forth the same in itself, after his kind; and the Gods saw that they were obeyed. And it came to pass that they numbered the days; from the evening until the morning they called night; and it came to pass, from the morning until the evening they called day; and it was the third time" (Abraham 4:11–13).

The major differences between the Genesis account and the Moses account is the use of "I, God" rather than "God," and the repeat of the origin of trees in the Moses account: "the fruit tree yielding fruit, after his kind, and the tree yielding fruit." There is no stated reason that such an addition was made. This portion of the book of Moses first appeared in June 1830 as page three of notes in the handwriting of Oliver Cowdery, as dictated by the Prophet Joseph Smith. There is no explanation for the specific additions, except, "On the third page of this manuscript, just before the beginning of the creation account, this revelation similarly declares that lost scriptural passages 'shall be had again among the Children of men.'" Otherwise, the handwriting flows through this portion of the Mosaic account with no other explanatory notes.[1]

The Abrahamic account of the creation of plants, based on Joseph Smith's translation of Egyptian papyri beginning in 1835, is quite different from the other two accounts. In this account, the creators are Gods—plural, not singular. There is no second mention of trees, as in the Mosaic account, and the earth was *prepared* to bring forth plants. This preparation was discussed in a previous chapter. Then there is a more explicit statement of trees only producing trees of their own kind "whose seed could only bring forth the same in itself, after his kind" (Abraham 4:12).

Modern research has demonstrated a similar fidelity in plant reproduction. Whereas trees and other plant don't precisely "bring forth the same in itself, after its kind," they come very close. The mutation rate for plants, as it turns out, is roughly one base pair change for every one hundred million base pairs per generation.[2] That is a reproductive accuracy rate of around 99.99999999 percent. Furthermore, most mutations that do occur end up causing non-viable or non-fertile offspring. However, that mutation rate of 0.000000001 percent, with several more zeros added before the 1 to account for the few mutations that are not detrimental, are enough for natural selection to work on over eons of time to bring about changes in the plant kingdom, and to create the beautiful and glorious diversity of plants we enjoy today.

Plants are defined primarily by their photosynthesis, involving the green, light-absorbing pigment chlorophyll. Modern science suggests that the first evidence of photosynthesis on earth, in bacteria, dates from about 3.4 billion years ago. Rather than absorbing visible light and giving off oxygen, as do modern plants, those early photosynthetic bacteria absorbed near-infrared light and produced sulfur and sulfate compounds. The first visible light-absorbing bacteria, called Cyanobacteria, which produced oxygen, first appeared about 2.7 billion years ago. The first evidence of rocks containing oxygen appeared about 2.4–2.3 billion years ago.[3] This seems like an excruciatingly slow process—much worse than watching grass grow—but we who were watching the grass grow were in an infinite, premortal state and, therefore, maybe the "time" passed relatively quickly.

We see a natural progression through time, in the earth strata, from primitive, single-celled plants to complex multicellular plants. More complex plants, with a nucleus and chloroplasts (structures inside the cell that closely resemble light-absorbing bacteria and contain chlorophyll), first appeared a little over a billion years ago. The first were red and brown algae. Green algae first appeared around 750 million years ago. The first land plants, including mosses and liverworts, which lack roots and stems, first appeared about 475 million years ago. The so-called vascular plants, such as grasses, herbs, and trees, first appeared on earth around 423 million years ago.[3] Those are the very plants referred to in Genesis, Moses, and Abraham. I'm sure we were all very excited at finally having the chance to watch grass grow—especially those of us who were preparing ourselves to be nerds when it was our time to come to earth. The rest of our fellow spirits probably had better things to do, although I can't imagine what.

Peat forms when wetland plants, such as mosses, sedges (grass-like plants), and shrubs die but don't fully decay under acidic and anaerobic (oxygen-free) conditions.[4] Most peat bogs existing today formed some 12,000 years ago at the end of the last major ice age.[5] Peat accumulates at a rate of approximately one millimeter per year—so the depth of peat blocks can be dated based on their thickness.[6] Those thicknesses can be confirmed by ages obtained by radiocarbon dating. Peat accumulates water to form bogs and ponds. In order to be used as fuel, peat must be extracted and stacked so that the water is forced out, allowing the peat to dry.

If peat is buried and compressed by an overburden of soil and rock, given enough time, the water is extruded, and the remaining organic matter can form coal. Around 300–100 million years ago, much of the earth was covered with bogs and primitive forests. As those plants died and sunk to the bottom of the bogs, under anaerobic conditions, they formed deep peat layers. As the water was extruded, under great pressure, the peat gradually became coal. Coal seams are typically 5–33 feet thick (some are as much as 200 feet thick) and typically lie under a 200–2700 foot thick overburden.[7]

Under even more pressure and heat, coal can become liquefied and even gasified to form oil and natural gas deposits. All of these fuels—coal, oil, and natural gas—are referred to as fossil fuels. The Industrial Revolution, which occurred between 1760 and 1840, was largely dependent upon coal. In 1860, the Belgian engineer Jean Lenoir invented a gas-fired internal combustion engine. We are now, especially in the US, highly dependent upon those internal combustion engines for transportation. In 2007, the US depended for our total energy sources on oil (petroleum) 36.0 percent, coal 27.4 percent, and natural gas 23.0 percent. Only 13.6 percent of our energy came from non-fossil fuel sources.[8] What a wonderful blessing from God that the earth was prepared in such a manner that we have so many benefits in our modern age.

A beautiful, poetic revelation concerning coal and gas deposits was given to the Prophet Joseph Smith at or near Kirtland, Ohio, on April 23, 1834: "For the earth is full, and there is enough and to spare; yea, I prepared all things, and have given unto the children of men to be agents unto themselves" (D&C 104:17). There is also a cautionary tale at the end of that revelation that we are "agents unto" ourselves and, thus, should be wise stewards over all these wonderful natural resources the Lord has provided. Fossil fuels are not limitless and burning them on a large scale has contributed to elevated CO_2 levels and global warming.

Especially in softer coal, the fossil remains of the plants living at the time the coal was formed can be seen in the layers. Based on examination of the fossil record, 96–98 percent of all plants that have ever lived are now extinct. Therefore, most of the fossil plants seen in coal beds, and most of the plants providing the coal, are now extinct.[9] Although we don't at present recall our premortal days when those coal-producing forests were growing, we probably had the breathtaking experience of seeing many gorgeous plants in real life before they went extinct. It is likely that we were privileged, as premortal, eternal spirit beings, to watch the greening of the earth. If such were the case, I'm sure we would have oohed and ahhed at the incredible beauty. I can imagine that we were especially touched by the beauty of the great giant ferns, giant club mosses (lycopsids), giant horsetail (calamites), conifers (cordaites), and other giant plants that were to form part of the coal beds and then become extinct.

Some coal mines have retained intact, standing tree trunks, with their unique bark patterns, dating from the Carboniferous period (359.2 to 299 million years ago). In other coal mines, such as the Vermilion Grove and Riola coal mines in eastern Illinois, fallen tree trunks and a jumble of other plants form what are called roof shales. In those coal mine roofs can be observed, "the largest intact fossil forest ever seen."[10] Around 307 million years ago, an earthquake in Vermilion Grove toppled the trees and suddenly dropped at least four square miles of swamp, where those plants were growing, by up to thirty feet. Mud and sand then rushed in, covering the plants and preserving them, first as peat and eventually as coal. The plants now lie some 230 feet below the surface—a time capsule of plant life preserved for over 300 million years. That preserved forest is now "a riot of intertwined tree trunks, leaves, fern fronds and twigs silhouetted black-on-gray on the clammy shale surface of the tunnel roof."[10]

In addition to fossil fuels, living plants provide the oxygen we require for survival. The atmosphere is approximately 20.95 percent oxygen, mainly in the form of free oxygen molecules (O_2). That is exactly the right percent of oxygen that optimizes our survival. Rainforest trees produce about one-third (28 percent) of the oxygen we breathe, but most of the oxygen (70 percent) in the atmosphere is produced by marine plants. The remaining 2 percent of oxygen in the atmosphere comes from other sources—such as the breakdown of oxygen-containing compounds in the atmosphere.[11]

Plants were critical to preparing the earth for human habitation—especially advanced human habitation—in which living plants and fossil fuels have played such vital roles. Just as one example, since the late 1970s, general conference has been broadcast by satellite to meetinghouses and homes around the world. Live broadcasts of conference "are digitized and sent a short distance via a custom-installed fiber optic line to the Triad Center in downtown Salt Lake where a cluster of satellite dishes send[s] the signals skyward. From there the broadcasts are picked up by a constellation of satellites"[12] As of 2012, general "conference is viewed in 175 countries and territories, and it is translated into 94 languages. About 595,000 households in North America tune in on television for the Sunday morning session."[13] Each satellite launched into orbit requires around 120 tons of fuel;[14] some of that is hydrogen, but the initial liftoff propellant is thousands of pounds of fossil fuel—created by those primeval forests that lived and died millions of years before we came to earth.

The stunning beauty of the earth is largely the result of the plants growing here. There are, today, approximately 400,000 species of plants living on earth.[15] We were, almost certainly as premortal spirits, excited and awed by the emergence of flowering plants and the breathtaking beauty they brought to the earth. These beautiful plants have played many roles over millions of years—during the process of the infinite Creation.

My wife, Kathleen, and I spent part of our honeymoon on Vancouver Island in British Columbia, Canada. One highlight of that visit was our trip to Butchart Gardens. I took a photograph of my gorgeous wife smelling a giant flower bloom as large as her head. We have since visited many beautiful gardens around the world—one of our favorite vacation activities—and constantly marvel at the beauty of the plants God has created. We have adorned our own home with myriad wonderful plans and love to spend our time visiting greenhouses, buying new plants, and working in our gardens. One day, a few years ago, not long after our youngest son died, I was walking in our garden in deep spiritual contemplation. As I passed by a specific locust tree, I could feel its spirit exuding love toward me, and tears welled up in my eyes.

One of my favorite hymns is "How Great Thou Art," originally written by the Swedish poet Carl Boberg in 1885 and then translated from the Russian hymn version into English by a British missionary, Stuart K. Hine in 1931. It is now hymn number 86 in our hymnal:

> When thru the woods and forest glades I wander,
> And hear the birds sing sweetly in the trees,
> When I look down from lofty mountain grandeur
> And hear the brook and feel the gentle breeze,
> Then sings my soul, my Savior God, to thee,
> How great thou art! How great thou art!

ENDNOTES

1. Old Testament Revision 1, 3. The Joseph Smith Papers, accessed Apr. 8, 2018, http://www.josephsmithpapers.org/paper-summary/old-testament-revision-1/5
2. Michael Lynch, "Evolution of the mutation rate," *Trends Genet.*, 26:345–352, 2010.
3. Nancy Y. Kiang, "The Color of Plants on Other Worlds," *Scientific American*, Apr. 2008.
4. Gorham, E., The development of peatlands, *Quarterly Review of Biology*, 32: 145–66, 1957
5. D. H. Vitt, L. A. Halsey, and B.J. Nicholson, "The Mackenzie River basin," 66–202 in L.H. Fraser and P.A. Keddy (eds.), *The World's Largest Wetlands: Ecology and Conservation* (Cambridge, UK: Cambridge University Press, Cambridge, 2005).
6. P. A. Keddy, *Wetland Ecology: Principles and Conservation*, 2nd edition (Cambridge, UK: Cambridge University Press, UK, 2010).
7. Snehendra Kumar Singh, "Extraction of Thick Coal Seam," Thesis, Department of Mining Engineering, National Institute of Technology, 201.
8. U.S. EIA International Energy Statistics
9. physics.tutorvista.com/earth-science/extinction-of-plants.html
10. Guy Gugliotta, "The World's Largest Fossil Wilderness," *Smithsonian Magazine*, July 2009.
11. nationalgeographic.org/activity/save-the-plankton-breathe-freely
12. news.hjnews.com/features/faith/broadcasting-to-the-world-technology-powers-lds-church-connections/article
13. lds.org/church/news/a-brief-history-of-general-conference
14. How much fuel is burned at a rocket launch?—do you know? youtube.com
15. bgci.org/policy/1521

CHAPTER 14

THE CREATION OF EARLY ANIMALS

I believe this chapter to be key to this entire book, for within our understanding of the creation of animals lies the key question to *The Infinite Creation*: is the variety of life on Earth the result of complex, mostly as yet undiscovered laws of biology, or is it primarily the result of chance historical events? Several prominent scientists have become convinced, sometimes for personal rather than scientific reasons, that the emergence of various life-forms, especially humans, on this planet was the result of purely historical events.

For example, the eminent US paleontologist George Gaylord Simpson stated in 1964, "The assumption, so freely made by astronomers, physicists, and some biochemists, that once life gets started anywhere, humanoids will eventually and inevitably appear is plainly false. The chance of duplicating man on any other planet is the same as the chance that the planet and its organisms have had a history identical in all essentials with that of the earth through some billions of years."[1]

The paleontologist and popular science writer Stephen Jay Gould stated in his 1989 book, *Wonderful Life*, "Wind back the tape of life to the early days . . . let it play again from an identical starting point, and the chance becomes vanishingly small that anything like human intelligence would grace the replay."[2]

The British evolutionary biologist and author Richard Dawkins stated in his 2009 book, *The Greatest Show on Earth*, "There is no evolutionary justification for the common assumption that evolution is somehow 'aimed' at humans, or that humans are 'evolution's last word.'"[3] I am in agreement with probably 99 percent of what Dawkins said in *The Greatest Show*, but the above statement is among the 1 percent with which I do not agree.

In 2002 the evolutionary biologist Ernst Mayr stated, "Evolution is a historical process that cannot be proven by the same arguments and methods by which purely physical or functional phenomena can be documented. Evolution as a whole, and the explanation of particular evolutionary events, must be inferred from observations."[4]

As a biologist myself, I consider the term "evolutionary biologist" to be an unnecessary duplication. I agree completely with the statement by Theodosius Dobzhansky that "nothing in biology makes sense except in the light of evolution."[5] Therefore, all biologists are, by our very discipline, evolutionary biologists. However, also as a biologist, I find Mayr's statement offensive, and I adamantly disagree that "evolution is a historical process that cannot be proven by the same arguments and methods by which purely physical or functional phenomena can be documented." If evolution is strictly historical and cannot be proven by scientific methods, then it is not science, and therefore, "evolutionary biologists" like Mayr were "stamp collectors," not scientists. I believe, however, that the laws governing the course of evolution are God-given scientific laws—set down before the foundation of the earth—most of which are yet to be discovered.

I am confident it was unjustified statements like Mayr's that prompted the 1968 Nobel Laurette in physics, Luis Alvarez, to denigrate paleontologists. In a 1988 telephone interview with Malcolm Browne of the *New York Times*, Alvarez stated, "I don't like to say bad things about paleontologists, but they're really not very good scientists. They're more like stamp collectors."[6] I think it is high time for biologists to quit acting like stamp collectors, or collectors of just-so history stories, and start acting like scientists. It's time for the next generation of biologists to start looking for, proposing, and then testing laws that govern the course of evolution. They are there; we just have to think outside the evolution-as-history box and start looking for them. Many molecular biologists and others are already doing the scientific research that can lead to identifying such laws of evolution.

Marine biologist Ronald L. Shimek appears to agree: "Until recently many of the discussions about evolutionary relationships have been exercises in logic based on limited evidence . . . such discussions were not really science, but more akin to science fiction. Recently, however, with the advent of techniques allowing for direct comparisons of the genetic code of organisms . . . the results are no longer in the realm of literature, but rather actually are 'real' science."[7]

In 2009, the US paleontologist and professor of geology at Mount Holyoke College, Mark McMenamin, stated,

> The late Stephen Jay Gould challenged natural selection from the standpoint of his emphasis on the importance of contingency in evolution. He argued that an overemphasis on adaptationisitic thought hampers our understanding of evolution. Ironically, Gould's rivals, some of whom take a highly deterministic view of evolutionary progress, also implicitly de-emphasize natural selection in the following way. If the same forms are going to reappear repeatedly, then natural selection is beside the point—the forms are going to appear anyway, via any number of a variety of processes. Some unknown process (evidently not natural selection) guides them to the same morphological destination time and time again.[8]

McMenamin has also proposed what he calls "Laws of Morphogenetic Evolution." He stated:

> It cannot merely be environmental constraint that sculpts these similar forms, but rather some kind of pattern for form, namely, a morphogenetic pattern. The answer, and this may be considered to be the key and most critical statement of this book [Paleotorus: The Laws of Morphogenetic Evolution] and its central thesis, may be stated as the first law of morphogenetic evolution:
>
> The same forces that control macroevolution control the observed high precision of convergent evolution. Both processes are associated with transformations of morphogenetic fields.[8]

Although our goal should be to place evolution under the purview of real science, our search for the laws of evolution needs be aided by our deep understanding of the historic events involved. The time when the stromatolite-building bacteria (prokaryotes—cells without nuclei) dominated the earth (4 to 2.5 billion years ago) is called the Archean Eon (Archean comes from the Greek word meaning the beginning or origin; the term was used by nineteenth century geologists to mean the earliest geological age; we now know that the Archean Eon was predated by an even older eon, called the Hadean, when the earth was being formed during the Solar Smashup). At first, geologists didn't realize that there was an abundance of microscopic life on Earth during the Archean Eon; just as soon as liquid water was available—no matter how hot; and called the next geological period the Proterozoic Eon (a term which comes from the Greek meaning earliest life), from 2.5 billion years to 541 million years ago. Microbes have certainly not gone away—in many ways they still dominate the earth today—including inside the human digestive system; but animals have also had their turn on the stage of life.

The beginning of the Proterozoic Eon is partly defined by the emergence of eukaryotes (cells with nuclei), which first appeared around 2.7 billion years ago. It must not have been a simple process to create eukaryotes, as it took some 1.3 billion years to go from prokaryotes to eukaryotes. Along the way, some prokaryotes apparently became incorporated into the cytoplasm of emerging eukaryotes—to become mitochondria, the powerhouses of the cell, without which eukaryotic cells cannot survive.

During most of the Proterozoic Eon, single-celled microorganisms (both prokaryotes to eukaryotes) continued to dominate the world, but beginning about 635 million years ago, a wonderful and extraordinary event began to unfold—an event which almost certainly was governed by many as yet undiscovered laws of nature and an event our eternal premortal spirits must have been anxiously awaiting for literally eons. Single eukaryotic cells began to stick together as colonies.[9] The adhesion molecules that held those colonies together have been inherited by *all* the descendants of those early colonies, implying that all living animals are descended from a common group of ancestral, colonial cells.[10]

From those early colonial cell clusters, life erupted into a beautiful, astonishing profusion of "big" multicellular creatures. I can imagine the oohs and ahhs that went up from the gallery of observing premortal spirits. Most of us, as mortals, love to attend aquaria and zoos where we ooh and ahh at God's wondrous creations that are living today. I'm sure we were even more excited to see the first of the complex life-forms appear.

Some of the best fossils from those 600–million-year-old creatures, which covered the earth, can be found today at a place called the Mistaken Point Ecological Reserve, Newfoundland. Unlike today's aquaria, where we can see fishes and other aquatic animals swimming about, the soft-bodied Proterozoic creatures had not yet evolved locomotion, but this was "the first time that life got big."[11] The strange life-forms that emerged at this time are now called Ediacarans and were first discovered in 1946 by Reginald Sprigg in the Ediacara Mines in southern Australia.[12] He thought some of them looked like jellyfish, but they were much older and had no movement.

Then in 1967, Shiva Misra discovered fossils at Newfoundland's Mistaken Point that looked a lot like Sprigg's "jellyfish." Other fossils at the site looked a bit like fern fronds, but others looked like creatures unknown to science. The volcanic ash layered in with the fossils contained traces of uranium, which allowed for precise radiometric dating of the site. In 1996, Mark McMenamin also discovered a layer of Ediacaran fossils in Sonora, Mexico.[13] Thanks to the Newfoundland, Australian, Mexican, and other sites, more than fifty different Ediacaran creatures have been identified so far—covering an age-range of nearly 100 million years, from 635 to 541 million years ago.[14]

Before this Proterozoic proliferation of large, multicellular life-forms, life on earth was microscopic, mainly kept from expanding by a shortage of oxygen. But marine bacteria were slowly generating the critical oxygen levels needed for more complex life-forms to evolve. Much of that oxygen, however, was escaping from the oceans into the atmosphere. Then around 717 to 635 million years ago, widespread glaciation took place—possibly covering the entire earth with thick layers of ice and snow. This "snowball earth" was probably the next critical phase in preparing the earth for more complex life. This frozen-earth state was a historic but perhaps inevitable event. The vital oxygen needed for complex life-forms was very likely trapped in the ice so that it was concentrated and its available levels began to rise. Then, around 635 million years ago, numerous volcanic eruptions spewed carbon dioxide into the atmosphere, causing a greenhouse effect, which warmed the planet and thawed the ice—releasing the trapped oxygen at high enough levels to prepare the earth to bring forth complex, multicellular life.[11]

Those Ediacaran creatures were structured very differently from modern organisms. They had a "quilted" body structure, unlike any living plant or animal today, and sort of resembled a variety of inflated mattresses. One paleontologist, Adolf Seilacher, has proposed to classify Ediacarans into a kingdom all their own, called Vendobiota, because of their unique, quilted body structure.[15] The quilting may have helped them collect nutrients from their environment as none of them seem to have had mouths or digestive systems, and they didn't move about like animals. Some of them were anchored to the sea floor by a knob or disc, called a holdfast, and the frond-like body wafted upward in the water column. But they don't appear to have been plants either, because many Ediacarans lived in very deep water, thousands of feet below the surface, where sunlight needed for photosynthesis did not penetrate.

Whereas most of the Ediacaran creatures were "quilted," one group called the cat's tongue (*Vendoglossa*) was not quilted. It had rows of tiny papillae, like those on a cat's, or other animal's tongue, and had an internal digestive system. The presence of an internal digestive tube was a huge step toward the formation of modern multicellular animals called metazoans, which are defined as having an outside layer (skin), an inside layer (the digestive tract), and a middle layer (muscle and, later, bone).[8]

Then, in 2010, Alex Liu and colleagues described something quite remarkable from the petrified mud that had covered the deep ocean floor 565 million years ago. Among the fossil Ediacarans at Mistaken Point, they found "trace-fossils," *trackways* left by something slithering through the mud. Something down there was moving! Liu and colleagues had discovered evidence for the very oldest known animals on Earth.[16]

Around 24 million years after the first slithering animals left traces on the deep sea floor, there was a veritable explosion of new animal forms—know literally as the Cambrian Explosion.[17] Imagine giving a premortal Sunbeam class modeling clay and telling each child to make an animal. Those clay models are then given to the premortal Very Early Animal Modeling Crew to build the actual living animals. What you would end up with is the vast array of very weird-looking animals similar to that found in the Burgess Clay deposits of western Canada.

An unusual name for some geographical feature often stimulates me to learn the story behind the name—such was the case for the Kicking Horse River in British Columbia. It turns out that in 1857, the British government and the Royal Geographical Society sent a team led by John Palliser, with geologist James Hector, to explore western Canada.[18] The following year, deep in the Canadian Rockies, in southeastern British Columbia, Hector was helping cross a stream. The expedition's journal account states: "In crossing a stream on the west side of the pass, near Lake Wapta, one of the pack animals, with instuments [sic] and records on its back, was getting into deep water. . . . [Dr. Hector] went in to turn it back. Coming out of the stream, with his clothes dripping with water, and going among the horses, one of them—probably frightened at his appearance—kicked him over the heart; Hector was insensible for so long that his party, supposing him to be dead, had dug his grave and were about to bury him when he showed some sign of life."[19]

As a result of the incident, the stream was named Kicking Horse River. Nearly thirty years later, the Kicking Horse Pass would be chosen as the route for the Trans-Canada railway through the Rockies.

The little town of Field, British Columbia, named for Cyrus Field, a US businessman being wooed by the Canadian Pacific Railroad to invest in the trans-Canadian Railway (he never did invest),[20] was built on the east bank of the river, at the base of the 10,000–foot Mount Stephen, named for George Stephen, president of the Canadian Pacific Railway. The town consisted originally of tents and shacks to house the railway construction workers, but Mt. Stephen House, built in Field in 1886, was the first hotel built in the Rockies.[20]

As the railway construction workers cut their way along the base of Mount Stephen, they discovered what they called "stone bugs" in the dark shale. In September 1886, the workers invited Richard McConnell, who was mapping the geology along the railway line for the Geological Survey of Canada, to examine the "bugs" in what was to become known as the trilobite beds.[21] Some of the fossils collected by McConnell made their way to Charles Walcott, secretary of the Smithsonian Institution, who correctly estimated their age to the Middle Cambrian (500–520 million years ago). Those samples whetted Walcott's appetite for additional exploration of the region, but it wasn't until 1907 that Walcott got the chance to visit Mount Stephen in person.[22]

Walcott's big discovery came in 1909 when he explored the slopes of Mount Field and Mount Burgess (named for Alexander MacKinnon Burgess, Deputy Minister of the Canadian Interior) on the west side of Kicking Horse River. The deposits there, now referred to as the Burgess Shale, are among the most famous in all of geology and paleontology.[23] The following year (1910), Walcott returned with his sons Stuart and Sidney. The shale he had examined the previous year had broken off and slid down the slope from a layer higher up on the mountain. Exploring farther up the slope, they finally discovered the fossil-rich layer. Between 1910 and 1924, Walcott and his sons returned many times and extracted more than 6,500 specimens from the fossil-bearing rock.[24]

What makes the Burgess Shale so remarkable is that the fine sediment deposited almost instantly over the entire ecosystem living 508 million years ago preserved the soft parts of the plants and animals in exceptional detail.[25] The pinpoint localization of the Burgess Shale fossils probably resulted from a mudslide, which slid them down an underwater slope and buried them in deep water away from the decay-causing oxygen.[2] Today, there is a total of over 225,000 Burgess Shale specimens in several collections around the world.[26]

Shale deposits around the world, like the Burgess Shale, were created as layer upon layer of mud accumulated over the various animals that had died in aquatic environments. Through the millennia, those mud layers hardened into rock, forming thin layers that can be separated by gentle tapping. The layers then open like the pages of a book—a 500–million-year-old book! Recently, I was invited by a geologist, L.J. Krumenacker, to visit the trilobite quarry in the 510,000 year-old Spence Shale just north of Bear Lake. I spent the day sitting on a ledge in the small quarry at the bend of a dry creek bed, digging shale from the side-hill and cracking open the layers. I felt like a young boy on Christmas morning, opening up those layers of shale and being the first person to ever lay eyes on the marvelous collection of animals that had lived and died in that mud so long ago. That day, I felt as close to God's creation as I ever have in my life.

Arthropods (the group of animals that now includes insects, spiders, crabs, and lobsters) were the most common animals in the Burgess Shale community (around 60 percent of the total). The most common arthropod (5,000 specimens) was a two-inch-long segmented bottom feeder named *Canadaspi,* with a pair of shells covering the body. The head exhibited four segmented antennae, eyes at the ends of stalks, and claws for feeding. Canadaspi had fifteen pairs of segmented legs, eight pairs of gills along the body, and a double, flattened, spiny tail.[27]

The wildest-looking little arthropod, and second most common in the Burgess Shale, was the one-inch-long *Marrella.* The head shield had four spines directed backward over the body—resembling some futuristic sports car. The head also had two very long antennae with thirty segments each, and two paddle-like appendages with lots of bushy hairs along the edges. This little bug was called a "lace crab" by Walcott because of the lacy gills above the twenty-six pairs of walking legs.[26]

The largest predator, gliding through the Burgess environment, was the over-three-foot-long *Anomalocaris.* One of the less common members of the community, and not at all impressive, was a two-inch-long fish-like animal named *Pikaia*.[26] Although, even now, there are millions of arthropods in the oceans and on land, the tiny, unimpressive *Pikaia*, and its kin, were destined to give rise to the vertebrates, which would eventually dominate the earth. *Pikaia* probably swam much like an eel and may have developed one of the first heads among the animals leading to the vertebrates. It had two antennae and six pairs of gill-like appendages. It also possessed a notochord and exhibited some thirty eight V-shaped muscular body segments.

Another fish-like animal from approximately the same time period (518 million years ago) was *Myllokunmingia*, discovered by Shu and colleagues in the Qiongzhusi Formation near Haikou, China. This inch-long animal was even more highly developed than *Pikaia*, with a skull and skeleton made of cartilage. The head had five or six gill arches and the trunk had twenty five V-shaped muscle segments. There was a notochord (forerunner of the backbone), pharynx, digestive tract, and possibly a pericardial cavity (the cavity around the heart). It had a sail-like dorsal fin and paired ventral fin folds toward the tail. In short, this animal had all the characteristics that have been predicted for an animal from which the vertebrates were created.[28]

Newer specimens from the Burgess Shale and elsewhere have allowed Simon Morris and Jean-Bernard Caron to describe yet another fish-like animal, *Metaspriggina*, with even more striking vertebrate characteristics. This primitive fish had a notochord; a head with camera-type eyes, a nose, and gills; W-shaped muscle segments; and a tail beyond an anus. According to Morris and Caron, "This primitive group of fish was cosmopolitan during Lower–Middle Cambrian times."[29]

This "cosmopolitan" distribution of several fish-like animals at the time of the Burgess Shale belies Gould's conclusion in *Wonderful Life* (literally the last page):

> Wind the tape of life back to Burgess times, and let it play again. If *Pikaia* does not survive in the replay, we are wiped out of future history—all of us, from the shark to robin to orangutan. . . . And so, if you wish to ask the question of the ages—why do humans exist?—a major part of the answer . . . must be: because *Pikaia* survived the Burgess decimation. This response does not cite a single law of nature; it embodies no statement about predictable evolutionary pathways, no calculation of probabilities based on general rules of anatomy or ecology.

> The survival of *Pikaia* was a contingency of 'just history.' . . . We are the offspring of history.[2]

Herein, Gould mentions and promptly dismisses a "law of nature" to explain vertebrate evolution and the origin of humans, but then claims unequivocally that we are "the offspring of history"—this sounds a lot like stamp collecting, not science. Conversely, I propose there were laws of nature governing the course of evolution—we simply haven't, as yet, given enough effort and creativity to find them.

For example, one rule of evolution might be that having a head may be an advantage to literally getting ahead in the evolution contest. Head formation in early animals has been proposed to have resulted from an elongated body, active swimming in search of food, and a mouth at the leading end. The search for food meant sensing the environment—such as smelling, feeling, and seeing—near the mouth. Concentration of nerves in the area of those sensory organs and nerve interactions for processing and responding to sensory information began the pathway toward a brain.[30]

There were also tiny sponges (porifera) and worms (annelids) in the Burgess Shale environment. Today, we are most familiar with the annelids we call earthworms. But there are also a gazillion marine annelids known as bristle worms, or polychaetes. There were five species of annelids in the Burgess Shale deposits, at least four of which were polychaetes. It turns out that the term "dominate the earth" is a relative, human-centered term—after all, humans coined the term "dominate" and the polychaetes didn't even have a vote. If you were a polychaete, you may have a different opinion of who dominates the earth.

It has been determined, for example, that in the mud of Tampa Bay, Florida, alone, there are about 13,000 polychaetes per square meter.[31] Tampa Bay covers roughly 400 square miles,[32] which is just over one billion square meters. Thus, the total number of polychaetes in Tampa Bay *alone* is roughly 13.5 trillion—or approximately 1,764 times as many polycaetes in Tampa Bay *alone* as there are humans on the *entire* earth. Furthermore, Tampa Bay doesn't even hold the record; in the mud off some New Zealand beaches, there are as many as 50,000 polychaetes per square meter.[33]

Most polychaetes have never even seen a human—and vice versa—they mainly encounter only other poychaetes mucking around in the same patch of ocean floor. But recently, some of their numbers have been experiencing severe health problems—weight loss and reduced burrowing times. And a few of them are becoming addicted to nicotine in the water. They don't know where the problem is coming from—but we do. We have known for years that "marine debris [produced by humans] is a global environmental issue." However, what may be news to most of us, as it turns out, of all things, is that "smoked cigarette filters are the predominant coastal litter item; 4.5 trillion cigarette butts are littered annually, presenting a source of bioplastic microfibres (cellulose acetate) and harmful toxicants [including nicotine] to marine environments." These items may be health hazards, especially if you are a polychaete ragworm (*Hediste diversicolor*) swimming in the coastal waters.[34]

Without question, the most famous account of the Burgess Shale, and perhaps its own major source of fame, was the 1989 book *Wonderful Life: The Burgess Shale and the Nature of History* by Stephen Jay Gould.[2] *Wonderful Life* made the *New York Times* bestseller list; my own 1990 paperback copy states on the front cover "National Bestseller." It won the 1991 Royal Society's Rhone-Poulenc Prize and the American Historical Association's Forkosch Award. It was also a finalist for the 1991 Pulitzer Prize.[35]

I obtained my copy of *Wonderful Life* soon after it was published, read it with relish, and disagreed with most of Gould's conclusions. I have read many of Gould's books and essays. I enjoy his writing and agree with about ninety percent of what he has written. His conclusions in *Wonderful Life* happen to be part of the other 10 percent. It is important here to address Gould's main point, as it is the very foundation of the evolution-is-history box that confines many otherwise-good biologists and the dismissal of God as Creator.

Gould challenged anyone reading the *Wonderful Life* to consider this: "I must be able to convince you—by actual example—that honorable, reasonable, and fascinating different alternatives could have produced a substantially divergent history of life not graced by human intelligence."[2] The "reasonable," "actual example" Gould came up with was a contest between polychaetes (segmented, marine bristle worms) and priapulids (unsegmented, smooth marine worms). Whereas both began in the Burgess Shale era, priapulids had the numerical advantage. However, polychaetes won out in the long run, having some eight thousand extant species today and priapulids lost, having only fifteen extant species. Gould claimed, "For some reason, priapulids do not rank among the success stories of modern biology."[2] He continued, "The entire modern world contains scarcely more genera of priapulids than the single Burgess fauna from one quarry in British Columbia, . . . Burgess priapulids occupied center stage. . . . What happened? We do not know. It is tempting to argue that polychaetes had some biological leverage. . . . But we have no idea what such an advantage might be."[2] How about polychaetes having *heads* and priapulids lacking the same? Would that make any difference? Is there a law of evolution that says, "If you have a head you have a great advantage over something without a head"? I'll take that challenge, Stephen, and I think your history hypothesis is losing out to laws of science.

Concerning priapulids, marine biologist Ronald Shimek stated, "These animals really don't have a defined head."[36] Furthermore, based upon genetic data, polychaetes exhibit a complete head to tail complement of *Hox* genes (developmental patterning genes, which will be discussed more in a later chapter), whereas priapulids show only caudal (tail) *Hox* genes—they exhibit no complete *Hox* gene sequences in what would be the head, if they had a head—which they do not.[37]

It turns out that many of the Burgess Shale animals had heads. Among their later crustacean descendants there were many independent lineages where anterior thoracic legs were transformed into feeding appendages, called maxillipeds. The expression of a *Hox* gene called *Ultrabithorax* (*Ubx*) is associated with thoracic legs but the expression is turned off in maxillipeds. Anastasios Pavlopoulos and colleagues at Cambridge, Iraklio, Crete, and Berkley have shown that when *Ubx* expression is suppressed in the thorax of a shrimp-like crustacean (*Parhyale hawaiensis), the legs become* maxillipeds.[38] Therefore, one might say that a law of development among crustaceans is that *Ubx* is involved in the formation of legs but its absence results in maxilliped formation. The earliest metazoans possessed a number of what might be considered pre-*Hox* genes. Sponges, which diverged from other metazoans around 580 million years ago, during the Ediacaran era, retained only those pre-*Hox* genes, and never developed full-fledged *Hox* genes—or bodies. Is there a law connecting the two? Shortly after the sponges diverged, the main-line metazoans did develop *Hox* genes—six or seven of them—in the common ancestor.[39] The creation of *Hox* genes by those early metazoans may have been the trigger that lead to the huge diversification of body plans known as the Cambrian explosion.[40] Another factor in the *Hox*-metazoan success story is the repeated duplication of *Hox* genes. By the time humans were created, there are more than two hundred genes in the *Hox* gene superfamily.[41]

Whereas modern polychaetes would feel right at home in the Burgess Shale community, insects would have felt out of place. Insects are defined primarily on the basis of having six legs—three pairs—and no animals in the Burgess Shale community had only six legs. Arthropods with six legs—that is the insects—first appeared about 28 million years after the Burgess Shale deposits, at around 480 million years ago.[42] All of the segmented Burgess Shale animals had simple *Hox* genes and simple body plans with a lot of similar segments. An increase in *Hox* gene number, function, and interactions in fewer segments allowed insects far more variety in creating various body structures.[43] Arthropods, including insects, first came onto land about 419 million years ago.[44] Today, one can find as many as 425 million tiny, creeping animals per acre of land (sample taken from Pennsylvania), and eighty percent (339 million) of those are arthropods.[45] Around 400 million years ago, one line of insects developed wings and radiated into even more niches.[42]

Insects are now the most common arthropods and are the most widely diversified living things on the entire earth, accounting for 80 percent of all living animal species. There are around 900,000 known species of living insects, and most experts agree that there are far more insect species yet to be described than there are known species—most suggest *at least* twice as many—estimates run as high as 30 million insect species not yet identified. There are around 10 quintillion (10,000,000,000,000,000,000) individual insects living in the world today.[45] That's about one billion insects for every living human being—far too many of them are mosquitoes. In the United States alone, there are around 23,700 species of beetles; 19,600 species of flies; 17,500 species of ants, bees, and wasps; and 11,500 species of moths and butterflies.[45]

The story of the creation of animals is one of multiple, rapid species explosions, followed, each in turn, by devastating extinctions. The great Cambrian explosion was followed by the Cambrian–Ordovician extinction 488 million years ago. That was followed, in turn, by the Ordovician expansion (485.4 to 443.8 million years ago, and named for, of all things, the Celtic tribe of Ordovices in north Wales, where rocks characterizing the era were first discovered), which saw the warm seas dominated by mollusks and arthropods, and the beginning of jawed fishes—the world's first true vertebrates. Life had not yet ventured onto land. During the

Ordovician, meteorites, resulting from an ancient asteroid collision 470 million years ago, plummeted the earth at a rate about one hundred times that seen today.[46] The Ordovician ended in the Ordovician-Silurian mass extinction 445 million years ago.[47]

Then there was the Devonian (419.2 to 358.9 million years ago, named for Devon, England, where sedimentary rocks from this era were first examined), when, wonder of wonders, life exploded onto land. Spore-producing vascular plants spread over the earth, forming massive forests. Those were followed by plants with leaves and true roots, and then by seed-bearing plants. Insects and other arthropods crawled out of the sea into the land—or flew over it. The seas saw the expansion of ammonites, trilobites, and coral reefs. But the seas were dominated by bony, ray-finned, and lobe-finned fishes. Large amounts of CO_2 in the atmosphere caused a greenhouse effect, resulting in a warm climate and elevated sea levels. The Devonian is called the "Age of Fishes," but it also could be called the "Age of Trees," which may have been the demise of the very era that saw their birth. Unlike their spore-bearing predecessor plants, which were less than one foot tall and whose rhizoids barely penetrated the earth, some of the new seed plants—the trees—grew up to one hundred feet. Those giant trees drove heavy, penetrating roots deep into the earth, pulverizing rocks into soil—to great depths. The massive forests absorbed the CO_2 and produced large quantities of oxygen. With the depletion of atmospheric CO_2, the environment began to cool, water was collected as ice at the poles, ocean levels fell, and the earth became much drier. The dried-out forests became susceptible to fire, and massive forest fires swept the land. Infrequent but sometimes deluginous rainstorms swept over the denuded and blackened loose soil—eroding black earth into the rivers and then the oceans. The end of the Devonian, 358.9 million years ago, which occurred in two waves of extinction, is marked by a layer of anoxic black shale, formed from the black mud covering and killing off as much as fifty percent of all the deep marine genera.[47]

The next era, the Permian (298.9 to 251.902 million years ago, and named for the city of Perm Krai, Russia, where the first fossils were discovered) witnessed the spread of large amphibians, mammals, turtles, snakes, lizards, crocodiles, and the ancestors of birds and dinosaurs. Sail-finned animals, including *Dimetrodons,* and other similar genera, appeared in the early Permian. Although *Dimetrodons* are often grouped with dinosaurs (and are almost always found in bags of toy dinosaurs), they were extinct forty million years before the dinosaurs appeared, and were more closely related to mammals than to reptiles or birds.[48] The Permian-Triassic mass extinction occurred 251.902 million years ago,[47] which provided the abundance of fossil fuels upon which we rely today. The Permian may also have ended in fire, possibly involving a combination of meteorites, volcanoes, and even coal and natural gas explosions.[49] The Permian-Triassic extinction is considered the most severe extinction event in all of Earth's creation history. Ninety-six percent of all marine species and seventy percent of all terrestrial vertebrate species died during the "Great Extinction." This was the one extinction when large numbers of insect species died out as well.[50] The extinction was so severe that it has been claimed that it took as much as ten million years for life on Earth to recover.[51]

The Triassic period (251.9 to 201.3 million years ago) was dominated by therapsids (ancestors to the mammals) and crocodiles. The earliest dinosaurs—many of them—began to appear toward the end of the period.[52] *Coelophysis* and *Herrerasaurus* were bipedal nine-foot long carnivorous dinosaurs.[53] *Liliensternus* were twice as large and also bipedal—they may have had feathers. *Isanosaurus* was one of the very first sauropod (walking on four legs) dinosaurs.[54] The Triassic-Jurassic mass extinction occurred over about an 18 million-year time period, ending about 201.3 million years ago.[47] Again, the period ended in fire. Climate change, volcanic eruptions, and, finally, an asteroid impact ended the Triassic; killing off, again, many amphibians, cephalopods, and marine reptiles—again roughly half of all animal species.[55]

The Jurassic period (201.3 to 145 million years ago; named for the Jura Mountains in the Alps) was called the "Age of Dinosaurs," the time when great numbers of dinosaurs, large and small, roamed the Earth. This was the age of *Diplodocus, Stegosaurus,* and *Allosaurus.* However, in spite of the movie *Jurassic Park,* the two most famous dinosaurs, *Triceratops* and *Tyrannosaurus rex,* did not appear until the Cretaceous (145 to 66 million years ago). The Cretaceous-Paleogene mass extinction occurred 66 million years ago.[47] Once again, the Cretaceous period may have been on the decline for quite some time. There was a major shift in climate and vegetation toward the end of the period, which may have led to a decline in the dinosaurs. Nonetheless, there is a thin layer of sediment, known as the K-Pg boundary, which covered the entire earth 66 million years ago. The sediment exhibits high levels of iridium, which is rare on Earth but common in asteroids.[56] It is estimated that around 75 percent of all plant and animal species died out in that extinction—when an asteroid hit the earth. With few exceptions, the only animals to survive were those weighing less than fifty-five pounds.[57]

ENDNOTES

1. G. G. Simpson, "The Nonprevalence of Humanoids," *Science*, 143:769–775, 1964.
2. Stephen Jay Gould, *Wonderful Life: The Burgess Shale and the Nature of History* (New York: Norton and Company, 1990).
3. Richard Dawkins, *The Greatest Show on Earth: The Evidence for Evolution* (London: Bantam Press, 2009).
4. Ernst Mayr, *What Evolution Is*, (New York: Basick Books, 2002), 13.
5. Theodosius Dobzhansky, "Nothing in Biology Makes Sense Except in the Light of Evolution," *American Biology Teacher*, 35:125–29, 1973.
6. Malcolm W. Browne, "The Debate Over Dinosaur Extinctions Takes an Unusually Rancorous Turn," *New York Times*, Jan. 19, 1988; nytimes.com/1988/01/19/science/the-debate-over-dinosaur-extinctions-takes-an-unusually-rancorous-turn.html
7. Ronald L. Shimek, "nvertebrate Strippers," 2003, reefkeeping.com/issues/2003–09/rs/index.htm
8. Mark A. A. McMenamin, *Paleotorus: The Laws of Morphogenetic Evolution* (South Hadley, MA: Meanma Press, 2009).
9. R. A. Dewel, "Colonial origin for Eumetazoa: Major morphological transitions and the origin of bilaterian complexity," *J. Morph.*, 243:35–74, 2000
10. W. E. G. Müller, "How was metazoan threshold crossed: The hypothetical Urmetazoa," *Comp. Biochem. Physiol. [A]*, 129:433–460, 2001.
11. David Quammen, "When Life Got Complicated," *National Geographic*, 88–107, Mar. 2018.
12. Australian Government National Heritage Places—Ediacara Fossil Site—Nilpena; environment.gov.au/heritage/places/national/ediacara
13. M. A. McMenamin, Ediacaran biota from Sonora, Mexico, *Proc Natl Acad Sci U S* A, 93:4990–4993, 1996.
14. A. H. Knoll, M. R. Walter, G. M. Narbonne, and N. Christie-Blick, "A new period for the geological time scale," *Science*, 305:621–22, 2004; see also Terence Monmaney, "Life on the edge," *Smithsonian*, 56–62, Apr. 2017.
15. A. Seilacher, "Vendobionta and Psammocorallia: lost constructions of Precambrian evolution," *Journal of the Geological Society, London*, 149:607–13, 1992.

16. Alexander G. Liu, Duncun Mcilroy, and Martin D. Brasier, "First evidence for locomotion in the Ediacara biota from the 565 Ma Mistaken Point Formation, Newfoundland," *Geology*, 38:123–126, 2010.
17. Andrey Zhuravlev and Robert Riding, *The Ecology of the Cambrian Radiation* (New York: Columbia University Press, 2000).
18. Irene M. Spry, *The Palliser Expedition: An Account of John Palliser's British North American Exploring Expedition 1857–1860* (Toronto: The Macmillan Company of Canada Limited, 1963).
19. Kicking Horse River, BC Geographical Names, *apps.gov.bc.ca/pub/bcgnws/names/40658.html*
20. field.ca/about
21. Desmond Collins, "Misadventures in the Burgess Shale," *Nature*, 460:952–953, 2009.
22. Desmond Collins, "A Brief History of Field Research on the Burgess Shale." In Jean-Bernard Caron and David Rudkin, *A Burgess Shale Primer—History, Geology and Research Highlights, The Burgess Shale Consortium*. International Conference on the Cambrian Explosion, 2009, 15–32.
23. Smithsonian Institute of Natural History: paleobiology.si.edu/burgess
24. E. L. Yochelson, "Discovery, Collection, and Description of the Middle Cambrian Burgess Shale Biota by Charles Doolittle Walcott," *Proceedings of the American Philosophical Society*, 140:469–545, 1996.
25. N. J. Butterfield, "Hooking some stem-group 'worms': fossil lophotrochozoans in the Burgess Shale," *BioEssays*, 28:1161–6, 2006.
26. Royal Ontario Museum, burgess-shale.rom.on.ca/en/science/burgess-shale/03–fossils.php
27. J. B. Caron and D. A. Jackson, "Paleoecology of the Greater Phyllopod Bed community, Burgess Shale." *Palaeogeography, Palaeoclimatology, Palaeoecology*, 258:222–256, 2008.
28. D. G. Shu, et al., "Lower Cambrian vertebrates from south China," *Nature, 402: 42,* doi:10.1038/46965, 1999.
29. Simon Morris and Jean-Bernard Caron, "A Primitive Fish from the Cambrian of North America," *Nature* 512:419–422, 2014.
30 D. Palmer, *The Atlas of the Prehistoric World*, (London: Marshall Publishing Ltd., 2000), 66–67.
31. George Karleskint, Richard Turner, and James Small, *Introduction to Marine Biology*, 4th ed. (Boston: Cengage Learning, 2012).
32. org/a_portrait_of_the_tampa_bay_estuary-fast_facts_about_tampa_bay.html
33. esolonline.tki.org.nz/content/download/16371/.../us17363_Marine_Worms.pdf
34. Stephanie L. Wright, et. al., "Bioaccumulation and biological effects of cigarette litter in marine worms," *Scientific Reports*, 5: 14119, 2015.

35. *Wonderful Life* (book); Wikipedia; wikipedia.org/wiki/Wonderful_Life_(book)
36. Ronald L. Shimek, "Invertebrate Strippers," 2003, reefkeeping.com/issues/2003–09/rs/index.htm
37. Renaud de Rosa, et al. "Hox genes in brachiopods and priapulids and protostome evolution, fig. 3," *Nature*, 399:772–776, 1999.
38. Anastasios Pavlopoulos, et al. "Probing the evolution of appendage specialization by Hox gene misexpression in an emerging model crustacean," *Proc. Natl. Acad. Sci.*, 106:13897–13902, 2009.
39. Patrick Goymer, "Genome evolution: How old are Hox genes?" *Nature Reviews Genetics*, 8:328, 2007.
40. W. E. G. Müller, et al. "The unique skeleton of siliceous sponges (*Porifera; Hexactinellida and Demospongiae*) that evolved first from the Urmetazoa during the Proterozoic: a review," *Biogeosciences*, 4:219–232, 2007.
41. Jongmin Nam and Masatoshi Nei, "Evolutionary Change of the Numbers of Homeobox Genes in Bilateral Animals," *Mol Biol Evol.*, 22: 2386–2394, 2005.
42. B. Misof, et al. "Phylogenomics resolves the timing and pattern of insect evolution," *Science*, 346:763–767, 2014.
43. Jennifer K. Grenier and Sean B. Carroll, "Functional evolution of the Ultrabithorax protein," *Proc. Natl. Acad. Sci.*, 97:704–709, 2000.
44. Russell J. Garwood and Greg Edgecombe, "Early Terrestrial Animals, Evolution, and Uncertainty," *Evolution, Education, and Outreach,* 4:489–501, 2011.
45. Smithsonian; si.edu/spotlight/buginfo/bugnos
46. New type of meteorite linked to ancient asteroid collision, *Science Daily,* 15 June 2016
47. R. V. Sole and M. Newman, "Extinctions and Biodiversity in the Fossil Record—Volume Two," *Encyclopedia of Global Environmental Change*, 297–391. John Wilely & Sons, 2002; Lauren Sallan and Andrew Galimberti, *Science* 350:812–815, 2015; Norman Myers and Andrew Knoll, *Proc. Natl. Acad. Sci.*, 98:5389–5392, 2001; *Whiteside, Jessica, et al., Proc. Natl. Acad. Sci.* 107:6721–6725, 2010.
48. K. D. Angielczyk, "Dimetrodon Is Not a Dinosaur: Using Tree Thinking to Understand the Ancient Relatives of Mammals and their Evolution," *Evolution: Education and Outreach,* 2:257–271, 2009.
49. Darcy E. Ogdena and Norman H. Sleep, "Explosive eruption of coal and basalt and the end-Permian mass extinction," *Proc. Natl. Acad. Sci., US,* 109:59–62, 2011.
50. M. J. Benton, *When life nearly died: the greatest mass extinction of all time* (London: Thames & Hudson, 2005).

51. "It Took Earth Ten Million Years to Recover from Greatest Mass Extinction," *Science Daily,* May 27, 2012.
52. S. L. Brusatte, M. J. Benton, M. Ruta, M., and G. T. Lloyd, "Superiority, Competition, and Opportunism in the Evolutionary Radiation of Dinosaurs," *Science, 321:1485–1488,* 2008.
53. K. T. Hollocher and O. A. Alcober, "Carnivore coprolites from the Upper Triassic Ischigualasto Formation, Argentina: chemistry, mineralogy, and evidence for rapid initial mineralization," *Palaios,* 20:51–63, 2005.
54. E. Buffetaut, et al., "The earliest known sauropod dinosaur," *Nature,* 407:72–74, 2000.
55. bbc.co.uk/nature/extinction_events/Triassic–Jurassic_extinction_event
56. Peter Schulte, "The Chicxulub Asteroid Impact and Mass Extinction at the Cretaceous-Paleogene Boundary," *Science,* 327:1214–1218, 2010.
57. David Muench, et al., *Primal Forces* (Portland: Graphic Arts Center Publishing, 2000).

CHAPTER 15

DINOSAURS: PART OF THE INFINITE CREATION

It was December 1991. My wife, Kathleen, had sent me out shopping for a few more last-minute Christmas food items, and I was standing in the Albertson's check-out line. There, on the "things you must have as you're checking out" rack was a white book with the black silhouette of a T-rex skeleton. The author's name was in red capital letters: MICHAEL CRICHTON. I had read several of Crichton's previous books and so picked this one up. It was *Jurassic Park*—just published in paperback. I bought the book, took it home, and devoured it during the Christmas break—underlining key passages. Although there were many obvious technical problems that Crichton had not cleaned up, the concept was intriguing, using dino-DNA to bring back those amazing extinct dinosaurs.

In April of 1993, we took our family to California for spring break. On the eighth, we visited Universal Studios and the *Jurassic Park* movie preview exhibit. We bought everyone *Jurassic Park* T-shirts and tickets to the actual park so that we would be ready if it ever opened. Then, on June 11, one of the ISU biology graduate students discovered that there was to be a sneak preview of the Steven Spielberg movie (screenplay by David Koepp), *Jurassic Park*, late that night. I took some of our family members, and we met eight biology grad students at the theater. We were nearly the only people there, so we were free to cheer at appropriate times in the movie and even chide the parts we didn't like.

In scene 15, we saw Alan Grant's (Sam Neill) and Ellie Sattler's (Laura Dern) moths simultaneously drop open as they gazed at a gigantic brachiosaur standing beside their jeep. We all broke out in wild cheers in the movie theater. And that was just a two-dimensional digital image on a screen. The closest I can find to this experience described in the scriptures is in the book of Job: "Where wast thou when I laid the foundations of the earth? . . . When the morning stars sang together, and all the sons of God shouted for joy?" (Job 38:4–7). Just imagine how thrilled we were then, and how we "shouted for joy," and high-fived each other, to see the real thing—a real live brachiosaur—walking majestically on the earth!

What was the purpose of dinosaurs? What was the purpose of the *Mona Lisa*? Personally, I'm glad I was there to see them.

Our prophet and president, Russell M. Nelson, stated in the April 2002 general conference, "Compared with the omniscience of our Creator, we know relatively little about dinosaurs or the details of the Creation, for example. But this we do know: 'Verily I say unto you, in that day when the Lord shall come, he shall reveal all things—things which have passed, and hidden things which no man knew, things of the earth, by which it was made, and the purpose and the end thereof—things most precious, things that are above, and things that are beneath, things that are in the earth, and upon the earth, and in heaven.' (D&C 101:32–34; see also D&C 121:29–32)."[1]

President Brigham Young admonished the Saints in Ogden, Utah, in 1860 that His people must prepare themselves before His Second Coming:

> This earth must become a paradise—must be purged of the sin that has been upon it for many generations, for all sin and iniquity must be swept from it, and a people be prepared for the coming of the Son of Man. He will prepare a people long before the earth is celestialized and prepared for the presence of God. The Saints will increase, the Spirit of wisdom and knowledge will increase, and every grace of the Spirit of the Lord Jesus Christ must increase upon the earth, until a people and place are so prepared that the Savior can come and finish the work given him to do, when he will present the kingdom to the Father.
>
> There is a great work for the Saints to do. Progress, and improve upon, and make beautiful everything around you. Cultivate the earth and cultivate your minds. Build cities, adorn your habitations, make

> gardens, orchards, and vineyards, and render the earth so pleasant that when you look upon your labors you may do so with pleasure, and that angels may delight to come and visit your beautiful locations. In the meantime, continually seek to adorn your minds with all the graces of the Spirit of Christ.[2]

We are also told in the Doctrine and Covenants that it is our duty to learn of those things and teach them in *preparation* for the Second Coming of the Lord: "And I give unto you a commandment that you shall teach one another the doctrine of the kingdom. Teach ye diligently and my grace shall attend you, that you may be instructed more perfectly in theory, in principle, in doctrine, in the law of the gospel, in all things that pertain unto the kingdom of God, that are expedient for you to understand; Of things both in heaven and in the earth, and under the earth; things which have been, things which are, things which must shortly come to pass; things which are at home, things which are abroad; the wars and the perplexities of the nations, and the judgments which are on the land; and a knowledge also of countries and of kingdoms" (D&C 88:77–79).

It is important to remember our charge to learn from other sources, including the earth itself: "And as all have not faith, seek ye diligently and teach one another words of wisdom; yea, seek ye out of the best books words of wisdom, seek learning even by study and also by faith" (D&C 109:7). Furthermore, we are told, "for the earth shall be full of the knowledge of the Lord" (Isaiah 11:9).

One person who has dug into the earth and taught about things that were "in the earth, and under the earth" for many years at Brigham Young University was Morris S. Petersen, professor of geology, and during part of his tenure, president of the Provo Utah East Stake. He wrote the following in an *Ensign* article in 1987:

> The different roles science and religion play is illustrated in a study of the dinosaurs. From the fossil record it is theorized that the dinosaurs were the dominant animals on earth between 225 and 67 million years ago. Some were meat-eating, others lived on plants. Some were small, while others were gigantic, weighing up to seventy-two metric tons and growing to lengths of more than twenty-seven meters.
>
> The existence of these animals is unquestionable, for their remains have been found in rocks all over the world. What eternal purpose they played in the creation and early history of the world is unknown. The

> scriptures do not discuss the subject of dinosaurs, and it is not the purpose of science to explain why they were here. We can only conclude, as Talmage did, that 'The whole series of chalk deposits and many of our deep-sea limestones contain the skeletal remains of animals. These lived and died, age after age, while the earth was not ready for human habitation.' . . .
>
> But this does not mean that science has no place in our eternal pursuit of truth. The more we learn of God's handiwork, the more we come to know him and love his works. As a Latter-day Saint geologist, I consider myself very fortunate to have the opportunity to study rocks and fossils as evidences of God's creation of our earth. Everything I have learned of the grandeur of the Creation has strengthened my resolve to learn more of our Heavenly Father and live as he would have me live.[3]

People have been collecting fossil bones since the earliest historic times, and probably even earlier. For example, several early Greek philosophers, including Herodotus, described fossilized marine organisms and concluded that the rocks containing the fossils must once have been under water. The fossilized femur of a woolly rhino, which became extinct during the last ice age, about 8,000 years ago, possibly revered as the thigh bone of an ancient mythic giant, was treasured in the acropolis at Nichoria, in southern Greece.[4]

In 1676, a huge femur was discovered in England by the Reverend Robert Plot, naturalist and professor of chemistry at the University of Oxford. As with the Greeks before him, Plot thought the bone was from an ancient "giant" human. The first recognized dinosaur skeleton scientifically described was a Megalosaurus, discovered in 1824 by the British clergyman and fossil hunter William Buckland.[5] In 1842, the paleontologist Richard Owen coined the term *dinosaur*, derived from the Greek words *deinos*, meaning "terrible" and *sauros*, meaning "lizard."[6]

Beginning in the last half of the nineteenth century, and continuing to the present day, paleontology and fossil hunting have been all the rage—generating huge prestige and wealth for major discoveries. In 1909, William Holland, Director of the Carnegie Museum of Natural History, hired the paleontologist, Earl Douglass to go out west and search for dinosaur bones. Searching east of Vernal, Utah, on August 17, 1909, Douglass hit the mother lode.[7] His discovery of the Vernal fossil beds, originally known as the Carnegie Quarry, and now called the Dinosaur

National Monument,[8,9] is considered one of the greatest discoveries in the history of paleontology. The site is now regarded as one of the most important fossil beds in the world. More than 700,000 tons of fossils were shipped back to the Carnegie Museum, producing twenty-three complete mounted skeletons. Bones were also sent to the National Museum and the University of Utah.[7] The quarry has remained active for more than 100 years and has continued to produce large numbers of high quality skeletons from hundreds of dinosaurs.

The rock layer containing the fossils in the main quarry is a sandstone and conglomerate deposit from a curve in an ancient river bed, known as the Morrison Formation, dating from the Jurassic Period, some 150 million years ago.[9] The dinosaurs and other extinct animals in the deposit were apparently washed downstream and dumped along the river bend during floods. The sandy sediments were eventually buried and compressed into solid rock. The main "dinosaur wall" at the quarry, which contains hundreds of dinosaur fossils, many articulated in place, was enclosed in 1957 and then remodeled in 2011. It is a partially excavated site revealing the complete skeletons of numerous dinosaurs, just as they lived and died 150 million years ago.[9] Anyone can walk by this spectacular display and see the ancient past come to life. Cheering there is optional.

The geology of the entire region is stunning. The entire monument contains rock strata dating from the Precambrian era, through the Mesozoic, and the Cenozoic, covering nearly the entire history of life on Earth.[9] Tectonic uplift events, which formed the Uinta Mountains, raised and cracked open the layers of sediment, exposing the fossils near the surface. Erosion then removed the surface layers allowing the fossil bones to be exposed.[9]

Another major Utah discovery was made in St. George in 2000 by optometrist Sheldon Johnson, who was leveling a hill on his property east of the city. About twenty feet below the surface, he unearthed a huge rock with dinosaur footprints on its under surface. More and more rocks were excavated, revealing, thousands of dinosaur and other animal footprints in the sandstone and mudstone. These had formed nearly 200 million years ago, during the Early Jurassic Period, on the shores of a shallow lake, now known as Lake Dixie, which covered much of southern Utah and northern Arizona.[10] The rocks containing the footprints now comprise the Dinosaur Discovery Site in St. George.

The dinosaur footprints imbedded in the mud of Lake Dixie were filled in with sand that drifted in, and over millions of years, both the mud and sand turned to rock, preserving the tracks to the extent that many look as fresh today as they did on the day they were made. The footprints show foot pads, claw marks, and even impressions of the scaly skin on the bottom of a dinosaur's foot. Lake Dixie and the surrounding area were close to the equator 200 million years ago and were nearly at sea level, as the Rocky Mountains had not yet begun to form.[10]

The presence of dinosaur bones and footprints in Utah and numerous other parts of the world testify that those magnificent beasts actually roamed *this* earth and lived and died *on this planet* 225 to 67 million years ago. The great antiquity of those populations testify to the power and majesty of God's infinite Creation.

In spite of the overwhelming evidence of their presence, there are still some people who doubt that dinosaurs existed as part of *our* world. One argument that I have heard, put forward in an attempt to explain away dinosaur fossils, is that this earth was made up of parts of other worlds that have passed away. Moses 1:35 and 38 appear to be the source of this proposition: "For behold, there are many worlds that have passed away by the word of my power. And there are many that now stand, and innumerable are they unto man; but all things are numbered unto me, for they are mine and I know them . . . And as one earth shall pass away, and the heavens thereof even so shall another come; and there is no end to my works, neither to my words" (Moses 1:35, 38).

First, although these two verses talk about worlds coming and going, they do not state that the new world is made from parts of the old. Second, we are given to understand that the earth was created from "matter unorganized."[11] Third, even if this earth was made from parts of others, dinosaur bones and tracks would not have survived the process of planet building to have been preserved from an earlier world.

Consider the following analogy: About 25 percent of the metal in your 2018 Honda Accord is made from recycled cars.[12] Perhaps part of that material came from a 1968 Ford Fairlane. Why can't you dig into the engine block of the Accord and find parts of the Fairlane buried there? Heat. It takes 1510° C (2750° F) to melt steel.[13] Whatever parts of the Fairlane that were recycled were first ground into small pieces and then disappeared into the molten mass that was poured into a mold to form the Accord engine block. No sign of the original Fairlane remains. The same would have been true for any chunk of another planet recycled to form the earth. Indeed, no "chunks" of planets remain but are pulverized into individual elements during any recycle event.

Why are dinosaurs not discussed in the scriptures? The short answer is we don't know. Elephants are never mentioned in the Old Testament either, although they are still living among us. Their only mention in all the scriptures is one rather odd verse in the book of Ether: "And they also had horses, and asses, and there were elephants and cureloms and cumoms; all of which were useful unto man, and more especially the elephants and cureloms and cumoms" (Ether 9:19). In no other scripture are elephants and cureloms and cumoms ever mentioned. I have often wondered why, when Moroni abridged the twenty-four plates found by the people of Limhi, he found it important to include this reference. I have also often wondered what Joseph Smith saw as he translated that verse. Someday I hope to ask him.

Beetles are mentioned only once in all the scriptures, in Leviticus: "Even these of them ye may eat; the locust after his kind, and the bald locust after his kind, and the beetle after his kind, and the grasshopper after his kind" (Leviticus 11:22). And then we are not told which of the 350,000 species of beetles may be eaten (there are many species of beetles that produce toxins to make them inedible). Leviticus suggests, apparently, that the edible beetles are only those that leap and have four legs (see 11:21), which seriously limits the selection, as the vast majority have six legs.

The most abundant animals on planet earth, the nematodes, are never mentioned even once in the scriptures.[14] Bacteria never come up, nor do amebae. Jellyfish, starfish, sea urchins, and not even clams find place in the scriptures. In short, most of the extant animal life on planet earth is never mentioned in the scriptures. Why would we expect extinct animal life to come up?

In pondering these issues, it is important to remember the counsel of James E. Talmage, who was an Apostle from 1911 to 1933: "The opening chapters of Genesis, and scriptures related thereto, were never intended as a textbook of geology, archaeology, earth-science, or man-science."[15] We can enhance our learning in those subjects by reading from the best books and by asking the earth itself to yield up its secrets about the infinite Creation.

ENDNOTES

1. Russell M. Nelson, "How Firm Our Foundation," April 2002 general conference.
2. Brigham Young, "Religion, Progress, and Privileges of the Saints, &c," *Journal of Discourses*, 8:83, 1860.
3. Morris S. Petersen, "Do we know how the earth's history as indicated from fossils fits with the earth's history as the scriptures present it?" *Ensign*, Sept. 1987.
4. Adrienne Mayor, *The First Fossil Hunters, Dinosaurs, Mammoths, and Myth in the Greek and Roman World: Tracing the History of Human Curiosity about Fossils* (Princeton, NJ: Princeton University Press, 2000, 2011).
5. nchantedlearning.com
6. livescience.com/3945–history-dinosaurs.html, Mar. 23, 2017.
7. Earl Douglass, US National Park Service. See nps.gov/dino/learn/historyculture/douglass.htm. Last retrieved 12 June 2020.
8. Dinosaur National Monument; US National Park Service. See nps.gov/dino. Last retrieved 12 June 2020.
9. Dinosaur National Monument. See nps.gov/dino/learn/nature/morrison-formation.htm. Last retrieved 12 June 2020.
10. Dinosaur Discovery Site, dinosite.org
11. c.f. M. Russell Ballard, *New Era*, June 1984.
12. "Benefits of Recycling Car Bodies," earth911.com
13. Brian Kross, jeffersonlab.org
14. huffingtonpost.com/2013/02/11/nematode-roundworm-parasite-earth_n_2657324.html
15. "The Earth and Man," address delivered Aug. 9, 1931, in the Salt Lake Tabernacle, 3. Copy in the Historical Department, The Church of Jesus Christ of Latter-day Saints.

CHAPTER 16

THE RISE OF BIRDS AND MAMMALS

Not long after I joined the faculty of Idaho State University (1981), I was asked by my good friend in the English department, Waller Wigginton, to participate in a debate at St. John's Catholic Student Center on the issue of evolution and creationism. Wigginton originally organized the debate between Doctors Ed House and Rufus Lyman (emeritus professor) of the biology department, Pastor Bill Knepper, of the Inkom Community Bible Church, and Pastor Mike Powell of the University Bible Church. Only a few days before the debate was scheduled to occur, Wigginton called me in some distress. It seemed that Knepper contracted cold feet and called in the "big creationist gun," Duane Gish, of the Institute for Creation Research, then located in Santee, California, to take his place. In protest of Knepper's move to elevate what was scheduled to be a "friendly" local debate to a large-scale debate involving a national creationist "celebrity," House withdrew from the debate. Wigginton called to ask if I would stand in for House. Not one to pass up an opportunity, even as a brand new faculty member, I agreed.

The night of the great debate arrived, and we assembled in the crowded basement lecture room of St. John's Catholic Student Center. First, Powell spoke in favor of creationism—essentially introducing Gish as a world-renowned creationist. (Mike and I have since become friends and have continued to enjoy a number of religious discussions.) Then Lyman spoke on the side of evolution. He arose and, as I recall, said something to the effect of, "Evolution is a well-established scientific principle, and it is a d--- waste of time to debate the propriety of creationism." Then he sat down. Five minutes into the debate, only Gish and I were left to speak.

I had read reviews of some of Gish's previous debates and was prepared for what he was about to say. His main point was that there are no transitional animals in the fossil record. It did take him quite some time to come to that point. Then it was my turn to speak. I had prepared two major points. One concerned the structure and amino acid sequence of the cytochrome c proteins—showing a clear evolutionary transition between a wide range of species. Molecular biology was in its infancy back then, and DNA sequence data were generally not available. The second point was to present all the anatomical features of the fossil animal *Archaeopteryx*, which was about the size of a pheasant and exhibited many features of birds and many features of reptiles—making it a perfect intermediate, transitional animal between two major classes.[1] Neither Lyman nor Powell had any closing comments. Gish again stood and stated that there are no transitional animals in the fossil record. He never even mentioned *Archaeopteryx*. In my turn, I pointed out that Gish had not addressed my principal points. That was it—the "great debate" was over. I was reminded of the Fourth of July back in Malta, Idaho, where I grew up. Each year, a small pig was smeared all over with grease and then released so that any child who wished to end up smeared in grease and dirt could chase after it. I had never chased after a greased pig—not until the night of the "great debate."

Even though the first *Archaeopteryx* fossil had been discovered near Langenaltheim, Germany, in 1861 (and eleven more specimens were subsequently found) for many years, *Archaeopteryx*, which had lived during the late Jurassic period, around 150 million years ago, remained essentially the only bird-dinosaur transition animal in the fossil record.[1] Then there was an explosion in China. Liaoning province in northeast China contains some of the finest sedimentary rock formations in the world. These formations preserve in exquisite detail not only bone structure but also feathers (some in color!) and even soft tissue details, including what the animal had eaten just before it died. The Liaoning area was volcanically active 131 to 120 million years ago, and huge plumes of volcanic dust repeatedly filled the air and covered the ground, instantly killing and burying every living thing in an anaerobic (without oxygen) environment where bacteria could not digest the flesh.[2] The first fossils were actually discovered there as early as 1920, but the finds remained largely unknown until the 1990s. In 1996, a small, feathered meat-eating dinosaur, *Sino-*

sauropteryx prima, made headlines around the world.[3] The fossil had been discovered by an enterprising farmer who found a rock slab with both mirror-image halves of the animal. He sold one half to one museum and the other half to another museum—thus doubling his income from the find. That discovery began a veritable fossil gold rush, which has yielded over forty remarkable transitional species to date.[4]

The finds include *Anchiornishuxleyi,* a chicken-sized animal with every feather preserved in living color. But, as once thought, it wasn't just the little guys who sported feathers. *Yutyrannus* was a ton-and-a-half bipedal behemoth richly adorned in feathers. The ash also preserved numerous other plants and animals. To date, in addition to the forty odd feathered dinosaurs, the region has yielded fifteen fish species, eight amphibian species, four species of turtle, twenty four non-feathered flying reptiles (pterosaurs), seventeen mammal species, and over fifty three bird species. There were lots of clams, snails, and crustaceans; as well as spiders and insects—right down to a bee with every minute detail preserved. There were also lots of plants: algae, mosses, ginkgo, cypress, and pine trees; and the earliest flowering plants.[4]

The timing of the Liaoning fossils is pivotal to our understanding of creation. The animals embedded there are a snapshot of history at the moment in time when modern birds were separating from feathered dinosaurs—developing new lifestyles—new ways of eating and flying.[4]

Speaking of the Liaoning fossils, Richard Conniff, a contributing author to *Smithsonian*, said, "These transitions have never been detailed in such abundance. The 150–million-year-old *Archaeopteryx* has been revered since 1861 as critical evidence for the evolution of birds from reptiles. But it's known from just a dozen fossils found in Germany. By contrast, Liaoning has produced so many specimens of some species that paleontologists study them not just microscopically but statistically."[4]

Archaeornithura is a full-fledged (literally) shorebird that lived in Liaoning around 130 million years ago. To date, it is the oldest "modern" bird ever discovered. It lacks the long vertebrae-packed tail of the bird-dinosaur transitional forms and, instead, it exhibits fan-shaped tail feathers typical of all modern birds. Its wings also exhibited several characteristics of modern, fully-flighted birds.[5] Of the two *Archaeornithura* fossils discovered so far, however, one has no wings, neck or head; and the other has everything except the beak—so there is no way of knowing if that genus had teeth or a smooth beak.

Among the fossils at Liaoning is the 120–125 million-year-old *Confuciusornis*, with a toothless modern bird beak, although other close relatives of modern birds living at the same time, such as *Hesperornis* and *Ichthyornis*, were still toothed.[6] One of those two toothed birds, however, *Ichthyornis,* had a different bird-beak innovation. The upper half of the beak was separate from the rest of the skull so that it could be lifted while the rest of the skull remained fixed. As a result of this innovation, which might seem trivial to us, most modern birds are able to use their beaks with great precision—much like having a surrogate hand there.[7]

Ancient birds, both toothed and non-toothed varieties, also walked the land in what is now Utah. In 1991, a good friend of mine, Steve Robison, described tracks he had found from three different types of shore birds living in the Late Cretaceous (72.1 to 83.6 million years ago) on two slabs of rock near old coal mines close to Huntington, and Orangeville, Utah. There were also frog or toad tracks on one of the slabs. The same strata of rocks from those areas also contain a "large number of dinosaur footprints in these rocks." The slabs Robison described also had many plant fragments, such as leafy redwood twigs and other angiosperm leaves, roots, and stems.[8]

With their highly mobile toothless beaks, their wings tuned to highly skilled, precise flight, and their fanned tail feathers, which aids considerably in their controlled flight, birds have done quite well for themselves. Today, there are around 18,000 to 20,000 bird species on earth, with between 100 billion and 400 billion individuals—apparently no one can get them to hold still long enough to make an accurate count. That means that there are somewhere between 13 and 53 times as many birds on earth as there are people—sort of brings Alfred Hitchcock's *The Birds* to mind.[9]

Recent research has shown that even though modern birds have lost their teeth in exchange for greater beak flexibility, they still have retained the genes for making teeth and can even make teeth under the right conditions.[10]

In 2014, Mark Springer and colleagues at the University of California—Riverside were interested in the absence in birds of dentin and enamel genes, which would function in toothed animals at later stages of tooth development. They wanted to know whether birds lost six genes involved in dentin and enamel production in a single event, suggesting that a common ancestor to all birds had lost all of those teeth genes, or whether loss of those tooth genes had happened separately in several different lines of birds throughout creation. They examined one dentin matrix gene (*dentin sialophosphoprotein*) and five enamel genes (*amelotin, ameloblastin, Enamelin, amelogenin,* and *enamelysin*) in forty-eight bird species, representing nearly all extant bird orders. They found the same inactivating mutations in those six dentin and enamel genes in all forty-eight species, suggesting a single, common ancestor of all living birds lost the genes to make enamel around 116 million years ago.[11]

The seventeen mammal species and fifty-three bird species in the Liaoning environment gives a ratio of three to one in favor of birds.[4] Interestingly enough, the ratio of more than 18,000 bird species living today[9] compared to the 5,416 species of mammals[12] is still about the same as it was 120 million years ago—just over a three to one ratio. It also is interesting to note that there were birds and mammals around 60 million years before *T. rex* ever set foot on the earth.

The earliest fossil mammal discovered in Liaoning, dating from around 125 million years ago, was about the size and shape of a mouse and has been named *Eomaia* ("dawn mother").[13] *Jeholodens* was a slightly larger nocturnal arboreal insectivore mammal with big eyes.[14] *Docofossor* looked and behaved like a modern mole, and *Volaticotherium* was like a modern flying squirrel. *Agilodocodon* gnawed through tree bark and fed on sap, whereas *Fruitafossor* was an anteater. *Castorocauda* was about the size of a prairie dog with webbed feet and a flattened tail—the earliest-known swimming mammal.[15] A mammal named *Repenomamus,* something like a wolverine, had just eaten a small dinosaur before being buried alive and preserved forever in volcanic ash.[4]

Ironically, ancient mammals were discovered *at the same time* as the first dinosaur, by William Buckland in a shale quarry in the English countryside in 1824. But whereas the dinosaur, named *Megalosaurus* ("big lizard") became famous, the mammals found in the same strata of the same quarry, which were only the size of mice, were soon forgotten in the now two-hundred-year-old human love affair with dinosaurs. Furthermore, very few additional fossil mammals were discovered until just the past fifteen years.[15]

Mammals actually came from cynodonts—transitional primitive animals with both mammal and reptile characteristics—around 210 million years ago, during the Late Triassic, when dinosaurs themselves were first appearing. The earliest mouse-sized mammals had developed a unique skull with a simple hinge joint to the lower jaw but with powerful, enlarged jaw muscles that could bring the teeth together in a massive bite—much more powerful than any other animal their size. The teeth were also specialized. The front teeth were for slicing, and the back molar teeth were for grinding. Another huge advantage to those tiny mammals was that females had developed modified sweat glands that produced milk for their infants, while the babies had delayed tooth emergence to facilitate nursing. Those developments, plus the growth of hair to cover their bodies and giving live birth to their young, gave mammals a huge advantage over other animals. All those factors ensured a higher survival rate for the young and allowed the young to grow faster and attain higher metabolic rates, thus allowing early mammals to survive in colder temperatures and at night when their competitors were not as active. Those characteristics also provided primitive mammals with increased intelligence and heightened sensory perception.[15]

New evidence has shown that during the Jurassic and Cretaceous periods, far from simply surviving by staying out of the way of dinosaurs, mammals were rapidly diversifying to fill numerous niches. Then a botanical event occurred that gave the mammals another edge. Angiosperms—plants with flowers—appeared, followed by seeds, fruits, and nuts. Insects, attracted to the flowers, were also an increasing food source. Mammals, with their grinding molars, were able to exploit these new resources, whereas their competitors, except for the birds that were also radiating and adapting, were unable to adapt to the new fare.[15] As angiosperms spread—in part because their seeds could be more widely dispersed than the more primitive spores produced by mosses, ferns, liverworts, and hornworts—they outcompeted and overcrowded the more primitive plants upon which many primitive animals, such as many herbivorous dinosaurs, depended for food. As a result, dinosaurs were on the decline even before the great Cretaceous-Paleogene mass extinction event occurred.[16]

Around 66 million years ago, an asteroid hit the earth, killing off nearly all large animals of every kind and further devastating, and nearly annihilating, the more primitive plants.[17] A new playing field was now open for an even greater expansion of the mammals, and they thrived in the post-apocalyptic era. Only 500,000 years after the asteroid struck, mammals were beginning to dominate the earth.[15] With the spread of grasslands across the fire-swept globe, the first hoofed ungulates appeared about 25 million years ago.[18] And around 63 million years ago, a tiny, wiry arboreal animal named *Torrejonia* appeared in New Mexico—the earliest known primate—a line that would eventually lead to us.[19]

ENDNOTES

1. British Museum of Natural History—specimen 'BMNH 37001'—the type specimen
2. Mark Norell, Eugene S. Gaffney, and Lowell Dingus, *Discovering Dinosaurs: Evolution, Extinction, and the Lessons of Prehistory* (Oakland, CA: University of California Press, 2000), 214–16.
3. P-J. Chen, Z-M. Dong, and S-N. Zhen, "An exceptionally well-preserved theropod dinosaur from the Yixian Formation of China," *Nature*, 391:14.–152, 1998.
4. Richard Conniff, "The great Sino Dino Boom," *Smithsonian*, 49:28–35, May 2018.
5. Elizabeth Quill, "The first flight plan," *Smithsonian*, 10, July–August 2016.
6. M. Ivanov, S. Hrdlickova, and R. Gregorova, *The Complete Encyclopedia of Fossils* (Netherlands, Rebo Publishers, 2001), 312.
7. Rebecca Hersher, "How Did Birds Lose Their Teeth And Get Their Beaks? Study Offers Clues, " National Public Radio, npr.org/sections/thetwo-way/2018/05/02/607117197/how-did-birds-lose-their-teeth-and-get-their-beaks-study-offers-clues, May 2, 2018; D. J. Field, et al., "Complete Ichthyornis skull illuminates mosaic assembly of the avian head," *Nature*, 557:96–100 ,2018.
8. Steven F. Robison, "Bird and Frog Tracks from the Late Cretaceous Blackhawk Formation in East-Central Utah," Geology of East-Central Utah 19: 325–334, 1991; archives.datapages.com/data/uga/data/061/061001/325_ugs610325.htm
9. American Museum of Natural History; amnh.org/about-the-museum/press-center/new-study-doubles-the-estimate-of-bird-species-in-the-world
10. M. P. Harris, S. m. Hasso, M. W. Ferguson, and J. F. Fallon, "The development of archosaurian first-generation teeth in a chicken mutant," *Curr. Biol.*, 16:371–7, 2006; David Biello, "Mutant Chicken Grows Alligatorlike Teeth," *Scientific American*, February 22, 2006. Students in my laboratory were also successful in growing one more structurally complete tooth in one chick embryo after implanting beads soaked in growth factors BMP4, FGF4, and FGF9.
11. R. W. Meredith, et al., "Evidence for a single loss of mineralized teeth in the common avian ancestor," *Science*, 346(6215):1254390. doi: 10.1126/science.1254390, 2014; Larua Geggel, "Why Birds Don't Have Teeth," livescience.com/49109–bird-teeth-common-ancestor.html
12. Don E. Wilson and Dee Ann M. Reeder, eds. *Mammal Species of the World: A Taxonomic and Geographic Reference*, 3rd edition (Baltimore: Johns Hopkins University Press, 2005).

13. Q. Ji, et al., "The earliest known eutherian mammal," *Nature,* 416:816–822, 2002.
14. J. Qiang, "A Chinese triconodont mammal and mosaic evolution of the mammalian skeleton," *Nature,* 398:326–30, 1999.
15. Stephen Brusatte and Zhe-Xi Luo, "Ascent of the Mammals," *Scientific American*, 28–35, June 2016.
16. Pallab Ghosh, "Dinosaurs were in decline before asteroid strike, study finds," BBC News, bbc.com/news/av/science-environment-36080555/dinosaurs-were-in-decline-before-asteroid-strike-study-finds, 2016
17. R. V. Sole and M. Newman, "Extinctions and Biodiversity in the Fossil Record—Volume Two," *Encyclopedia of Global Environmental Change* (John Wiley & Sons, 2002), 297–391; Lauren Sallan and Andrew Galimberti, *Science* 350:812–815, 2015; Norman Myers and Andrew Knoll, *Proc. Natl. Acad. Sci.*, 98:5389–5392, 2001; Jessica Whiteside, et al., *Proc. Natl. Acad. Sci.* 107:6721–6725, 2010.
18. Caroline A. E. Strömberg, "Dung Fossils Suggest Dinosaurs Ate Grass," National Geographic News, news.nationalgeographic.com/news/2005/11/1118_051118_grass_dinos_2.html, 2005
19. Brusatte, ibid.

CHAPTER 17

WHO IS GOD?

During the winter of 1834–1835, the Prophet Joseph Smith and/or Sidney Rigdon gave seven lectures on faith as a course of instruction to the School of the Elders assembled in the Kirtland printing office. Part of Lecture Fourth states: "Correct ideas of the character of God are necessary in order to the exercise of faith in him unto life and salvation, and . . . without correct ideas of his character, the minds of men could not have sufficient power with God to the exercise of faith necessary to the enjoyment of eternal life, and that correct ideas of his character lay a foundation as far as his character is concerned, for the exercise of faith, so as to enjoy the fulness of the blessing of the gospel of Jesus Christ, even that of eternal glory"[1]

Whereas the goal of early Church leaders was to teach the true character and nature of God and thus establish true faith among Christians, many of God's characteristics and attributes could not have been appreciated at that early date. Modern scientific advances have contributed immensely to our understanding of the scriptures describing the characteristics of God and Jesus Christ.

As recorded in Luke 24, after His resurrection, Christ appeared to His Apostles in a closed room. He told them to do two things: First, handle Him to see that He has a body of flesh and bones. He said, "Behold my hands and my feet, that it is I myself: handle me, and see; for a spirit hath not flesh and bones, as ye see me have" (Luke 24:39). Second, He told his Apostles to bring Him fish and honeycomb to eat. "And while they yet believed not for joy, and wondered, he said unto them, Have ye here any meat?" (Luke 24:41) Why would Christ demonstrate to the Apostles that He could eat? What does the resurrected Christ eating tell us about resurrected bodies? It appears to me that there is an infinity of information packed into that demonstration—information that could not have been comprehended before the past one hundred years.

After the Last Supper and after Judas had departed to betray the Savior, Jesus prayed to the Father in behalf of the remaining eleven Apostles. During that prayer He said, "And this is life eternal, that they might know thee the only true God, and Jesus Christ, whom thou hast sent." (John 17:3) In the conversation leading up to that prayer, speaking to Thomas, the Savior said, "If ye had known me, ye should have known my Father also: and from henceforth ye know him, and have seen him. Philip saith unto him, Lord, shew us the Father, and it sufficeth us. Jesus saith unto him, Have I been so long time with you, and yet hast thou not known me, Philip? he that hath seen me hath seen the Father; and how sayest thou then, Shew us the Father?" (John 14:7–9)

Unfortunately, that scripture, perhaps more than any other, has caused an enormous amount of misunderstanding throughout the history of Christianity. The confusion caused by taking this scripture literally rather than metaphorically has led to the abominable creed of the Trinity (see Joseph Smith—History 1:19).

When Joseph Smith entered the grove of trees near his family home in the early spring of 1820 to ask the questions, "Who of all these parties are right; or, are they all wrong together? If any one of them be right, which is it, and how shall I know it?" (Joseph Smith History 1:10). He was apparently not questioning the common Christian belief in the Trinity; but what he saw would change forever our understanding of the Godhead: "I saw a pillar of light exactly over my head, above the brightness of the sun, which descended gradually until it fell upon me . . . When the light rested upon me I saw two Personages, whose brightness and glory defy all description, standing above me in the air. One of them spake unto me, calling me by name and said, pointing to the other—This is My Beloved Son. Hear Him!" (Joseph Smith History 1:16–17) In several other accounts of this vision, Joseph said that the two looked identical to each other.[2] There is little wonder, then that Jesus would say to His apostles in Jerusalem, "he that hath seen me hath seen the Father."

In our ordinary lives, it is common for a son to be "the spitting image" of his father. When I attend my family reunions, many of my cousins delight in calling me Ray—my father's name—because I look very much like him when he was older. I politely reply, "Thank you." I recently attended my fiftieth high school reunion and greeted several classmates I had not seen since graduation day. More than one of them commented, "You look more like your father than you do yourself." I could easily say to a stranger I meet, "If you want to know what my father looked like, just look at me. If you've seen me you've seen my father."

The brother of Jared had a unique experience in human history:

> And it came to pass that when the brother of Jared had said these words, behold, the Lord stretched forth his hand and touched the stones one by one with his finger. And the veil was taken from off the eyes of the brother of Jared, and he saw the finger of the Lord; and it was as the finger of a man, like unto flesh and blood; and the brother of Jared fell down before the Lord, for he was struck with fear. And the Lord saw that the brother of Jared had fallen to the earth; and the Lord said unto him: Arise, why hast thou fallen? And he saith unto the Lord: I saw the finger of the Lord, and I feared lest he should smite me; for I knew not that the Lord had flesh and blood. And the Lord said unto him: Because of thy faith thou hast seen that I shall take upon me flesh and blood; and never has man come before me with such exceeding faith as thou hast; for were it not so ye could not have seen my finger. Sawest thou more than this? (Ether 3:6–9)

The brother of Jared "saw the finger of the Lord, . . . [which had the appearance of] flesh and blood." The Lord told him, "Thou hast seen that I shall take upon me flesh and blood." It is obvious from this scripture that the brother of Jared saw what Christ would look like when He came to the earth. But what did the brother of Jared actually see at the time? Did he see only what would be, or did he also see what actually was at the time—the spirit Christ? Maybe the answer is yes. Maybe he was seeing the present *and* the future at the same time—such, perhaps, is the nature of infinity. Maybe Christ's spirit finger looked *exactly* like what his mortal finger would look.

The Prophet Joseph Smith gave the following instruction to the Saints gathered at Ramus, Illinois, on April 2, 1843: "The Father has a body of flesh and bones as tangible as man's; the Son also; but the Holy Ghost has not a body of flesh and bones, but is a personage of Spirit. Were it not so, the Holy Ghost could not dwell in us" (D&C 130:22). Therefore, we can look to the characteristics of Jesus's resurrected, immortal body in order to understand God's eternal, immortal body.

In order to understand Christ's resurrected body, we may ponder Luke's accounts of Christ's appearances to His disciples following His resurrection. He first appeared to two disciples as they journeyed to Emmaus. We read that after they reached Emmaus, the following occurred: "And it came to pass, as he sat at meat with them, he took bread, and blessed it, and brake, and gave to them. And their eyes were opened, and they knew him; and he vanished out of their sight" (Luke 24:30–31).

While Christ "sat at meat" with His two disciples at Emmaus, did he eat the "meat," or did He just watch them eat? We are not told for certain, but we can logically assume that He ate with the disciples. A later encounter, however, leaves no question about Christ's ability to consume food. Furthermore, on that occasion, Christ specifically *demonstrated* that He *could* eat food. After Christ appeared to the Apostles, "he said unto them, Have ye here any meat? And they gave him a piece of a broiled fish, and of an honeycomb. And he took it, and did eat before them" (Luke 24:41–43).

It appears that Christ ate the fish and honeycomb specifically to prove to the Apostles that he *could* eat—He ate before them—as in a demonstration. Was Christ just performing some sort of "trick" to "prove" He could eat—to what purpose? It doesn't seem reasonable that Christ would just swallow food to prove that He could without His intending for us to ponder the implications of that event. I believe He consumed food to teach us important, eternal truths about resurrected beings—with huge implications. To me, Christ's purposeful gastrological demonstration provides critical data to our understanding the resurrection. Those data, apparently, tell us that the resurrected Savior's digestive tract was intact and functional. The implications of those data could not have been understood by any of His disciples or their contemporaries, nor could the implications have been fully understood by anyone living more than a hundred years or so ago.

The Savior told His disciples, "I can of mine own self do nothing . . . I seek not mine own will, but the will of the Father which hath sent me" (John 5:30). Therefore, it appears that God *told* Jesus to demonstrate to the Apostles that He could eat. It, therefore, appears that it is significant to God to let us know that the risen Christ could eat food. Christ told us that by seeing Him we are seeing God. Therefore, His gastrological demonstration must teach us that God, as an immortal, resurrected being with a body of flesh and bones, can consume food. It is obviously important to God that we know this truth about Him, as He commanded His son, after His resurrection, to eat fish and honeycomb before the disciples—and that this event was recorded in the scriptures (see Luke 24:41–43).

Furthermore, we have been told that the resurrected Savior can still partake of food and drink—at least that will be the case at the time of His Second Coming. He has told us: "Behold, this is wisdom in me; wherefore, marvel not, for the hour cometh that I will drink of the fruit of the vine with you on the earth, and with Moroni, whom I have sent unto you to reveal the Book of Mormon, containing the fulness of my everlasting gospel, to whom I have committed the keys of the record of the stick of Ephraim" (D&C 27:5).

Of course, it is entirely possible that consuming and processing food by a resurrected, immortal body is completely different from the way it is consumed and processed by mortals. At least two issues, however, argue against that proposition. First, the resurrected Christ apparently had the same body configuration as when he was mortal—including at least lips, teeth, and tongue. He apparently produced speech in the same manner he had done previously. His closest disciples could not distinguish His resurrected body from a mortal body—even though, in several cases, they didn't quite recognize him as the Jesus they had known. The disciples on the road to Emmaus seem to have thought Him to be a stranger, whereas, Mary thought He was a gardener. Maybe He appeared to be a different age, very likely with white hair rather than the dark hair they knew; or perhaps there was some other characteristic than the Jesus they knew. But there seems no doubt that He looked completely human. His apostles in the closed room thought they had seen a spirit, but He invited them to handle Him. Second, formal logic and the scientific method teach us the principal of parsimony, which states that without sufficient evidence to the contrary, the simplest explanation is most likely the correct explanation.

With these ides in mind, let us assume that Christ's digestive tract was much the same after the resurrection as it was before, and then discuss what we now know about digestion. The data from the resurrected

Christ's gastrological demonstration strongly suggest that resurrected beings have digestive systems where food is pulverized—by the teeth—mixed with digestive enzymes, and where individual nutrient molecules are absorbed through the intestinal cells lining the alimentary canal. In mortals, those nutrients then pass into the intestinal blood supply and are disbursed throughout the body by the heart where they are broken down to provide energy for cellular metabolism. Hemoglobin in the blood also carries oxygen from the lungs to the tissues, where metabolism takes place. None of this information was known by any human before the mid-nineteenth century. Before then, breathing, digestion, and blood functions were mysteries. The possibility certainly exists that the liquid transport medium in mortals (blood) may be replaced by some other liquid in resurrected beings. At present, we simply have too little information to propose such an alternative, and parsimony tells us, at the present time at least, to continue using the story of blood.

Paul said to the Corinthians, "Now this I say, brethren, that flesh and blood cannot inherit the kingdom of God; neither doth corruption inherit incorruption" (1 Corinthians 15:50). Many people seem to take this phrase literally, believing that in heaven we will have bodies of flesh and bone but not flesh and blood. It is much more likely, however, that Paul was speaking metaphorically—describing the human condition. He said to the Galatians, "To reveal his Son in me, that I might preach him among the heathen; immediately I conferred not with flesh and blood: Neither went I up to Jerusalem to them which were apostles before me; but I went into Arabia, and returned again unto Damascus" (Galatians 1:16–17). And to the Ephesians, "For we wrestle not against flesh and blood, but against principalities, against powers, against the rulers of the darkness of this world, against spiritual wickedness in high places" (Ephesians 6:12). In these last two scriptures, Paul seems to be using the term "flesh and blood" to refer to people in general.

Furthermore, if neither Paul nor anyone else of his era had any idea what blood actually did, why would they be so specific about there being no blood in heaven? Ancient people believed for thousands of years that blood was the corrupting principle in the body but did not know why. They reasoned that if no corruption could enter heaven, then that must include blood. They also had no idea what the heart actually did—they believed it was the mind—it was the source of love and devotion and courage. They thought the brain was simply the body's cooling system

They had no idea that the heart was actually a pump that propelled blood throughout the body. Therefore, if there is no blood in heaven, then there would be no need for hearts there either. Do resurrected beings have no hearts? People seem to find it easier to believe there is no blood in heaven than that there are no hearts in heaven. Of course, if blood is replaced by some other fluid that is "immortal" but has all the same functions as blood, then the resurrected, immortal heart may pump that immortal fluid. In any event, it seems likely that the resurrected heart will pump *something*. We simply haven't sufficient information to even hazard an intelligent guess at this time as to what that something might be—if not blood.

Glycolysis, also known as the Embden–Meyerhof pathway, which explains how humans break down carbon compounds from food to produce the energy necessary for life, was not worked out until the 1920s and 1930s, in Germany, by Gustav Embden and Otto Meyerhof—the culmination of over one hundred years of research by many people.[3] Still, many people today have never even heard of glycolysis or Embden-Meyerhof. Those of us who have studied this critical pathway know that the last breakdown product of the Embden–Meyerhof pathway feeds into the citric acid cycle, which, in turn, feeds into the electron transport chain. The last step in the electron transport chain, which transfers the energy stored in hydrogen bonds (electrons) to produce ATP (adenosine triphosphate, the energy currency of the body), is the transfer of an electron to oxygen.[4] Without oxygen as the terminal receptor in this long chain of events, the whole system comes to a screeching halt, not enough ATP is produced to sustain life, and the person dies within a matter of about six minutes.

Whereas a small portion of oxygen is dissolved in the plasma, most of the oxygen transported to the tissues (98.5 percent) is attached to hemoglobin molecules inside red blood cells—it's the iron inside the hemoglobin molecule, bound to oxygen, that gives blood its red color. The connection between hemoglobin and oxygen was first proposed by the French physiologist Claude Bernard around 1870.[5] Just as critical as the delivery of oxygen to tissues is the removal of CO_2, the waste product of glycolysis, from the tissues. If CO_2 accumulates in cells, glycolysis slows down or stops completely and death follows. Veins carry CO_2, dissolved in the blood, back to the lungs, where it is exhaled and a new breath of oxygen-containing air is inhaled. Arteries then carry the fresh supply of oxygen-containing blood to the tissues.

The problem is that oxygen is a double-edged sword. On the one hand, our very lives depend upon it, but on the other hand, it is one of the most dangerous elements on earth and even in space. Oxidation is named for the processes involving oxygen. The rusting of metal, fruit turning dark, the aging process, and general deterioration throughout the world are often the result of oxidation. It is critical within our bodies that oxygen is kept away from most tissues. That is why it is held captive within hemoglobin molecules, inside red blood cells, until it can be transferred to the mitochondria inside tissue cells where it is employed in the electron transport chain. If oxygen leaks out of the blood, such as occurs in a cerebral hemorrhage, oxygen in the blood will destroy the neurons with which it comes in contact. This double function of oxygen, life and death, is probably the greatest irony of mortality.

One way to combat oxidation is by means of antioxidants. We are constantly seeking, in our modern world, the perfect antioxidants to help combat disease and put off the aging process. Maybe, from an eternal perspective, antioxidants are the secret to immortality. Perhaps that was the function of the tree of life in the Garden of Eden. We are also told that there will be trees of life in the paradise of God (see Revelation 2:7; 22:2). Perhaps those trees of life will be the secret of our future immortality. But dependence on some outside source, such as the tree of life, for our immortality would appear to make that immortality conditional—yet as we contemplate immortality, such a condition seems counterintuitive.

Perhaps another solution to accomplishing immortality would be to get rid of our dependence on oxygen all together. The Savior said, "Lay not up for yourselves treasures upon earth, where moth and rust doth corrupt. . . . But lay up for yourselves treasures in heaven, where neither moth nor rust doth corrupt" (Matthew 6:19–20). Possibly, the main difference between a mortal and an immortal being is that the oxygen-containing blood is replaced by some "spiritual" fluid in our veins and arteries that carry some other terminal receptor molecule for the electron transport chain. Or maybe, the entire Embden–Meyerhof pathway—citric acid cycle—electron transport chain system will be replaced by some other enzymatic pathway in resurrected beings. At present, we cannot propose what the elemental basis of such fluid might be. Oxygen occupies a unique position on the periodic table of the elements, and there is no place, that we know of at present, for any other element to perform the task performed by oxygen. Furthermore, at present, parsimony argues that it is far more likely that the mortal and immortal systems are more the same rather than different. If God has a heart, which I believe He has, then He has blood or some other fluid pumped by that heart throughout His body.

In our modern society, researchers are already looking for other fluids that can either supplement or even replace blood in our circulatory systems. The main reason for such a search is to eliminate the technical problems and medical risks of blood transfusions. The ultimate goal of such research is to discover or create fluids that are alternative oxygen-transport systems. To date, however, no acceptable oxygen-carrying blood substitutes have been discovered, although some hemoglobin-based carriers and non-hemoglobin, perfluorocarbon-based carriers are under investigation.[6] There, are however, liquid volume expanders widely available for medical cases where only volume recovery is necessary. Those systems still rely on the oxygen-carrying capacity of hemoglobin.

After the Resurrection we may possibly look forward to life without the double-edged sword of oxygen, which is both life-giving and life-limiting. Our immortal "spiritual" blood will apparently transport absorbed nutrients (Jesus demonstrated that resurrected beings can eat) to the cells of our bodies. Within those cells, the Embden–Meyerhof pathway, citric acid cycle, and electron transport chain (or some equivalent system) will break down those nutrients to produce ATP (or some equivalent energy storage molecule). Critically, at the end of a series of enzymatic steps, some very efficient electron receptor will be there to accept that electron and keep the energy-producing system flowing smoothly. At present, we have no clue what that electron acceptor might be—if not oxygen.

Here, as often occurs in that gap between science and religion, we may either choose to stand firmly on the rock of proven scientific knowledge or to take a leap of faith and discover a previously invisible bridge leading across the chasm to the cave of the Holy Grail. What marvelous wonders may await the inquisitive mind that ventures into that cave of grails? Who knows, by thinking outside the box concerning terminal electron receptors, some young person may be *the* person who discovers the ultimate oxygen substitute—the Holy Grail of blood chemistry—and wins the Nobel Prize in chemistry and medicine for such a life-saving discovery. Religious belief can often provide the needed faith to go beyond conventional knowledge and open whole new vistas of research.

What we can learn about God from this one demonstration of Christ's ability to eat is, in my opinion, enormous. Putting the discussion of oxygen aside, the other implications of Christ's eating fish and honeycomb lead us to conclude that immortal, resurrected life is based on cellular life. Before cells were discovered in the seventeenth through nineteenth centuries, people could believe that they, as well as resurrected beings, were some sort of single, indivisible entity. Today, we have a difficult time even identifying with this belief for mortal humans. We now know that we are each composed of more than thirty trillion cells—one hundred times more cells in a single human body than there are stars in the Milky Way Galaxy. But most people have not applied that same information to the condition of a resurrected body. How would one build such a body without employing the individual building blocks of that body? How does one make a body of flesh and bone without muscle cells and bone cells? How does one make resurrected muscles pull on resurrected bones without causing individual muscle cells to contract—a process that depends on ATP? To me, the logical conclusion is that God is cellular. This discovery—or proposal, if you will—in my mind does not detract from God's infinity, or omniscience, or omnipotence. But it does enhance our understanding of "the only true God" that we might have "life eternal" (John 17:3).

Actually, many of the complex sugars we eat are broken down by bacterial enzymes in our gut, not by our own enzymes, which accounts for as much as 30 percent of our total digestion.[7] It turns out that the bacterial cells in our bodies are roughly equal in number to our own cells, and many are critical to our normal healthy digestive functions.[8] So, if resurrected bodies can consume food, are our bacteria resurrected with us? Are there bacteria in heaven, or is the celestial kingdom sterile? If we are eating food in the celestial kingdom, where does that food come from? If there is food there, then there must be death of something, and that something—be it fauna or flora—must parish in the process of being eaten. Christ demonstrated that He could not only eat honeycomb but that He could eat fish as well. And if we consume food in heaven, there must be elimination of waste . . .

It's only been over the past twenty years or so that we've begun to appreciate the microbiome living inside us and the vital role it plays in our own health, and we still have a long way to go. Yet compared to what people understood only fifty years ago, we have come a long way. As with everything else, the more we learn, the more questions are generated. As a result, our meager understanding of and questions about the Resurrection were much simpler fifty or one hundred years ago—without the cells and the bacteria—than they are now. Nonetheless, even though many questions persist and other questions arise, we now know much more about the nature of God than anyone has ever known before.

Another important clue to the characteristics of God is that He is the biological father of Jesus. In order for that to be the case, God would have had to contribute twenty-three chromosomes and one copy of each of approximately twenty thousand genes toward Jesus's genetic composition. The implications of God contributing just the right number of chromosomes and twenty thousand genes in the correct order may be the subject of its own entire book.

Mark's gospel emphasized the real-life, human, forty-six-chromosome-twenty-thousand-gene nature of Christ when His neighbors inquired, "Is not this the carpenter, the son of Mary, the brother of James, and Joses, and of Juda, and Simon? and are not his sisters here with us? And they were offended at him" (Mark 6:3). For most of human history since Jesus lived, people could believe that Christ was human because of some magical sleight of hand, much like a fairy turning the wooden Pinocchio into a real boy. Today, however, with our understanding of cells and chromosomes and genes, we understand that that age-old story of Pinocchio is just a fairytale. We must re-examine our understanding of the biological nature of Jesus Christ and His eternal Father. In my opinion, removing Christ from the Pinocchio paradigm in no way decreases His holiness or reality. Quite the contrary. To me, Christ becomes much more a real person who we can better understand, identify with, have faith in, and emulate.

In addition, throughout most of human history, the virgin birth paradox was unexplained away as one of the mysteries that we shouldn't delve into. Today we have enough background knowledge to, at least partially, begin to solve some of those mysteries. And we are expected to solve them to the best of our mental capacity if we are to "know . . . the only true

God, and Jesus Christ whom thou hast sent" (John 17:3). Let it suffice to say here concerning the virgin birth that I grew up on a dairy farm where we milked about seventy-five cows at any given time. We never once had a bull set foot on our farm; every cow we owned was a virgin throughout her entire life. Yet each year, each of those seventy-five cows gave birth to a calf by artificial insemination. If we, with our limited, finite knowledge of reproduction can accomplish such a minor feat, God, with His infinite knowledge, could certainly accomplish something similar or, indeed, much greater—not by magic but by the application of higher laws, laws that we are only now discovering.

As a result of modern revelation, the virgin birth paradox has moved away from the notion of some Pinocchio-like character being born to a a virgin to an understanding of Christ's necessary cellular composition and the possibility of Mary's conception following artificial insemination of some sort, toward a paradox of trying to grasp how God, therefore, must have twenty-three pairs of chromosomes and twenty thousand gene pairs in light of what we think we know about the randomness of evolution. An alternative explanation is that God is way ahead of our modern molecular technology. We have only recently discovered a natural process called CRISPR, which we are beginning to employ with amazing results in molecular biology. God's infinite knowledge of that, and other molecular techniques, puts Him light years ahead of us in knowing how to manipulate genes and chromosomes to accomplish His ends.

However, just like digestion and all other body functions, reproduction is a cellular event: a single cell from the male and a single cell from the female unite to form a new and unique human zygote—a single cell, which will develop, through time, into the thirty-trillion-celled adult human being. Jesus Christ went through the same development process as every other human being (see Luke 2:40). He is able to lead the way for us into eternity because He is, for the most part, one of us. The part of His being that was unlike us—the part that was divine from the beginning—is the part we have not as yet discovered and probably never will. Faith, after all, is a necessary part of our progress into infinity (see Hebrews 11).

ENDNOTES

1. *Lectures on Faith*, Lecture Fourth, The Attributes of God, item 1; http://lecturesonfaith.com

2. josephsmithpapers.org/site/accounts-of-the-first-vision
3. *Microbiology—Embden-Meyerhof Pathway/Krebs Cycle* (Philadelphia, PA: Lippincott Williams & Wilkins, 1992).
4. R. R. Seeley, T. D. Stephens, and P. Tate, *Anatomy and Physiology*, 8th edition (Dubuque: McGraw-Hill, 2007).
5. Claude Bernard, *Experimental Medicine* (New Brunswick, NJ: Transaction Publishers, 1999).
6. T. Henkel-Honke, M. Oleck, "Artificial oxygen carriers: A current review," *AANA Journal,* 75: 205–11, 2007.
7. 2010–08–exploring-role-gut-bacteria-digestion, phys.org, 2010
8. R. Sender, S. Fuchs, and R. Milo, "Revised Estimates for the Number of Human and Bacteria Cells in the Body," *PLoS Biol*, 19:14: e1002533, Aug. 19, 2016.

CHAPTER 18

THE CREATION OF MAN

We read the following about the Creation in Genesis 1 and Moses 2 (the text in brackets is what was added or replaced in the Joseph Smith translation, as we read in Moses 2:26):

> And [I,] God, said [unto mine Only Begotten, which was with me from the beginning:] Let us make man in our image, after our likeness; [and it was so. And I, God, said:] Let them have dominion over the fishes of the sea, and over the fowl of the air, and over the cattle, and over all the earth, and over every creeping thing that creepeth upon the earth. [And I,] God, created man in mine own image, in the image of [mine Only Begotten] created I him; male and female created [I] them. And [I,] God, blessed them, and said unto them: Be fruitful, and multiply, and replenish the earth, and subdue it, and have dominion over the fish of the sea, and over the fowl of the air, and over every living thing that moveth upon the earth. And [I,] God, said [unto man:] Behold, I have given you every herb bearing seed, which is upon the face of all the earth, and every tree in the which [shall be] the fruit of a tree yielding seed; to you it shall be for meat. And to every beast of the earth, and to every fowl of the air, and to everything that creepeth upon the earth, wherein [I grant] life, [there shall be] given every clean herb for meat; and it was so, [even as I spake.] And [I,] God, saw everything that I had made, and, behold, [all things which I had made were] very good; and the evening and the morning were the sixth day. (Moses 2:26–31)

The main difference between the Genesis and Mosaic accounts is reference to "mine Only Begotten." We are told in Moses 3 that all of chapter 2 described a spiritual creation: "For I, the Lord God, created all things, of which I have spoken, spiritually, before they were naturally upon the face of the earth. For I, the Lord God, had not caused it to rain upon the face of the earth. And I, the Lord God, had created all the children of men; and not yet a man to till the ground; for in heaven created I them; and there was not yet flesh upon the earth, neither in the water, neither in the air; But I, the Lord God, spake, and there went up a mist from the earth, and watered the whole face of the ground" (Moses 3:5–6).

It is not entirely clear why the creation of mankind is connected in these verses to rain and mist coming up from the earth. The environment from which the creation traditions emerged was a desert environment, so people living in that environment would have placed great importance to rain and mists. The human origins spoken of in these verses are still, at least from a scriptural perspective, much shrouded in mists. Before the advent of modern anthropology, Bible-believing people were comfortable with the story of a single man, Adam, being molded from the dust of the earth to become the progenitor of all humans, a mere six thousand years ago. Today, as more and more anthropological data accumulate, the picture of a simple creation from the mists and clay of the earth become much more complicated, and a science-religion reconciliation must be resolved, at least for those of us who value both scientific and religious truth.

During the April 2003 general conference of the Church, President Gordon B. Hinckley stated, "Every man or woman who ever walked the earth, even the Lord Jesus, was once a boy or girl like you. They grew according to the pattern they followed. If that pattern was good, then they became good men and women.

"Never forget, my dear young friends, that you really are a child of God who has inherited something of His divine nature."[1]

Does such a statement that "every man or woman who ever walked the earth . . . was once a boy or girl like you" also include Adam and Eve? I believe it does. In this chapter, I will discuss human origins as understood from the scientific data and then discuss what the scriptures say about Adam as the first man.

Before discussing human origins, I would remind the reader concerning the accuracy of and regard for radiometric dating as discussed in chapter 12. In 1954, Henry Eyring, the internationally renowned chemist, active member of the Church, and father of President Henry B. Eyring, wrote a note to Adam S. Bennion in response to the latter's question about determining the age of the earth. Because of its importance to our understanding of human origins, I would recommend the reader to reconsider that letter. Since 1954, our ability to read the radioactive clocks described by Dr. Eyring has vastly improved. We currently have more than a dozen different radiometric clocks, as well as many additional methods, that can be used to determine and then verify the age of a given sample. Furthermore, the accuracy with which such samples can be measured is now often between 1 and 3 percent,[2] compared to 10 percent back in 1954.

About fifty years ago the remains of two anatomically modern humans (*Homo sapiens*) with some primitive characteristics were discovered near the Omo River, in what is now Omo National Park, in southwest Ethiopia. The stratigraphic layer from which the bones were recovered were argon 40—argon 39 dated (another of the radioactive clocks) in 2005 to 195,000 years ago (± 5,000 years).[3] Then, in 2017, Jean-Jacques Hublin and colleagues at the Max Planck Institute, Leipzig, Germany, reported that recently discovered human fossils (*Homo sapiens*) at Jebel Irhoud, Morocco, have been dated by thermoluminescence flint dating to 315,000 (± 34,000) years ago. From the fossilized human remains, Hublin and his team identified several anatomically modern human features—including facial, mandibular, and tooth morphology—but the skulls also exhibited more primitive, not quite modern human brain case morphology.[4]

Our remote ancestors (*Homo habilis*) had been flint knapping to make stone tools for at least 2.5 million years,[5] and they had controlled fire since as many as one million years ago (*Homo erectus*).[6] Often the flint knapping occurred around firepits, and many flint flakes ended up in the fire. If a given flake was heated by the fire to at least 450°C, the time when it was chipped off the core piece of flint can be thermoluminescently dated.[7] (A bonfire, by the way, can reach temperatures of over 1,000°C.)[8]

The earth is constantly bombarded by radiation and photons, which can accumulate through time in certain materials, such as stones and clays. When the stone or clay is heated in a fire to over 450°C, the accumulated radiation and photons are driven out and the thermoluminescence clock is reset to zero. Then, over subsequent years, more radiation and photons accumulate in the material. When samples of such material are properly prepared and then subjected to high temperatures, they become luminescent (light up). The amount of the thermoluminescence in the sample is proportional to the age of the sample and inversely proportional to the radiation exposure of the sample since it was in the fire. By this method, scientists can determine fairly accurately (± 10.8 percent) how long ago a given flint flake, for example, was chipped off into a fire.[9]

A comparable, although slightly younger, date of 286,000 (± 32,000) years ago was obtained through uranium radiocarbon dating of a tooth from one of the Jebel Irhoud fossils. This age of approximately 300,000 thousand years ago (average of the two dating methods) for the Jebel Irhoud fossils was also consistent with the type and ages of the rodent fossils obtained from the same site.[10] A research team headed by Mattias Jakobsson of Uppsala University in Sweden has recently obtained DNA genome sequence data that also place the oldest known *Homo sapiens* in Africa as a separate species around 260,000 to 350,000 years ago.[11]

With these scientific data in mind, we can now turn to the scriptural statements about Adam. The phrase "Adam, who was the first man" (D&C 84:16; see also Moses 1:34, 3:7; Abraham 1:3) may have at least five meanings:

1. Adam may have been literally, chronologically the first man.
2. The term "first man" may be a title.
3. Adam may have been the first man to hold the priesthood.
4. Adam may be the head of the human family, in the same sense as Abraham.
5. The term "Adam" means mankind.

1. Adam may have been literally, chronologically the first man.

This first definition is certainly how the relevant scriptures seem to have been interpreted down through the years. It may come as a surprise to some people that the phrase "first man" is never used in Genesis. Indeed, only once is the phrase used in the Old Testament. In Job we read, "Art thou the first man that was born? or wast thou made before the hills?" (Job 15:7). Here, Adam is not referred to as the "first man." Rather, Job is being asked if he was the first man born—born to whom, if he was the *first* man? The phrase "first man" appears twice in the New Testament, both in 1 Corinthians: "And so it is written, The *first man* Adam was made a living soul; the last Adam was made a quickening spirit. Howbeit that was not first which is spiritual, but that which is natural; and afterward that which is spiritual. The *first man* is of the earth, earthy: the second man is the Lord from heaven" (1 Corinthians 15:45–47).

If the phrase "first man" is taken literally in 1 Corinthians, then "the last Adam" must also be taken literally, which meaning is not clear. Furthermore, if "the first man Adam" is taken literally, then the "second man" is the Lord, Jesus Christ. We know that Jesus Christ was not literally the second man ever born. Clearly, therefore, the term "first man Adam" must be taken metaphorically in this scripture as is obviously meant by the "last Adam" and the "second man . . . Lord." A metaphorical interpretation of this scripture makes perfect sense in what Paul was saying to the Corinthians about the Resurrection. Therefore, one must conclude that nowhere in ancient scripture is the phrase "first man" in reference to Adam meant to be taken literally.

The phrase "first man" in reference to Adam appears five times in modern scripture—three times in the Pearl of Great Price and twice in the Doctrine and Covenants. Our first encounter with this phrase is in Moses 1:34: "And the first man of all men have I called Adam, which is many." Here, the phrase "which is many" seems a bit odd and will be discussed in more detail later. The second appearance is also in Moses: "And I, the Lord God, formed man from the dust of the ground, and breathed into his nostrils the breath of life; and man became a living soul, the first flesh upon the earth, the first man also; nevertheless, all things were before created; but spiritually were they created and made according to my word" (Moses 3:7).

Adam is not mentioned in this verse as its object, but if the implied Adam is literally the "first man," he is also the "first flesh." The term "spiritually . . . created" in this verse suggests that this verse isn't even talking about the earthly creation. The use of "first flesh" and "first man" here, therefore, may refer only to the spiritual creation. The only citation in Abraham is in reference to the priesthood, which will be discussed later: "It [the priesthood] was conferred upon me from the fathers; it came down from the fathers, from the beginning of time, yea, even from the beginning, or before the foundation of the earth, down to the present time, even the right of the firstborn, or the first man, who is Adam, or first father, through the fathers unto me" (Abraham 1:3).

The two references in the Doctrine and Covenants are either in reference to the priesthood, "And from Enoch to Abel, who was slain by the conspiracy of his brother, who received the priesthood by the commandments of God, by the hand of his father Adam, who was the first man" (D&C 84:16) or a quote of 1 Corinthians 15:45–47 (D&C 128:14).

2. The term "first man" may be a title.

The English language is full of metaphors to which we pay little or no attention; "first" is one of them. For example, the president of the United States and his family are called the First Family. The president's wife is called the First Lady. It is obvious here that "first" has no chronological implication, and it would be ridiculous to believe that the First Family or the First Lady were the first people to ever live on Earth. There are many other examples of "firsts," such as First Presidency, First Knight, First Lieutenant, or First Boy. Adam, for a number of reasons, holds a very important position in the human family, for which "first man" is a fitting title.

3. Adam may have been the first man to hold the priesthood.

Two of the verses cited above (Abraham 1:3 and Doctrine and Covenants 84:16) are references to the priesthood. It is entirely possible that, for whatever reason, Adam was the first person given the priesthood and that *Homo sapiens* living before him were not given that right. Doctrine and Covenants 84:16 certainly suggests that we need not trace the priesthood beyond Adam. We do not as yet understand the reasons for withholding the priesthood until the time of Adam. However, when the twelve tribes of Israel were organized and exited Egypt, only the Levites were given the priesthood—and that only the Aaronic. Furthermore, we do not understand why most black male members of the Church were not given the priesthood before 1978.

4. Adam may be the head of the human family, in the same sense as Abraham.

Abraham was foreordained to his calling: "And God . . . said unto me: Abraham . . . thou wast chosen before thou wast born" (Abraham 3:23). We are not specifically told in the scriptures that Adam was also foreordained. However, we are told that all who receive the priesthood are "called and prepared from the foundation of the world according to the foreknowledge of God, on account of their exceeding faith and good works" (Alma 13:3). Abraham's calling was to be the father of all who accept the gospel, whether his biological children or not, "as many as receive this Gospel shall be called after thy name, and shall be accounted thy seed, and shall rise up and bless thee, as their father" (Abraham 2:10). We are further told in Galatians, "And if ye be Christ's, then are ye Abraham's seed, and heirs according to the promise" (Galatians 3:29). We are told in the Doctrine and Covenants that this Abrahamic promise, this covenant, was an eternal covenant, "and as touching Abraham and his seed . . . both in the world and out of the world should they continue as innumerable as the stars...and the promise was made unto Abraham; and by this law is the continuation of the works of my Father, wherein he glorifieth himself" (D&C 132:30–31). Abraham would not even be aware of all those who would fall under his covenant. "Doubtless thou art our father, though Abraham be ignorant of us, and Israel acknowledge us not: thou, O Lord, art our father, our redeemer; thy name is from everlasting" (Isaiah 63:16).

By extension, the Abrahamic covenant also includes all of Abraham's righteous ancestors, all the way back to Adam—the first man by whom this covenant exists in eternity. Paradoxically, the Abrahamic covenant even includes Adam as a son of Abraham because of his accepting Christ and being baptized after the Fall (see Moses 5:14–15 and 6:51–69). God appeared to Adam and his posterity in the valley of Adam-ondi-Ahman: "And the Lord administered comfort unto Adam, and said unto him: I have set thee to be at the head; a multitude of nations shall come of thee, and thou art a prince over them forever" (D&C 107:53, 55). Why would such a blessing be given to Adam if he were already the biological father of *every* living human being? This blessing sounds very similar to the Abrahamic covenant, and it could be called the Adamic covenant. This covenant, like the later Abrahamic covenant, is timeless, eternal. We all agreed to this covenant in the great premortal council. Therefore, it was of no importance whether or not Adam was literally the first man and all humans were descended from him. The consequence of the Adamic covenant was that all people are his children and all people are partakers of his fall, whether his direct biological offspring or not.

Abraham discusses the right of the "firstborn" in Abraham 1:3. He says, "It [the high priesthood] was conferred upon me from the fathers; it came down from the fathers, from the beginning of time, yea, even from the beginning, or before the foundation of the earth, down to the present time, even the right of the firstborn, or the first man, who is Adam, or first father, through the fathers unto me" (Abraham 1:3). This right of the firstborn, the high priesthood, is not confined to only the literal firstborn. Rather, it is conferred upon all worthy sons of Adam and sons of Abraham. It is clear that the term "firstborn" in this context is a metaphorical title. As in Doctrine and Covenants 93:22, "And all those who are begotten through me are partakers of the glory of the same, and are the church of the Firstborn."

5. The term Adam means mankind.

The name Adam has two meanings. One refers to a specific man, Adam. The other is a metaphorical name referring to *all* humans, male and female alike. We are told in the scriptures, "Male and female created he them; and blessed them, and called their name Adam, in the day when they were created" (Genesis 5:2; see also Moses 6:9). Therefore, any *Homo sapiens* is an Adam, no matter how long ago he or she was born. We can therefore say, by this scriptural definition, that the very first *Homo sapiens*, born in Africa some 315 thousand years ago, was Adam.

Adam is a Hebrew word (מָדָא) meaning "man," "mankind," or "human." Not coincidentally, it is closely connected to the Hebrew word *adamah* meaning the "earth," specifically red earth or clay, from which the Hebrews believed Adam was specifically taken. We find the Hebrew word מָדָא used in Genesis in all of its meanings: collectively as "mankind," (Genesis 1:27) gender nonspecific, (Genesis 5:1, 2) and male specific. (Genesis 2:23–24)[12] The notion that Adam can be translated "mankind" seems to help Moses 1:34 make more sense: "And the first man of all men have I called Adam (i.e, mankind), which is many." Thus, mankind was the first man, which is many.

As we evaluate the term "first man" in the scriptures in light of the five possible meanings just presented, and possibly more, we can ask the question, which of these interpretations are compatible with the first *Homo sapiens* appearing some 300,000 years ago? It turns out that only the first definition of Adam, as the "first man" taken literally and chronologically is in conflict with the scientific data. Definitions 2 through 5, taken collectively or individually, are all compatible with the scientific data. Therefore, what appears on the surface to be a simple choice between these two options of a literal, chronological "first man" or the term "first man" being a title, having reference to the first priesthood holder, head of the human family, and/or the symbol of mankind—a mere flip of the coin, if you will—has a huge impact on how we understand the relationship between science and religion. If we choose the literal, chronological option, we create a huge gulf between the two, and we are forced to reject either science or religion by doggedly adhering to the other. In making such a choice, science is not the loser. It is impartial; it doesn't care whether or not it has converts. The truths of science can continue without any believers because belief in science has no impact on the truths it reveals. Religion, on the other hand, requires faith (see Hebrews 11), for without faith, there is no religion. Without faith, it is impossible to please God (see Hebrews 11:6). But faith is difficult enough without forcing oneself to abandon all common sense. We should not be prepared to demonstrate our "faith" by throwing away the truths revealed by science in favor of accepting as literal terms in the scriptures that were meant to be metaphorical. Personally, I reserve my faith for more fundamentally important issues such as the plan of salvation, the Atonement of Jesus Christ, and our potential glorious future in the presence of our Heavenly Father.

As new frontiers of science are reached, some religious concepts may require re-evaluation in the new scientific context. At the same time, the limitations of science have to be realized so that we don't "throw out the baby with the bathwater." Science is a powerful source of truth concerning the human body but is very limited concerning what it can say about the human spirit and infinity. Religion, on the other hand, may provide metaphorical stories about human origins but is critical to our understanding of our infinite nature.

ENDNOTES

1. Gordon B. Hinckley, "ou Are a Child of God," April 2003 general conference.
2. G. Brent Dalrymple, *The Age of the Earth* (Stanford, CA: Stanford University Press, 1994).
3. Ian Mcdougall, F. H. Brown, and J. G. Fleagle, "Stratigraphic placement and age of modern humans from Kibish, Ethiopia," *Nature,* 433:733–736, 2005.
4. Jean-Jacques Hublin, et al., "New fossils from Jebel Irhoud, Morocco and the pan-African origin of *Homo sapiens*," *Nature*, 546:289–292, 2017. (Daniel Richter, et al. "The age of the hominin fossils from Jebel Irhoud, Morocco, and the origins of the Middle Stone Age," *Nature*, 546:293–296, 2017.)
5. Briana Pobiner, "The First Butchers," sapiens.org/evolution/homo-sapiens-and-tool-making, 2016.
6. F. Berna, P. Goldberg, L. K. Horwitz, J. Brink, S. Holt, M. Bamford, and M. Chazan, "Microstratigraphic evidence of in situ fire in the Acheulean strata of Wonderwerk Cave, Northern Cape province, South Africa," *Proceedings of the National Academy of Sciences*, 109:E1215–1220, 2012.
7. H. Valladas, "Thermoluminescence dating of flint," *Quaternary Science Reviews* 11:1–5, 1992.
8. Gaby Munoz, "How Hot Is a Bonfire?," sciencing.com, 2018.

9. University of Notre Dame Physics, nd.edu/~nsl/Lectures/phys10262_2014/art-chap5–4.pdf
10. Denis Geraads, et al. "The rodents from the late Middle Pleistocene hominid-bearing site of J'bel Irhoud, Morocco, and their chronological and paleoenvironmental implications," *Quaternary Research,* 80:552–561, 2013.
11. C. M. Schlebusch, et al., "Southern Africa ancient genomes estimate modern human divergence to 350,000 to 260,000 years ago," *Science,* 358:652–655, 2017.
12. Ronald S. Hendel, et al., *Eerdmans Dictionary of the Bible* (Grand Rapids, MI: Wm B. Eerdmans Publishing Co., 2000).

CHAPTER 19

THE CREATION OF WOMAN

We are told in the books of Moses and Genesis: "And Adam gave names to all cattle, and to the fowl of the air, and to every beast of the field; but as for Adam, there was not found an help meet for him. And I, the Lord God, caused a deep sleep to fall upon Adam; and he slept, and I took one of his ribs and closed up the flesh in the stead thereof; And the rib which I, the Lord God, had taken from man, made I a woman, and brought her unto the man. And Adam said: This I know now is bone of my bones, and flesh of my flesh; she shall be called Woman, because she was taken out of man. Therefore shall a man leave his father and his mother, and shall cleave unto his wife; and they shall be one flesh. And they were both naked, the man and his wife, and were not ashamed" (Moses 3:20–25; see also Genesis 2:20–25).

In a 1976 *Ensign* article entitled "The Blessings and Responsibilities of Womanhood," President Spencer W. Kimball stated, "'And I, God, created man in mine own image, in the image of mine Only Begotten created I him; male and female created I them.' [The story of the rib, of course, is figurative.]"[1] The scriptures don't add any additional information concerning the creation of woman—but mitochondria do.

Mitochondria are tiny, bacterial-size inclusions in most eukaryotic cells, numbering up to as many as one thousand to two thousand per cell and accounting for as much as one-fifth the total cell volume.[2] They are the powerhouses of the cell, responsible for most of the cell's energy production. Mitochondria have their own circular, unpaired DNA, allowing for that DNA to be traced to the most remote points of human history.

They are inherited through the egg cells of mothers of every human being who has ever lived, a process known as matrilineal inheritance.

When Rebecca Cann entered UC Berkeley in the fall of 1977 to work on her PhD in biochemistry under the supervision of Allan Wilson, she had a dream. She believed she could trace the matrilineal line of all females back to a first common ancestor using racial mutation differences in mitochondrial DNA (mtDNA). She already had experience in constructing phylogenetic trees—she had spent five years working at Cutter Laboratories in Berkeley, constructing such trees using macaque (Old World monkeys) serum proteins. She collected cell samples and extracted mtDNA from women of African, European, Asian, and South Pacific descent. Another graduate student working in Wilson's lab, Mark Stoneking, added the mtDNA from Australian aboriginal and New Guinea women.

Wesley Brown, also in the biochemistry department at UC Berkeley, however, beat the Cann team to the punch, publishing the first estimate of the most recent common female ancestor at 180,000 years ago, based on twenty-one mtDNA samples, in 1980.[3]

Cann graduated with her PhD from UC Berkeley in 1982, and five years later, she, Stoneking, and Wilson published their research in the journal *Nature*. They had mapped mtDNA from a total of 147 women and concluded, "All these mitochondrial DNAs stem from one woman who is postulated to have lived about 200,000 years ago, probably in Africa."[4] That "one woman" identified by Cann, Stoneking, and Wilson, became known as "Mitochondrial Eve," a term apparently coined by Wilson. Their research also laid the foundation for the "Out of Africa" theory of human origins.

What Cann and her colleagues were doing in the late 1970s was the same thing AncestryDNA and other DNA research companies do today (except today mtDNA is usually not done in general screening, but can be done for an extra fee)—except that they pushed the research back to the most recent female common ancestor—identifying an unbroken line from mother to mother back some ten thousand generations.

As of 2013, fine tuning, based on additional data and using newer techniques, has placed the date of the most recent common female ancestor at about 150,000 years ago.[5] Y chromosome data, which follows the patrilineal, male-male line, gives about the same result of 150,000 years ago.[6] Those data also match very closely the data obtained from the fossil record, as described in chapter 21.

I find this scientific information, as I do all scientific information, to be exciting—but also challenging. I always have to re-evaluate my prior knowledge base, whether secular or spiritual, and do some slight tweaking, or perhaps even major adjusting. I have been pondering the relationship between the "Mitochondrial Eve" and Mother Eve for at least the past thirty years, since the Cann et al. paper was published.

We are given to understand from pondering the scriptures, and from other sources, that Adam and Eve lived on the earth some six thousand years ago. Yet there are overwhelming data from numerous scientific sources that tell us *Homo sapiens* were living on this earth long before then—more than 200,000 years earlier. How do we reconcile this vast disparity?

We are told in the scriptures that Eve is the "mother of all living" and the "first of all women" (Moses 4:26). If we consider these references in light of the infinite Creation, even though we are not told explicitly in the scriptures, we can be quite certain that Eve was foreordained to that noble calling, even before the foundations of the earth. We also can assume that we all sustained Eve in her calling, just as we did Adam in his calling as the first man. Therefore, in the infinite perspective, it matters not one whit when Eve was actually born. She was destined to become "the mother of all living" and the "first of all women" in all our calculations of the human family. We honor her in that noble position—even though generations of women lived and died before her.

But why aren't we told these things explicitly in the scriptures? I have pondered this question most of my life.

President Dallin Oaks, first counselor in the First Presidency, in his address given at the "Be One" celebration marking the fortieth anniversary of the revelation on the priesthood, at the Conference Center in Salt Lake City, June 1, 2018, provided his understanding of God's instructions to his children. He stated, "As part of my prayerful study, I learned that, in general, the Lord rarely gives reasons for the commandments and directions He gives to His servants."[7] Apparently, God has left to us to discover most of the thrilling truths concerning the infinite Creation. Even though President Nelson felt revelation from God distilling upon him while conducting open heart surgery,[8] he had to spend years of his time and enormous effort each day to learn the scientific basis behind and the dexterity required to perform that surgery.

Along with Oliver Cowdery, we are instructed, "Behold, you have not understood; you have supposed that I would give it unto you, when you took no thought save it was to ask me. But, behold, I say unto you, that you must study it out in your mind; then you must ask me if it be right, and if it is right I will cause that your bosom shall burn within you; therefore, you shall feel that it is right. But if it be not right you shall have no such feelings, but you shall have a stupor of thought that shall cause you to forget the thing which is wrong; therefore, you cannot write that which is sacred save it be given you from me" (D&C 9:7–9). It may require a lifetime of pondering, research, and prayer to gain an understanding of Eve's place in the infinite Creation.

In the October 1987 women's conference, Russell M. Nelson stated, "Without women, the whole purpose of the creation of this world would be in vain. . . . All the purposes of the world and all that was in the world would be brought to naught without woman—a keystone in the priesthood arch of creation."[8] Then, as President of the Quorum of the Twelve Apostles, he stated in the October 2015 general conference, "We know that the culminating act of all creation was the creation of woman!"[9]

In the October 1996 general conference, President Gordon B. Hinckley stated:

> Without you the plan could not function. Without you the entire program would be frustrated. As I have said before from this pulpit, when the process of creation occurred, Jehovah, the Creator, under instruction from His Father, first divided the light from the darkness and then separated the land from the waters. There followed the creation of plant life, followed by the creation of animal life. Then came the creation of man, and culminating that act of divinity came the crowning act, the creation of woman.
>
> Each of you is a daughter of God, endowed with a divine birthright. You need no defense of that position.[10]

In 2004, President Hinckley also stated, "Eve became God's final creation, the grand summation of all of the marvelous work that had gone before."[11]

ENDNOTES

1. Spencer W. Kimball, "The Blessings and Responsibilities of Womanhood," *Ensign*, Mar. 1976; lds.org/ensign/1976/03/the-blessings-and-responsibilities-of-womanhood?lang=eng
2. B. Alberts, A. Johnson, J. Lewis, M. Raff, K. Roberts, K., and P. Walter, *Molecular Biology of the Cell* (New York: Garland Publishing Inc., 1994).

3. W. M. Brown, "Polymorphism in mitochondrial DNA of humans as revealed by restriction endonuclease analysis," *Proc Natl Acad Sci USA,* 77:3605–09, 1980.
4. Rebecca L. Cann, Mark Stoneking, and Allan Wilson, "Mitochondrial DNA and human evolution," *Nature,* 325:31–36, 1987.
5. Q. Fu, et al., "A revised timescale for human evolution based on ancient mitochondrial genomes," *Current Biology,* 23: 553–59, 2013.
6. G. D. Poznik, et al., "Sequencing Y chromosomes resolves discrepancy in time to common ancestor of males versus females," *Science,* 341:562–65, 2013.
7. Dallin H. Oaks, An address given at the "Be One" celebration marking the 40th anniversary celebration of the revelation on the priesthood at the Conference Center in Salt Lake City, June 1, 2018.
8. Russell M. Nelson, "Lessons from Eve," October 1987 general conerence.
9. Ibid., "A Plea to My Sisters," October 2015 general conference.
10. Gordon B. Hinckley,"Women of the Church," October 1996 general conference.
11. Ibid., "The Women in Our Lives," *Ensign,* Nov. 2004, 83.

CHAPTER 20

CHROMOSOMES AND MOLECULAR CONSTRAINT

I have a book in my library—one of my treasured possessions actually—entitled *An Atlas of Chromosome Numbers in Animals* by Sajiro Makino of Hokkaido University in Sapporo, Japan. It is the "Second Edition (FIRST American Edition), Revised and enlarged from the original Tokyo edition." It was published at the Iowa State College Press, Ames, Iowa, in 1951. Inside the front cover, in blue ink, is my printed name and the date, "Feb. 10, 1965." I was sixteen.

In the preface to the second edition, Makino stated, "It represents a revised and enlarged list indexed with the chromosome numbers of 3317 species of animals, namely 2754 species of invertebrates and 563 species of vertebrates, together with the pertinent references." The book is one big, long *table* of chromosome numbers in animals. There is no text except for the forewords and preface. I found the book at King's Variety Store in Burley, Idaho. I have reflected many times why King's Variety Store in Burley, Idaho, would carry such a book. I am quite likely one of the few people on Earth who owns a copy of it. I am quite certain I was the only sixteen-year-old to ever buy a copy.

My intent in purchasing the book was to test my hypothesis of a "chromosome barrier to evolution." I reasoned that if evolution was correct, then one should see a gradual increase in chromosome number from simpler to more complex animals—as the number of genes increased. If such a correlation did not exist, then that would be a powerful argument against evolution. I meticulously went through all 290 pages of the atlas and wrote in pencil at the top of each page the average number of chromosomes listed for a given genus. Then I plotted the results on a piece of poster board. As I expected, the chromosome numbers showed no pattern but rather varied all over the board. I had the evidence I needed—all I had to do was write the paper.

I entered BYU in the fall of 1966 with two goals: disprove evolution and be the first person to map a chromosome. My big chance came in the spring of 1967 when I was assigned to spend the second half of my freshman English class writing a thesis. I plunged into the project with great enthusiasm and immersed myself in the library. I soon discovered that my two goals were untenable. First, I discovered that Alfred Sturtevant, a student of Thomas Hunt Morgan, had already mapped the chromosomes of the fruit fly (*Drosophila melanogaster*) in 1913. Morgan won the 1933 Nobel Prize for his work on genes and chromosomes. Sturtevant was awarded the 1967 National Medal of Science—almost exactly the same time I was beginning my research. Thus, I had been beaten to my second goal by fifty-three years.

I also quickly discovered that my first goal, disproving evolution, was going to be a problem. I came across a recent paper (1965) by Hampton Carson, then at Washington University in St. Louis. In that paper, Carson had shown, quite elegantly, that of the some one thousand species of Drosophila in the Hawaiian Islands, the newer species, with the most extreme divergence in morphology and behavior, lived on the younger islands of the archipelago. More important, to me, Carson was able to show changes in chromosome structure that accompanied (indeed would have preceded) the morphological and behavioral changes.[1] Carson's work clearly demonstrated that the evolution of the Hawaiian *Drosophila* could be mapped by changes in their chromosome structure—as reflected by specific changes in their banding pattern. It was clear to me at that point that chromosome patterns *supported* the theory of evolution. That single paper caused me to do a 180 in my thinking about evolution.

I could think of no way to make additional contributions to our understanding of genes and chromosomes, so I selected some new goals—determining what causes limbs to form where they do on a vertebrate animal and elucidating the mechanism of action of the drug thalidomide in causing numerous human birth defects of the limbs. I have been moderately successful in accomplishing both goals. Another goal was to find a way to reconcile my new-found knowledge concerning the power of evolution with what I have read in the scriptures about the Creation and what I believe to be true. That goal has been a lifelong quest.

In my opinion, little additional progress has been made in our understanding of the relationship between chromosomes, genes, and evolution beyond what Carson demonstrated in 1965. Indeed, that work is not even cited in a 2011 biography as being among his most noted accomplishments.[2] In 2010, Mark Kirkpatrick observed, "Alfred Sturtevant, who invented genetic mapping while still an undergraduate, published the first evidence of a chromosomal inversion in 1921. . . . Starting in the 1970s, this rich literature largely sank from view with the rise of biochemical and then molecular genetics. . . . Despite the importance of inversions as a major mechanism for reorganizing the genome, we are still struggling to understand how and why they evolve almost a century after Sturtevant's discovery."[3]

I tinkered for quite a while with the notion of forcing a chromosome inversion in the laboratory. My idea was to start with *Drosophila melanogaster* and compare the chromosome banding pattern to a close sister species, *Drosophila simulans*, then produce the same banding pattern in *Drosophila melanogaster* chromosomes as that seen in *Drosophila simulans* by forced inversions in the laboratory, thus transforming one species into another—a feat which had to that point never been accomplished—producing a new species in the laboratory. The problem was, I could never figure out how to force such inversions in a laboratory setting. To date, no one else has solved that technical problem either.

Examination of the G-banding patterns (obtained by a specific staining technique using giemsa stain) in chimpanzee and human chromosomes reveals somewhere around nine inversions distinguishing the two, which can be seen under the microscope. However, genetic sequence analysis has revealed as many as 1,576 small inversions. Many of the longer inversions are flanked by segment duplications. There are also at least three small inversion polymorphisms among humans, indicating that inversions are more common than previously realized.[4] Mark Kirkpatrick commented, "chromosomes are far more structurally fluid" than had been previously believed.[3]

These chromosome patterns, molecular data, and fossil evidence indicate that around six to eight million years ago, the last common ancestor of gorillas, chimpanzees, and humans may have been an animal like *Nakalipithecus*, whose fossils have been found in Kenya, or *Ouranopithecus*, whose fossils were found in Greece.[5] Molecular evidence suggests that gorillas first branched from the line leading to humans, around eight million years ago, followed by chimpanzees around six million years ago. The DNA among humans of all races is about 99.9 percent identical. Our DNA differs from that of chimpanzees by only 1.2 percent (98.8 percent identical).[6] The fossil record indicates that one of the first defining human traits, bipedalism, the ability to walk on two legs, first appeared around four million years ago in the genus *Australopithecus*.[7]

In comparing the G-banding pattern in chimpanzee and human chromosome 4, we can identify a large inversion, but we have no idea what that particular inversion does. Is it responsible for our bipedalism, our greater intelligence, or our scarcity of hair? We simply do not know. How critical is that particular inversion to making us human? Without that inversion in chromosome 4 would we even be human?

Then there is the question of why we have twenty-three pairs of chromosomes. Eighteen of our twenty-three pairs of chromosomes are identical to chimpanzee, gorilla, and orangutan. The major difference among chromosomes is that chimpanzees, gorillas, and orangutans have twenty-four pairs—what chromosome 2 is in humans is actually two chromosomes in the other three primates. Does that make us human?[8]

We are well aware that humans are in trouble, not just if we are missing one pair of chromosomes or have an extra pair of chromosomes, but if we are even missing or have an extra *half* a pair. This condition, called aneuploidy (having an abnormal number of chromosomes, such as forty-five or forty-seven rather than forty-six), is usually lethal. Examination of miscarriages reveals that half of all early miscarriages show aneuploidy. Of those, 44–64 percent are autosomal (any chromosome but the X and Y chromosomes) trisomy and 10–40 percent are monosomy X. Another 10–14 percent are other aneuploidies.[9] There are probably many more trisomies and monosomies that never even develop far enough to implant and therefore never show up as miscarriages.

Although many monosomy X embryos die, some survive to term and even adulthood. The condition is called Turner syndrome and is mainly characterized by webbing of the neck—resulting from abnormal lymphatic development as a fetus. We have no idea how missing one X chromosome so dramatically affects the developing lymphatic system. The most common trisomy that survives to birth is trisomy 21, Down syndrome. One interesting issue with Down syndrome is that that extra chromosome 21 changes even the fingerprint pattern (dermatoglyphics), so that the fingerprints of Down syndrome cases resemble each other more than they resemble other members of their own family.[10] We have no idea how an extra chromosome 21 results in the typical characteristics we see—right down to the fingerprints. This condition tells us that we have a long way to go in understanding how chromosomes work in making us who we are.

We know, therefore, that the number of forty-six chromosomes is literally vital to our normal development and survival, but we really don't know much beyond that. This is an area of research that may reveal many laws of humanness and is in dire need of study.

In 1894, William Bateson coined the term *Homœosis* and defined it as "something has been changed into the likeness of something else."[11] Bateson stated that whereas Homœosis is "common in flowering plants," it is "rare in animals." He wrote, "The occurrence of Homœosis among the appendages of Arthropoda is illustrated by a small but compact body of evidence." He described and illustrated a case in *Cimbex axillaris* where the right antenna was normal but the left antenna ended in a well-formed foot (after Kraatz, 1876).[12] Bateson appreciated the importance of these Meristic, Homœosic variations. He stated, "Variation comparable perhaps with that which the phenomena of the prism held in the study of the nature of Light. They furnish a test, an elenchus, which any hypothesis professing to deal with the nature of organic Repetition and Meristic Division must needs endure."[13] The genetics of this condition, however, were unknown to Bateson, or to anyone else of his time.

The first evidence of a genetic basis for Homœosis came in 1915 from Calvin Bridges, a student working in Thomas Hunt Morgan's famous "fly room" at Columbia University. Bridges discovered a fruit fly (*Drosophila melanogaster*) in which the thorax had been partially duplicated. This fly mutation became known as *bithorax* (*bx*), the first homeotic mutant to be described.[14] Then, in 1948, Jean Le Calvez identified *Antennapedia* (*Antp*^{LC}) in the fruit fly (*Drosophila melanogaster*)—the same sort of homeotic transformation described by Bateson in 1894.[15]

I worked in the *Drosophila* genetics laboratory at BYU, affectionately called "Fanny Farkle's Fantastic Fly Factory," with Duane Jeffery at the helm, for a couple of years as an undergraduate. In 1972, I wrote a paper on the importance of homeotic mutants to evolution and then moved on to other areas of research in developmental biology because nobody was doing much work with homeotic mutants at that time. Gene sequencing was in its infancy. The next year, Edward B. Lewis, at Caltech, discovered that *Drosophila* homeotic genes are organized in a "cluster" of genes, now known as the Bithorax complex, which is organized in the same sequence in the chromosome as their functional sequence from head to tail in the developing embryo, a concept called collinearity—not just in *Drosophila*, but in other animals as well—including humans.[16] Lewis founded the research field of evolutionary developmental biology, and laid the foundation for our modern understanding of the universal, evolutionarily conserved gene patterning and functions controlling animal development and morphology. Lewis was awarded the 1995 Nobel Prize.

Two different groups of researchers in the laboratories of Walter Jakob Gehring at the University of Basel in Switzerland, and Thomas Kaufman at Indiana University in Bloomington sequenced the homeotic domains of *Antennapedia* and *bithorax* in 1983. They discovered a 180 base-pair sequence common to both genes, which became known as the homeobox (*Hox*).[17]

Hox genes can help us scientifically approach questions such as why polychaetes have heads, whereas priapulids do not. We can also begin to understand when each *Hox* gene first appeared and in what regions of which animals. We still have a long way to go, however, in understanding the laws governing the emergence of *Hox* genes and how they guided subsequent evolution. We do know that the first *Hox* genes appeared very early in the creation of animals. They control the sequence and identities of various body segments, but we still have a long way to go in fully understanding their molecular functions.

In July 2016, William Martin and colleagues at the Institute of Molecular Evolution, Heinrich Heine University Düsseldorf, Germany identified 355 genes common to all living organisms on Earth, inherited from a Last Universal Common Ancestor (LUCA).[18] Those basic genes have changed very little over the past 3.5 to 3.8 billion years.

Three scientists, Leland Hartwell, Paul Nurse, and Tim Hunt, shared the 2001 Nobel Prize for disentangling the role of various genes in controlling the cell cycle. Hartwell found that yeast (*Saccharomyces cerevisiae)* and humans have common genes with more-or-less the same functions in the cell cycle, and identified one hundred such genes. These genes have remained relatively unchanged in both structure and function, over the past 3.8 billion years.[19] Nurse discovered a master control gene of the cell cycle, called *cdc2* in yeast and *Cdk1* in humans. This CDK (Cyclin-Dependent Protein Kinases) family of proteins signals the cell that it is prepared to move into the next stage of the cell cycle.[20] In the 1980s Hunt discovered the protein cyclin, which binds to and controls CDK molecules during the cell cycle. Cyclins are formed and then broken down during each cell cycle. The discoveries of Hartwell, Nurse, Hunt, and others have demonstrated that cell division is controlled by universal mechanisms in all eukaryotic cells—which have existed throughout the entire history of life's creation.

In his 1802 book *Natural Theology or Evidences of the Existence and Attributes of the Deity*, William Paley introduced the watchmaker analogy. Paley stated, "Suppose I had found a *watch* upon the ground . . . when we come to inspect the watch, we perceive . . . that its several parts are framed and put together for a purpose . . . the inference, we think, is inevitable; that the watch must have had a maker" Likewise, Paley argued, the human eye, which resembles a telescope, must have been created by design: "There is precisely the same proof that the eye was made for vision, as there is that the telescope was made for assisting it."[21] The analogy may have been perfectly sensible back in 1802, and it has seen a lot of press over the past more than two hundred years. But we have come a long way since then in our understanding of biological complexity—and it is probably wise not to flippantly invoke the watchmaker without knowing a lot more about the "watch."

Richard Dawkins, in his 1986 *The Blind Watchmaker: Why the Evidence of Evolution Reveals a Universe without Design*, attacked Paley nearly as blindly as the title of his book—and as blindly as Paley's watchmaker analogy is still cited by many today.[22] It is my opinion that reality lies nearly midway between Paley's and Dawkins' myopic views of life. I propose that God made laws to govern creation but did not, thereafter, micro-manage the process.

I will take two examples, neither of which was even known in Paley's day, and neither of which seem to have occurred to Dawkins, who stated, "Evolution has no long-term goal. There is no long-distance target, no final perfection to serve as a criterion for selection."[22] The first example is a protein called cytochrome c, which transports a single electron within the electron transport chain inside mitochondria.[23] Actually cytochrome c attaches heme c, a specifically shaped small molecule, which, in turn, attaches the electron.[24] In fact, cytochrome c is a "target." It is a protein of approximately one hundred amino acids, only five of which (three being invariable) make up the "bull's-eye," to which the heme c attaches in the center of the coiled protein.

The rest of the cytochrome c protein amino acid sequence can vary, within strict limits. Among over thirty species examined, 34 of the 104 amino acids are identical. But even among species with as much as fifty percent amino acid difference, such as humans and wheat, the cytochromes are cross-reacting.[25] Therefore, the shape of cytochrome c can be viewed as an evolutionary target, whose functions are critical to the cell and also critically related to its shape. Thus, its shape cannot be modified significantly without disrupting its function. And, therefore, in the evolution of cytochrome c there indeed was a specific target—making a small protein that can specifically bond heme c, which is a small molecule with a very specific shape.

An even more dramatic example of strictly conserved structure among proteins are those proteins containing the so-called homeodomains—a highly conserved sixty amino acid sequence with a very specific association to DNA. This amino acid sequence supercoils into precisely the right pattern to fit exactly into the major helix of the DNA molecule. DNA is constrained by its molecular nature into a very specific shape. Thus, the structure of proteins directly interacting with DNA to regulate its function, are structurally highly constrained. Therefore, the *homeobox* (*Hox*) genes, which code for the homeodomain proteins, although first appearing very early in evolutionary history, have remained highly conserved throughout all of creation. These genes play a critical role in organizing the embryo into specific patterns. Animals with very simple structures, such as sponges, lack *Hox* genes, simpler animals have few genes, whereas more and more complex animals have more and more *Hox* genes. Humans have 235 *Hox* genes and another 65 similar pseudogenes (structurally similar genes but without function).[26]

The structure of *Hox* genes is not random. The 60–base homeodomain is a key that has to fit into a specific DNA lock with a specific structure. Proteins are not developed in a vacuum. They must interact with other molecules to be useful. Genes are also arranged in a collinear fashion in the chromosomes. All of these pieces of information tell us that there must be still, as yet, undiscovered laws that govern the creation of animals. More research into the conservation of protein structure based on specific structure-related functions may in the future open new doors into understanding laws governing such structure-function relations. Castoe and colleagues have stated, "This result [molecular convergence] implies that the protein adaptive landscape is sometimes highly constrained." And , therefore, "careful genome-wide assays for convergent molecular evolution are warranted."[27]

In his 1944 book *What is Life?*, the Austrian Nobel Prize-winning quantum physicist Erwin Schrödinger proposed that the macroscopic organization seen in living organisms was the result of laws and order at the quantum level. He suggested that, at that level, life was uniquely different from the non-living world.[28] Concerning Schrödinger's ideas of quantum biology, Jim Al-Khalili, a British theoretical physicist, and Johnjoe McFadden, an Anglo-Irish molecular geneticist, both at the University of Surrey, stated in 2014:

> Schrödinger's argument was based on the paradoxical fact that the laws of classical physics, such as those of Newtonian mechanics and thermodynamics, are ultimately based on disorder. Consider a balloon. It is filled with trillions of molecules of air all moving entirely randomly, bumping into one another and the inside wall of the balloon. Each molecule is governed by orderly quantum laws, but when you add up the random motions of all the molecules and average them out, their individual quantum behaviour washes out and you are left with the gas laws that predict, for example, that the balloon will expand by a precise amount when heated. This is because heat energy makes the air molecules move a little bit faster, so that they bump into the walls of the balloon with a bit more force, pushing the walls outward a little bit further. Schrödinger called this kind of law 'order from disorder' to reflect the fact that this apparent macroscopic regularity depends on random motion at the level of individual particles.[29]

Al-Khalili and McFadden continued, "Schrödinger pointed out that many of life's properties, such as heredity, depend of molecules made of comparatively few particles—certainly too few to benefit from the order-from-disorder rules of thermodynamics. But life was clearly orderly. Where did this orderliness come from? Schrödinger suggested that life was based on a novel physical principle whereby its macroscopic order is a reflection of quantum-level order, rather than the molecular disorder that characterises the inanimate world. He called this new principle 'order from order.'"[29]

Al-Khalili and McFadden stated, "The signs of quantum mechanical behaviour in the building blocks of life are becoming increasingly apparent. Recent research indicates that some of life's most fundamental processes do indeed depend on weirdness welling up from the quantum undercurrent of reality."[29]

Al-Khalili and McFadden presented several examples of quantum activity in living systems. One they provide is the function of enzymes—which catalyze reactions within cells that can occur in milliseconds. Left to themselves, without enzymes, those reactions could take up to thousands of years to occur on their own. "Life would be impossible without them. But how they accelerate chemical reactions by such enormous factors, often more than a trillion-fold, has been an enigma. Experiments over the past few decades, however, have shown that enzymes make use of a remarkable trick called quantum tunnelling to accelerate biochemical reactions. Essentially, the enzyme encourages electrons and protons to vanish from one position in a biomolecule and instantly rematerialise in another, without passing through the gap in between—a kind of quantum teleportation."[29]

Al-Khalili and McFadden concluded by stating, "Just as Schrödinger predicted, life seems to be balanced on the boundary between the sensible everyday world of the large and the weird and wonderful quantum world, a discovery that is opening up an exciting new field of 21st-century science."[29]

Al-Khalili said that senior colleagues tried to dissuade him from this line of research, calling it "wacky," but he stated, "I have since realized that some of the best ideas come out of seemingly crazy thoughts, because otherwise they wouldn't be new."[30]

We are told in the scriptures, "So God created man in his own image, in the image of God created he him; male and female created he them" (Genesis 1:27; compare Moses 2:27). But we are not told *how* He created us. For hundreds, if not thousands, of years, people have apparently believed that He made us by some magic trick—like pulling a rabbit out of a hat—in a single twenty-four–hour day. When William Paley compared us to a watch in 1802, neither he nor anyone else at the time had any idea the complexity of the human body—with its roughly thirty five trillion cells, nearly five billion miles of DNA, and three hundred heptillion proteins (3×10^{23}).

A watch may take a year or more to build from scratch. It has taken 3.8 billion years to make us. The separate line leading specifically to us, compared to a chimpanzee, emerged some six million years ago. Who are we to question *how* God created us—without taking the time to study the whole creation process? Many people may not like the answers we are receiving. What were you expecting—a rabbit out of a hat? In the infinite space of creation, what difference does it make how long it took to make us or by what process we were created?

We know that our bodies are temples (see 1 Corinthians 3:16), but our spirits are the offspring of God. Our temples were prepared over the space of creation to house those spirits. We can make an analogy with the Salt Lake Temple, whose granite was hewn from the walls of Little Cottonwood Canyon. The oldest rocks there are 1.6 billion years old.[31] It took that long to create the walls of the temple, which houses the spirit of the Lord. Likewise, it has taken 3.8 billion years to build our walls to house our spirits.

In his 1998 book *Perfection Pending*, then Apostle Russell M. Nelson stated, "Temporal or physical laws that relate to our divine creation often have a spiritual application. This should come as no surprise, because 'all [of God's] kingdoms have a law given. . . . And unto every kingdom is given a law; and unto every law there are certain bounds also and conditions.'"[32]

ENDNOTES

1. Carson, H.L. Chromosome morphism in geographically widespread species of Drosophila, In: Barker, H.G. and Stebbins, G.L. (eds), *The Genetics of Colonizing Species*, Academic, New York, 503–531, 1965.
2. Templeton, Alan R., Hampton Lawrence Carson 1914–2004, A Biographical Memoir, National Academy of Sciences, Washington, D.C., 2011.
3. Kirkpatrick, M., How and Why Chromosome Inversions Evolve, *PLoS Biol* 8: e1000501, 2010.
4. Feuk, L, MacDonald, J. R, Tang,T, Carson, A. R, Li M, et al., Discovery of human inversion polymorphisms by comparative analysis of human and chimpanzee DNA sequence assemblies, *PLoS Genet*, 1: e56, 2005.
5. Kunimatsu, Yutaka; Nakatsukasa, Masato; Sawada, Yoshihiro; Sakai, Tetsuya; Hyodo, Masayuki; Hyodo, Hironobu; Itaya, Tetsumaru; Nakaya, Hideo; Saegusa, Haruo; Mazurier, Arnaud; Saneyoshi, Mototaka; Tsujikawa, Hiroshi; Yamamoto, Ayumi; and Mbua, Emma; A new Late Miocene great ape from Kenya and

its implications for the origins of African great apes and humans, *Proceedings of the National Academy of Sciences,* 104:19220–19225, 2007; de Bonis, Louis, and Melentis, J., Les primates hominoides du Vallesien de Macedoine (Grece): etude de la machoine inferieure, *Geobios,* 10:849–855, 1977.

6. American Museum of Natural History; amnh.org/exhibitions/permanent-exhibitions/human-origins-and-cultural-halls/anne-and-bernard-spitzer-hall-of-human-origins/understanding-our-past/dna-comparing-humans-and-chimps.
7. Smithsonian National Museum of Natural History; humanorigins.si.edu/education /introduction-human-evolution.
8. Yunis, J.J., Prakash, O., The origin of man: A chromosomal pictorial legacy, *Science,* 215: 1525–1530, 1982.
9. Kajii, T., Ferrier, A., Niikawa, N., Takahara, H., Ohama, K., and Avirachan, S., Anatomic and chromosomal anomalies in 639 spontaneous abortuses, *Human Genetics,* 55: 87–98, 1980.
10. Stephens, T.D., and Shepard, T.H., The Down Syndrome in the fetus, *Teratology,* 22, 37–41, 1980.
11. Bateson, William, *Materials for the Study of Variation, Treated with Especial Regard to Discontinuities in the Origin of Species,* p. 85, Macmillan, New York, 1894.
12. Bateson, William, *Materials for the Study of Variation, Treated with Especial Regard to Discontinuities in the Origin of Species,* p. 146–147, Macmillan, New York, 1894.
13. Bateson, William, *Materials for the Study of Variation, Treated with Especial Regard to Discontinuities in the Origin of Species,* p. 146, Macmillan, New York, 1894.
14. Lindsley, Dan L. and Grell, E.H., *Genetic Variations of Drosophila melanogaster,* p. 43, Carnegie Institution of Washington, Washington, D.C., 1968.
15. Lindsley, Dan L. and Grell, E.H., *Genetic Variations of Drosophila melanogaster,* p. 16, Carnegie Institution of Washington, Washington, D.C., 1968.
16. Lewis, E., A gene complex controlling segmentation in Drosophila, *Nature,* 277:565–570, 1978.
17. McGinnis, W., Levine, M.S., Hafen, E., Kuroiwa, A., and Gehring, W.J., A conserved DNA sequence in homoeotic genes of the Drosophila Antennapedia and bithorax complexes, *Nature,* 308:428–433, 1984; Scott, M.P., and Weiner, A.J., Structural relationships among genes that control development: sequence homology between the Antennapedia, Ultrabithorax, and fushi tarazu loci of Drosophila, *Proc. Natl. Acad. Sci., US, 81:4115–9, 1984;* Heuer, J.G. and Kaufman, T.C., Homeotic genes have specific functional roles in the establishment of the Drosophila embryonic peripheral nervous system, *Development,* 115:35–47, 1992.

18. Weiss, Madeline C., Sousa, Filipa L., Mrnjavac, Natalia, Neukirchen, Sinje, Roettger, Mayo, Nelson-Sathi, Shijulal, and Martin, William F., The physiology and habitat of the last universal common ancestor, *Nature Microbiology*, 1(9):16116. doi: 10.1038/nmicrobiol.2016.116.; see also Wade, Nicholas, Meet Luca, the Ancestor of All Living Things, *New York Times*, 25 July 2016.
19. yourgenome.org/stories/using-yeast-in-biology.
20. sparknotes.com/biology/cellreproduction/cellcycle/section3.
21. Paley, William, *Natural Theology or Evidences of the Existence and Attributes of the Deity*, 1802, books.google.com/books?id=Oag-uAAAAYAAJ&pg= PR1&source=kp_read_button#v= onepage&q&f=false; italics in the original.
22. Dawkins, Richard, *The Blind Watchmaker: Why the Evidence of Evolution Reveals a Universe without Design*, W. W. Norton & Company, New York, *1986*.
23. Seeley, R.R., Stephens, T.D., and Tate, P., *Anatomy and Physiology*, McGraw-Hill, Dubuque, 8th edition, 2007.
24. Mavridou, D.A., Ferguson, S.J., and Stevens, J.M., Cytochrome c assembly, *IUBMB Life*, 65:209–16, 2013.
25. Stryer, L., *Biochemistry*, p. 362, W.H. Freeman and Company, San Francisco, 1975.
26. ghr.nlm.nih.gov/primer/genefamily/homeoboxes.
27. Castoe, T.A., de Koning, A.P., and Pollock, D.D., Adaptive molecular convergence: Molecular evolution versus molecular phylogenetics, Commun Integr Biol., 3:67–9, 2010.
28. Schrödinger, Erwin, *What is Life*? Cambridge Univ. Press, Cambridge, UK, 1944.
29. Al-Khalili, Jim, and McFadden, Johnjoe, You're powered by quantum mechanics. No, really . . . *The Guardian*, 25 Oct 2014; theguardian.com/science/2014/oct/26/youre-powered-by-quantum-mechanics-biology; see also McFadden, Johnjoe, and Al-Khalili, Jim, *Life on the Edge: The Coming of Age of Quantum Biology*, Bantam Press, 2014.
30. Merali, Zeeya, Solving Biology's Mysteries Using Quantum Mechanics, *Discover*, December 2014.
31. geology.utah.gov/popular/places-to-go/geologic-guides/virtual-tour-central-wasatch-front-canyons/little-cottonwood-canyon.
32. Nelson, Russell M., *Perfection Pending*, Deseret Book, Salt Lake City, Utah, 1998.

CHAPTER 21

OUT OF AFRICA

For Father's Day in 2017, one of my daughters gave me an Ancestry DNA kit. It turns out, according to Ancestry DNA, that I am 65 percent Great Britain, 13 percent Scandinavian, 9 percent Ireland, 6 percent Europe West, 2 percent Italy/Greece, 2 percent Iberian Peninsula, 2 percent Finland/Northwest Russia, and 1 percent Europe East. I was told by Ancestry that these connections were "thousands of years ago."

Then in February 2018, my wife and I attended the general session of RootsTech at the Salt Palace in Salt Lake City. There 23andMe were offering their $199 kits for $100. So we bought two of the kits. It turns out, based on 23andMe DNA analysis, that I am 55.1 percent British and Irish, 27.8 percent French and German, 13.1 percent Broadly Northwestern European (Scandinavian), 3 percent Iberian, 0.2 percent Broadly Southern European, and 0.8 percent Broadly European. I was also told I am about 1.95 percent Neanderthal.

Whereas the Ancestry DNA and 23andMe DNA data are broadly compatible, indicating that I am mainly of western European descent, the two data sets differ considerably in the details. What appears considerable, however, is not all that considerable when the details are examined more closely. Both tests say I'm about 13 percent Scandinavian and 2–3 percent Iberian. Ancestry says I'm 80 percent British, Irish, French, and German. The results from 23andMe says I'm 82.9 percent British, Irish, French, and German. The difference is whether the scale tips more toward the British-Irish side (Ancestry) or the French-German side (23andMe). In order to keep the costs down in these DNA tests, companies doing DNA testing use a shotgun approach, which leaves quite a few blank spots (referred to as "no calls"). A computer program then fills in the blank spots based on the surrounding DNA. In one case, the computer may see more adjacent British DNA and call the blank spot British. In another run, even from the same DNA, the computer may see more adjacent German DNA and call the blank spot German—thus the difference between 27.8 percent French and German from 23andMe and 6 percent from Ancestry.[1] My actual family history data tend to align more with the 23andMe data, suggesting a higher percent French and German.

The International Society of Genetic Genealogy lists thirty-five DNA testing companies.[2] DNA testing is the hottest new rage. According to a June 2018 *Deseret News* report, more than 17 million people have already had their DNA ancestral test run, over half of those with Ancestry DNA.[3] If you haven't had yours done yet, you will soon be in the minority. You need to keep up with the Joneses or the Smiths or the Stephenses—whatever your family name. I am still amazed that some of the major TV advertisements now include Ancestry.com, Ancestry DNA, and 23andMe. Who would have believed it twenty years ago?

The Human Genome Project was an audacious undertaking begun in 1990 in numerous laboratories around the world, with a projected completion date of 2005. An announcement was released February 12, 2001, to correspond with the 192nd birthday of Charles Darwin, that the project was 90 percent complete. The February 16, 2001, issue of *Science* referred to the human genome as the "Book of Life" and included an approximately four-foot by four-foot fold-out poster of the human genome. I hung my copy of the poster on my office wall, where it remained until my retirement. Then on April 25, 2003, to correspond with the fiftieth anniversary of Watson and Crick's historic paper in *Nature* describing the structure of DNA, also known as International DNA Day, an official statement was released stating that the human genome project was 100 percent complete.

Since that historic date, numerous other genome projects have been completed. As of January 2018, the genomes of about 2,500 species have been sequenced.[4] By 2014, the complete genomes of sixteen extinct species had been sequenced, including the passenger pigeon, three species of moa, an extinct species of zebra, an extinct horse species, two species of extinct bears, the Tasmanian wolf, the woolly rhinoceros, the American mastodon, two species of mammoths, and three species or subspecies of extinct humans: *Homo heidelbergensis*, *Homo sapiens neanderthalensis*, and

Homo sapiens ssp Denisova.[5] One of those genomes, reported in 2014, was the complete genome sequence of a Neanderthal woman (*Homo sapiens neanderthalensis)* who lived about fifty to one hundred thousand years ago. The DNA was extracted from a bone fragment discovered in a cave in the Altai Mountains in Siberia.[6]

That cave, named Denisova Cave for a hermit named Dionisij (Denis) who lived in the cave in the eighteenth century, also called Bear Rock by the locals, has turned out to be one of the holy grails of anthropology. Artifacts showing human habitation going back to about 125,000 years have been discovered in the cave and dated by thermoluminescence dating of fired objects in the sediments and by radiocarbon dating of charcoal. Fragments of a stone bracelet made of polished dark green chloritolite stone with drilled holes, as well as pendants, have been discovered in the cave. Bone tools have also been found, including awls and small needles with drilled eyes, the latter dating to 50,000 years ago, making them the oldest needles ever discovered.[7,8] Bones have been discovered in the cave from three different types of humans: *Homo sapiens sapiens* (us), *Homo sapiens neanderthalensis*, and *Homo sapiens ssp Denisova.*

In his tenth edition of *Systema Naturae* (1758), Carl Linnaeus, the father of modern taxonomy, proposed five subspecies for humans: *Homo sapiens sapiens* (pure humans, apparently Linnaeus himself, in all humility), *Homo sapiens europaeus* (other people living in Europe), *Homo sapiens americanus* (people living in America), *Homo sapiens asiaticus* (people living in Asia), and *Homo sapiens* after (people living in Africa). He distinguished the four subspecies by behavior, in the very European-centric manner of the time: "europaeus was 'governed by laws,' americanus was governed 'by customs,' asiaticus 'by opinions,' and after 'by impulse.'"[9] In his new human nomenclature, Linnaeus also proposed three fanciful human subspecies: *Homo sapiens ferus* (wild man), *Homo sapiens monstrosus* (monstrous human), and *Homo sapiens troglodytes* (caveman).[10]

Wild men have existed on the fringes of society for hundreds of years. They were depicted in medieval heraldic art as covered entirely with hair,[11] likely inspired, at least in part, by the very real human genetic disorder Hypertrichosis.[12] Cavemen became a popular literary genre in the early twentieth century with books such as Arthur Conan Doyle's *The Lost World* (1912) and Edgar Rice Burroughs *The Land That Time Forgot* (1918).

Although the human subspecies that Linnaeus proposed were eventually debunked, there were fossil remains that looked somewhat human but exhibited characteristics that were decidedly not modern human. In 1864, William King wrote, "It has long been known that human bones, belonging to an extinct race have been found in the limestone fissures or caverns of the lofty precipices which overhang the river Meuse, in Belgium" King further stated, "that the Neanderthal fossil had not belonged to a human being," and that, "the Neanderthal skull is at once observed to be singularly different from all others which admittedly belong to the human species"[13] Then in 1856, the type specimen (the specimen that defines a species or subspecies) was described. It was found in the Neanderthal (Neander Valley) in the German Rhineland, and thus the subspecies was eventually named *Homo sapiens neanderthalensis*.[14]

In 2017, Jean-Jacques Hublin and colleagues at the Max Planck Society, Leiden University, proposed that *Homo sapiens* was wide spread across Africa by 300,000 years ago.[15] The first archaic humans, *Homo erectus*, began to migrate out of Africa about two million years ago and then, *Homo heidelbergensis*, the likely ancestor of both *Homo sapiens sapiens* and *Homo sapiens neanderthalensis*, began to leave Africa around 500,000 years ago.[16]

Neanderthals appear to have left Africa about 400,000 years ago, when they first appear in the fossil record of Southern Europe.[15] Modern humans (*Homo sapiens sapiens*) apparently left East Africa around 70,000 years ago. They first spread along the southern coast of Asia and then into Oceania by about 50,000 years ago and then into Europe about 40,000 years ago.[16]

A preliminary draft of the Neanderthal genome was published by Svante Pääbo and colleagues at the Max Planck Institute for Evolutionary Anthropology in two consecutive papers in the May 7, 2010, issue of *Science*. The data from those studies revealed Neanderthal DNA admixture in both European and Asian populations but not in African populations. The most reasonable explanation for those data is that Neanderthals and modern humans were interbreeding in Europe and Asia (around 40,000 to 60,000 years ago), but because Neanderthals apparently did not enter Africa in significant numbers, there was little if any interbreeding with African modern humans.[17] Then, about 30,000 years ago, Neanderthals disappeared from the fossil record all over Europe, Asia, and the Middle East—they had gone extinct as a unique subspecies.[18]

In Denisova Cave, in addition to the remains of Neanderthal and modern humans, were the finger bone, toe bone and two teeth which did not belong to either of those known subspecies. The bones were broad and heavy, like Neanderthal, but the teeth were unique and shared, "no derived morphological features with Neanderthal or modern humans."[19]

The completed mitochondrial DNA (mtDNA) sequence of the finger bone from a girl who died in the cave 41,000 years ago was accomplished by Svante Pääbo's group at the Max Planck Institute in 2010. The group reported in the journal *Nature*, "It represents a hitherto unknown type of hominin mtDNA that shares a common ancestor with anatomically modern human and Neanderthal mtDNAs about 1.0 million years ago. This indicates that it derives from a hominin migration out of Africa distinct from that of the ancestors of Neanderthals and of modern humans. The stratigraphy of the cave where the bone was found suggests that the Denisova hominin lived close in time and space with Neanderthals as well as with modern humans.[20]

The team also concluded, from the teeth samples, that this newly discovered hominin group had been in that cave at least 110,000 years ago. They named this new subspecies *Homo sapiens ssp Denisova*, after the cave where the bones and teeth were found. So far, this is the only place on Earth where this previously unknown subspecies has ever been found.[20] A more extensive DNA study conducted by Pääbo's group in 2016, found that Neanderthals had interbred with early modern humans multiple times, but that they had only interbred with Denisovans once.[21]

Very little of this new, dazzling information about our remote ancestors was known even thirty years ago, before the age of sophisticated DNA sequencing. Radiometric dating did not exist before the twentieth century.[22] The first ancient human fossil was discovered in 1848 at a quarry on the Rock of Gibraltar by a Captain Edmund Flint, a British officer in the Royal Navy. Had the significance of the skull discovered at Gibraltar been recognized, this line of humans would have been named the Gibraltar man, rather than the Neanderthal man—for the discovery in the Neander Valley eight years later. The skull was labeled, "an ancient human, died before the universal flood," and was placed into a cupboard to be forgotten for years. Whereas the Gibraltar Neanderthal skull was the first discovered, it may have belonged to the last surviving Neanderthal, some 28,000 years ago, having been pushed from most of Europe onto the Iberian Peninsula, and finally onto Gibraltar—before becoming extinct.[23]

One of the most astonishing discoveries of the nineteenth century was that in 1868 of Altamira Cave located near Santillana del Mar, Spain, by a hunter named Modesto Peres. The cave had been sealed, like a time capsule, by a rock slide some 13,000 years earlier. Then, in 1879, the cave was explored by the amateur archaeologist Marcelino Sanz de Sautuola. His eight-year-old daughter Maria, who accompanied her father on some of his trips to the cave, discovered that the ceiling in part of the cave was covered by paintings of now extinct steppe bison.[24] Even more amazingly, it was discovered in 2012 that the paintings ranged in age from 35,600 years ago to 15,600 years ago, covering a period of some 20,000 years—during which time several artists rendered those magnificent pieces of art.[25]

The talent exhibited by the unknown artists who created those bison masterpieces over the millennia was stunning. The bison images were rendered by the ancient artists in charcoal and ochre, often diluting pigments to produce variations in hue. Their technique is now called the chiaroscuro effect—using strong tonal contrasts of light and dark to create the illusion of three dimensions—a technique that would not be used again until the Renaissance some 35,000 to 15,000 years later. The cave artists had also exploited the natural contours of the ceiling to further enhance the three-dimensional effect. Those amazing paintings were so modern in composition that de Sautuola was accused of creating a fraud. No primitive art of such quality had ever been previously discovered. Even though the cave was also explored by Juan Vilanova y Piera, archaeologist at the University of Madrid, and their joint findings were published in 1880, de Sautuola and Piera were violently attacked by the "experts" of the time. This virulent attack, with accusations of forgery and hoax, was led by the French archaeologists and anthropologists Gabriel de Mortillet and Emile Cartaillac. The accusations came to a head at the Prehistorical Congress, Lisbon, Spain, in 1889.[24] Sautuola had died the previous year, his reputation and spirit shattered. Then, by 1902, it was Mortillet and Cartaillac's turn to have their reputations tarnished, as several additional caves with paintings like those in Altamira Cave had been discovered. By that time, Mortillet had died, but Emile Cartailhac published *Mea culpa d'un sceptique* ("Acknowledging my fault as a skeptic") in the journal *L'Anthropologie*. Altamira was the first of what is now seventeen Paleolithic mural caves designated in 1985 as a UNESCO (The United Nations Educational, Scientific and Cultural Organization) designated site of Cave of Altamira and Paleolithic Cave Art of Northern Spain.[26]

I, personally, was so impressed when I first encountered pictures of the Altamira Cave paintings in the early 1980s that I painted in oil a copy of one of the bison. I first mixed fine parakeet gravel into gesso and applied the mixture to a canvas, giving it a rough surface. I then rendered the bison in burnt sienna and raw umber, matching as closely as I could the color and design of the original. That painting hung for nearly thirty years in my university office, until my retirement in 2011.

On December 18, 1994, three cave explorers, Eliette Brunel-Deschamps, Christian Hillaire, and Jean-Marie Chauvet, discovered another remarkable cave along the Ardèche River in southern France, now named the Chauvet Cave after one of the discoverers.[27] The original Chauvet Cave entrance collapsed in a rock slide some 29,000 years ago, sealing the cave as a time capsule until its discovery in 1994. Carbon 14 and other dating techniques put the paintings in Chauvet Cave at 30,000 to 32,000 years ago. The 1994 access to the cave was only through a narrow passage in the roof. The opening was so narrow that the original explorers could barely squeeze through and then drop vertically into the main cave, which was nearly a quarter mile long with several chambers opening from it.[27]

The deepest, darkest chambers of the cave house a unique, spectacular gallery of art. Mostly rendered in charcoal and red ochre, the paintings on the cave walls depict at least thirteen different animal species—many of them now long-since extinct—in such remarkable detail that the artists clearly had first-hand knowledge of those animals. Several hundred animal paintings have been catalogued in the cave, including many carnivores, such as bears, lions, leopards, wolves, foxes, and hyenas. Herbivores such as wooly rhino, deer, rain deer, bison, ibex, horses, and antelope are also depicted. An extinct female cave lion is shown snarling at her mate. A horse, of a species now extinct, is depicted with its mouth open as though it was winded from running. Several paintings show animals in motion, as though seen in time-lapse drawings, such as a rhino with several horns. There are also numerous ochre hand prints, many from one artist, found in several places throughout the cave, who was about six feet tall and had a crooked little finger (the tip of the left little finger is bent toward the ring finger). Those hand prints were made by placing the hand against the stone and then blowing ochre through a hollow tube, such as a hollow bird bone, making a negative of the hand surrounded by red ochre.[27]

More than eighty separate radiocarbon tests have been conducted on material taken from the cave, including animal bones, charcoal from the cave floor, torch soot on the ceilings, and samples from the paintings themselves. Radiocarbon dating of organic material on the rock slide surfaces at the cave's original entrance confirm the slide date at approximately 29,000 years ago. The radiocarbon dating is further confirmed by the fact that some paintings are coated with a type of crystal speleothem called flowstone, which takes thousands of years to form from minerals carried in by water dripping over the walls. The artists themselves never saw the speleothems formed by the dripping water, as those cave features did not begin to form until after the cave was sealed by the rock slide. Other paintings have been scratched over by cave bears, which became extinct some 24,000 years ago. There is also a cave bear skull on the floor of the cave, covered with flowstone to the point that is looks like a piece of porcelain.[27]

Without a doubt, for most people, the most spectacular painting in the cave is called the panel of the horses or the horse panel. The somewhat overlapping heads of four different horses are depicted, mainly in charcoal, with stiff mains like modern zebras. While true to life, there is a certain amount of abstraction and artistic flare to the paintings. These are not the work of some unskilled amateur artist. The sensitivity, the humanity, the individuality of the art is stunning. This is a piece of highly sophisticated work worthy of any world-class art museum. Indeed, this panel of the horses is timeless and ranks among the greatest works of art in the world today. In technique, in quality, in artistic ability, it ranks among the best works of art ever created.[28]

The Altamira and Chauvet Caves are not isolated incidents in human history. It has been estimated that there are more than two hundred Paleolithic caves with paintings worldwide, with thousands of individual paintings. In reference to the Altamira and Paleolithic Cave Art of Northern Spain, the UNESCO website states, "The caves are inscribed as masterpieces of creative genius and as the humanity's earliest accomplished art. They are also inscribed as exceptional testimonies to a cultural tradition and as outstanding illustrations of a significant stage in human history."[29] John Pfeiffer has called this phenomenon a "Creative Explosion" and has stated in 1982,

"Nothing in the twentieth century can match the Upper Paleolithic for its combination of art and setting, content and context. Nowhere in our lives are there comparable concentrations of modern art with a purpose. . . . The works in caves speak together, individual styles but with an underlying unity, singing in unison like a chorus of individual voices expressing collective feelings, collective goals. That is their special power."[30]

In addition to painting, modern music emerged about the same time. A tiny bone flute, made from a vulture radius and contemporary with the Chauvet Cave art has been found in a German cave, not far from Chauvet. Its music is based on a pentatonic musical scale and can play the same notes that we use in composing music today.[27]

Then there was some person keeping numerical track of something by cutting notches in a baboon fibula in the Lebombo Mountains between South Africa and Swaziland, some 43,000 to 44,200 years ago.[31] Those so-called tally marks; on stone, bone, or sticks; may have been used for counting such things as elapsed time: days or lunar cycles; or for keeping track of quantities, such as of animals.[32]

These people who were painting in caves, playing flutes, and making tally marks were still hunter-gatherers, but their sophistication should not be underestimated. In 2012, Jayne Wilkins and colleagues in the Department of Anthropology, University of Toronto, discovered that our ancestors have been making bone or stone-tipped spears since around 500,000 years ago.[33] Then, about 30,000 years ago, spear-throwing technology took a giant leap forward. Someone invented a device called a spearthrower, or atlatl, which is a stick or bone with a notch cut into it to hold the butt end of the spear. This device increased the throwing range of a spear to more than one hundred meters.[34]

The hunter-gatherer societies continued for another seventeen thousand years. Then, around 13,000 years ago, there is evidence at Abu Hureyra, Syria, that people were cultivating and selecting better varieties of rye from the wild type.[35] Around 3,000 years later (10,000 years ago) people in the Ganj Dareh ("Treasure Valley"), in the central Zagros Mountains of Persia, established a settlement and began domesticating goats and barley.[36] In order to keep track of the number of goats a given person had, they made round clay tokens with a plus sign baked into each of them representing one goat. A token with a different symbol represented ten goats. If a person had twenty three goats he would hold two "ten" tokens and three "one" tokens. By about 6,000 years ago, the tokens were made with holes and were strung onto a string—thus the first known abacus.[37]

The early tally sticks and clay discs were telling people how many they had, but they did not specify *what* they were counting. Around five thousand years ago, people living in Uruk, Sumer, in Mesopotamia (in present-day Iraq), began making wedge-shaped marks in soft clay discs, cylinders, and tablets; called cuneiform text (meaning wedge-shaped) to convey information about things and events. Marc Van De Mieroop said of Uruk, Sumer, "Uruk was an enormous city, perhaps some 5.5 square kilometers in size, with majestic temples, monumental art, a society with unprecedented complexity and social hierarchy, which required a method of record keeping that was sufficiently flexible to represent the spoken language."[38] Somewhere between half a million and two million cuneiform tablets have been excavated to date, of which some 30,000—100,000 have been translated. The British Museum, alone, holds some 130,000.[39]

Fifty-five years ago, when I first became interested in human origins as a young high school student, the complete hominin fossil record could fit in a shoebox. There were no DNA data showing any relatedness between those fossils and us. I was convinced at that time that those primitive cavemen had no connection to us. Today, I have no idea how many hominin fossils are in various museums and research centers around the world. The Smithsonian's National Museum of Natural History alone holds the hominin fossil remains of more than six thousand individuals living before ten thousand years ago.[40] The pace of discovery is now so great that no one is keeping track of the total. Every year, anthropologists are unearthing hundreds of new hominin fossils—pushing the knowledge of our roots ever deeper and broader. Modern DNA data leave little doubt of how closely all of humanity is related and how closely we are related to those remote ancestors who left Africa—or stayed in Africa—some 500,000 years ago.

An editorial starting on the front page of the June 3, 2018, *Deseret News* (Douglas Wilks editor) states, "With the introduction of autosomal DNA testing (which gleans information from both maternal and paternal lines), which Ancestry started doing in 2012, they've tapped into a burgeoning science that can reveal much more, including information people don't want to know."[41] The type of information "people don't want to know" referred to in the newspaper article included information such as having a different father from the one who raised them. But some of the information pouring out of modern

DNA research that some people don't want to know includes that fact that we, *Homo sapiens*, are 99.9 percent related to each other; and that includes being related to *Homo sapiens* living 300,000 years ago in Africa. Our genomes are also 99.7 percent identical to *Homo sapiens neanderthalensis*, and most of us—those whose ancestors left Africa—carry several Neanderthal genes in our genome.[42]

It turns out, apparently, that around six thousand years ago, Adam and Eve were plucked out of an early agrarian civilization, probably Mesopotamian, and were in some way transported (perhaps by some conduit system) (Joseph Smith—History 1:43) to Missouri, on the North American Continent. Missouri was apparently very sparsely populated at the time—if populated at all. Carbon-14 dating places the oldest human ever discovered in the region, the so-called Lansing Man, discovered in February 1902, within the loess bank of the Missouri River near Lansing, Kansas, at 3579 BC (roughly 5,597 years ago)—about the time Adam and Eve were isolated in the Garden of Eden.[43]

The place chosen by God, somewhere eastward in Eden for the Garden (see Genesis 2:8), where the next major act of the infinite creation-fall-atonement was to be played out, was apparently at or near Spring Hill, in what is now Daviess County, Missouri (see D&C 107:53; 116:1). There, Adam and Eve would represent all mankind by enacting the infinite Fall, which would be critical to our testing and eventual eternal salvation.

ENDNOTES

1. Barry Starr, "Ancestry," genetics.thetech.org/ask-a-geneticist/same-dna-different-ancestry-results, 2013.
2. isogg.org/wiki/List_of_DNA_testing_companies
3. Douglas H. Wilks, ed., "DNA Dilemma," *Deseret News*, 7:1, 10–11, June 3, 2018.
4. economist.com /science-and-technology/2018/01/23/sequencing-the-world
5. Rebecca Kaßner, quora.com/Which-extinct-species-have-had-their-genome-sequenced, data obtained from GenBank, 2014.
6. Kay Prüfer, et al., "The complete genome sequence of a Neanderthal from the Altai Mountains," *Nature*, 505:43–49, 2014.
7. Hirst K Kris, Denisova Cave—Only Evidence of the Denisovan People, thoughtco.com/denisova-cave-only-evidence-denisovan-people-170604, 2017

8. siberiantimes.com/science/casestudy/news/n0711–worlds-oldest-needle-found-in-siberian-cave-that-stitches-together-human-history
9. David Notton and Chris Stringer, "Who is the type of Homo sapiens?," *International Commission on Zoological Nomenclature*, iczn. org /content/who-type-homo-sapiens, 2011.
10. Carl Linnaeus,*Systema Naturae*, 10 ed, 20–24, archive.org/stream/cbarchive_53979_linnaeus1758systemanaturae1758, 1758
11. For example, as depicted in the side panels of a portrait by Albrecht Dürer, in the Alte Pinakothek, Munich, 1499.
12. See for example, Joris Hoefnagel, *Animalia Rationalia et Insecta (Ignis)—Plate I*, National Gallery of Art Washington.
13. William King, "The Reputed Fossil Man of the Neanderthal," *Quarterly Journal of Science*, 1:88–97, 1864.
14. Wilhelm Gieseler, "Die Schreibung des Lemmas," *Neandertal 1* folgt, Germany, *In*, Kenneth P. Oakley et al., *Catalogue of Fossil Hominids: Europe Pt. 2.*, Smithsonian Institution Proceedings, 198–199, 1971.
15. Jean-Jacques Hublin, et al., "New fossils from Jebel Irhoud, Morocco and the pan-African origin of *Homo sapiens*," *Nature*, 546:289–292, 2017.
16. Carina M. Schlebusch, et al, "Southern African ancient genomes estimate modern human divergence to 350,000 to 260,000 years ago," *Science*, 358:652–655, 2017.
17. R. E. Green RE, et al, "A draft sequence of the Neandertal genome," *Science*, 328:710–722, 2010.
18. C. Finlayson, et al., "Late survival of Neanderthals at the southernmost extreme of Europe," *Nature*, 19:850–853, 2006.
19. David Reich, et al., "Genetic history of an archaic hominin group from Denisova Cave in Siberia," *Nature*, 468:1053–1060, 2010.
20. J. Krause, et al., "The complete mitochondrial DNA genome of an unknown hominin from southern Siberia," *Nature*, 464:894–897, 2010.
21. B. Vernot, et al., "Excavating Neandertal and Denisovan DNA from the genomes of Melanesian individuals," *Science*, 352: 235–239, 2016.
22. Bertram Boltwood, "The Ultimate Disintegration Products of the Radio-active Elements. Part II. The disintegration products of uranium," *American Journal of Science*, 23:77–88, 1907.
23. C. Finlayson, et al., "Late survival of Neanderthals at the southernmost extreme of Europe," *Nature*, 443:850–853, 2006.
24. Breves apuntes sobre algunos objetos prehistóricos de la provincia de Santander por Don Marcelino de Santuola. Real Academia de la Historia. 1880; José Luis López-Linares and Olivia Hetreed, *Finding Altamira*, 2016 film, directed by Hugh Hudson, Eagle Films; Samuel Goldwyn Films

25. A. Pike, et al., "U-series dating of Paleolithic art in 11 caves in Spain," *Science*, 336:1409–1413, 2012.
26. unesco.org/World Heritage List
27. *Cave of Forgotten Dreams*, History Films, Creative Differences Production; written, directed, and narrated by Werner Herzog; Produced by Erik Nelson and Adrienne Ciuffo, 2010; with supplementation from other sources, such as UNESCO/culture/World Heritage Center/The List/World Heritage List; see also Jean-Marie Chauvet et al., Dawn of Art: The Chauvet Cave, English translation by Paul G. Bahn from the French edition La Grotte Chauvet (New York: Harry Abram, 1996).
28. bradshawfoundation.com/chauvet/fighting_rhino_four_horses.php
29. UNESCO/culture/World Heritage Center/The List/World Heritage List
30. John Pfeiffer, "Was Europe's Fabulous Cave Art the Start of the Information Age?" *Smithsonian*, 14: 36–45, April 1983; see also Pfeiffer, *The Creative Explosion: An Inquiry into the Origins of Art and Religion* (New York Harper & Row, 1982).
31. d'Errico Francesco, et al, "Early evidence of San material culture represented by organic artifacts from Border Cave, South Africa," *Proc. Natl. Acad. Sci.* 109: 13214–13219, 2012.
32. Geroges Ifrah, "The Universal History of Numbers: From Prehistory to the Invention of the Computer," Wiley, Hoboken, NJ, 2000.
33. J. Wilkins, et al, "Evidence for early hafted hunting technology," *Science*, 338:942–6, 2012.
34. James E. McClellan III and Harold Dorn, *Science and Technology in World History: An Introduction* (Baltimore, MD: Johns Hopkins University Press, 2006).
35. G. Hillman, et al, "New evidence of Lateglacial cereal cultivation at Abu Hureyra on the Euphrates," *Holocene*, 11:383–393, 2001.
36. Melinda A. Zeder and Brian Hesse, "The Initial Domestication of Goats (Capra hircus) in the Zagros Mountains 10,000 Years Ago," *Science*, 287: 2254, 2000.
37. Denise Schmandt-Besserat, *How Writing Came About* (Austin, TX: University of Texas Press, 1996).
38. Marc Van De Mieroop, *Cuneiform Texts and Writing of History* (London: Routledge, 1999).
39. William W. Hallo, "Before Tea Leaves: Divination in Ancient Babylonia; sidebar: Cuneiform Tablets: Who's Got What?," *Biblical Archaeology Review*, 31:2, 2005.
40. John Hawks, medium.com/ @johnhawks/how-much-evidence-have-scientists-found-for-human-evolution, 2017
41. Douglas H. Wilks, ed., "DNA Dilemma," *Deseret News*, 7:1, 10–11, 3 June 2018.

42. Ker Than, "Neanderthals, Humans Interbred—First Solid DNA Evidence," *National Geographic,* May 6, 2010.
43. W. H. Holmes, "Fossil Human Remains Found near Lansing, Kansas," *American Anthropologist,* 4: 743–752, 1902; William M. Bass, "Lansing Man: A half century later," *American Journal of Physical Anthropology,* 38: 99–104, 1973.

CHAPTER 22

OUR ROLE IN CREATION

In 1911 J. M. Barrie wrote, "She [Mrs. Darling] returned to the nursery, and found Nana with something in her mouth, which proved to be the boy's shadow. As he [Peter Pan] leapt at the window Nana had closed it quickly, too late to catch him, but his shadow had not had time to get out; slam went the window and snapped it off."[1] Like Peter Pan's shadow, we might ask, how do we keep our spirits attached to our bodies without Wendy Darling to sew them back on if they are caught in a window? What are our spirits and how do they relate to our bodies? People tend to think of spirits as some sort of ethereal fog that is loosely associated with our bodies, sort of like Peter Pan's shadow, then drifts off into space after we die.

What if our spirits are far more complex than we have ever imagined? We are told that our spirits are the literal offspring of God (see Acts 17:29). To what extent were our spirits so created, so organized, so birthed? Is it possible that our spirits are as complex as our physical bodies? In chapter 17, I proposed that God and Christ's resurrected bodies are cellular bodies—just as complex as our physical bodies. I also proposed that Christ's spirit body looks exactly like his physical body (see Ether 3:6–9). What if Christ's spirit body looks exactly like His physical body right down to the cellular level, right down to the protein level, right down to the subatomic level?

In chapter 2, I discussed the possibility that spirit matter may be something like dark matter. Whereas spirit may be some other, as yet undiscovered matter, let us suppose for the sake of discussion that it is some subset of dark matter. It has been proposed that there is roughly five and a half times as much dark matter in the universe as regular matter.[2] That means there is enough dark matter to match every particle of regular matter in our bodies without even making a dent in the total.

Quantum physicists and astrophysicists have been discussing the concept of multiverses and parallel universes for quite some time—ever since Hugh Everett first proposed the notion in 1957.[3] It has been calculated that there may be $10^{10\wedge 122}$ distinct possibilities of particle configurations in multiple universes.[4] For our purposes here, we don't need that many possibilities—only one: what if every particle of matter on this earth, including every particle in each of us, had a parallel in what science calls dark matter, but which religion calls spirit? We are told in Moses that every single living thing on earth, right down to every herb has a spirit: "And every plant of the field before it was in the earth, and every herb of the field before it grew. For I, the Lord God, created all things, of which I have spoken, spiritually, before they were naturally upon the face of the earth. For I, the Lord God, had not caused it to rain upon the face of the earth. And I, the Lord God, had created all the children of men; and not yet a man to till the ground; for in heaven created I them; and there was not yet flesh upon the earth, neither in the water, neither in the air" (Moses 3:5).

The entire creation described in Genesis 1 and Moses 2 are describing the creation of spirits. That creation appears to be exact, complete, detailed—and declared "good"—compared to the physical creation, which occurred later.

If our spirits are identical to our bodies, right down to the subatomic level, if we were part of the creation, and if our spirits are intimately connected to our bodies, then it is possible that each of us was involved in organizing our own earthly bodies. One exception may be birth defects, where our physical bodies fall short of the perfection of our spirits. As then Apostle Russell M. Nelson stated in the October 2013 general conference, "Stellar spirits are often housed in imperfect bodies."[5]

We are told in the Doctrine and Covenants, "For by the power of my Spirit created I them; yea, all things both spiritual and temporal—First spiritual, secondly temporal, which is the beginning of my work; and again, first temporal, and secondly spiritual, which is the last of my work" (D&C 29:31–32). And further, "That which is spiritual being in the likeness of that which is temporal; and that which is temporal in the likeness of that which is spiritual; the spirit of man in the likeness of his person, as also the spirit of the beast, and every other creature which God has created" (D&C 77:2).

How are our bodies and spirits connected or associated? Perhaps they are so connected at the subatomic level that their interaction falls into what is known in quantum physics as entanglement.

The English physicist Thomas Young performed his famous double-slit experiment in 1807, showing that light passing through two slits either add together or cancel each other, resulting in interference patterns, or polarization, which can only be explained if light travels in waves.[6] In 1900, Max Planck coined the term *quanta* to describe the relationship between the temperature of an object and the radiation the object emits. He proposed that energy is composed of small, discrete units called quanta. Thus, the Young data and the Planck data, taken together, demonstrated that light has characteristics of both particles and waves. This concept falls well outside the realm of classical physics—within the realm of metaphysics and quantum physics.[7]

During the 1920s, a group of German physicists including Max Born, Werner Heisenberg, and Wolfgang Pauli, all of whom would become famously associated with the concepts of this strange new field, began using the term *quantum mechanics* to describe this duality of nature.[8]

In 1935, Albert Einstein, Boris Podolsky, and Nathan Rosen published a paper in the journal *Physical Review* proposing that something was missing from the theory of quantum mechanics—that the concept of a wave function for light and energy does not provide a complete description of physical reality. This dilemma became known as the EPR paradox. In essence, contrary to predictions, in some instances, two particles can interact in such a way that it is possible to measure both their position and momentum simultaneously—as though measuring one particle instantaneously affects the measurement of the other, no matter how far apart, even across the universe—which would involve information being transmitted from one particle to the other faster than the speed of light—contrary to the theory of special relativity. Einstein, Podolsky, and Rosen concluded, "We are thus forced to conclude that the quantum-mechanical description of physical reality given by wave functions is not complete."[9] Einstein called this concept "spooky action at a distance."[10]

In response to the EPR paper and proposed paradox, Erwin Schrödinger first wrote to Einstein and then published his own paper in *Mathematical Proceedings of the Cambridge Philosophical Society,* wherein he called this strange phenomenon "entanglement." In his paper, Schrödinger stated, "I would not call [entanglement] *one* but rather *the* characteristic trait of quantum mechanics, the one that enforces its entire departure from classical lines of thought."[11]

An example of entanglement is given as follows: "Imagine . . . that you leave home with a single glove because you forgot the other one at home. Before searching your pocket, you do not know whether you have the left or right glove. Once you see that you have the right-hand glove, though, you will immediately know that the one at home is the lefty."[12]

Recent experiments (2016) have suggested that ions within a crystal, for example, the sodium and chloride ions comprising a salt crystal, are entangled. As a result, the position of any given ion within the crystal can be predicted by knowing the position of the other ions.[13] One of the "states" of DNA is also crystalline, which enabled Maurice Wilkins and Rosalind Franklin, at King's College, London, to obtain X-ray diffraction pictures of the molecule. Examination of those photographs lead James Watson and Francis Crick, at the Cavendish Laboratory, Cambridge, to correctly deduce the structure of DNA.[14] By discovering the structure of DNA, Watson and Crick unlocked the secret of inheritance. The major key to that lock is that the two strands of the DNA double helix are entangled.[15] By knowing the nucleotide sequence of one strand, one can exactly predict the sequence of nucleotides in the complimentary strand. This occurs because of a four-part code whose interactions are binomial, just like the binomial (1,0) system in all computer programs. Adenine (A) in one strand can only bind to thymine (T) in the complimentary strand, producing say the 1 in the binomial system. Likewise, guanine (G) can only bind to cytosine (C), producing say the 0 in the binomial system.[16] What makes DNA so much more powerful than any existing computer is that, in current computers, there is no entanglement behind the binomial system. Computer geniuses are currently working on "quantum computers" where entanglement will be in integral part of computer functions—increasing their speed and reliability by several orders of magnitude.[17]

Now imagine a similar scenario to the glove analogy of entanglement, described above, at a molecular level: what if you have the right half of a DNA molecule in your pocket, rather than your right glove? You not only know that you left the left half of the DNA double helix back home, but you also know the *exact* sequence of nucleotides on that DNA strand—no matter how long the strand and how far away.

The DNA sequence in our roughly 20,000 genes, however, appears to be quite random. Herein lies a paradox that requires solution: how can we be created in God's image if our creation resulted from random mutations in our DNA sequence? This paradox lies at the very heart of the science-religion controversy. Is there any way that the random DNA sequence in the human genome can in some way be determinate rather than purely random?

A solution to that paradox may already exist. In 2010, William Poirier, professor of chemistry and biochemistry and joint professor of physics at Texas Tech University, was investigating the quantum mechanics of complex molecules. His research led him into a strange new parallel universes that may be "poking through into our own." In his research, Poirier "found a completely new way to draw quantum landscapes. Instead of waves, his medium became parallel universes."[18] Poirier's theory has become known as "Many Interacting Worlds." John Davis (TTU Communications Office) made the following comment about this theory: "In his theory, Poirier postulates that small particles from many worlds seep through to interact with our own, and their interaction accounts for the strange phenomena of quantum mechanics. Such phenomena include particles that seem to be in more than one place at a time, or to communicate with each other over great distances without explanations . . . quantum communication of faraway particles . . . [entanglement] is actually due to interaction of nearby worlds."[19]

Davis quoted Poirier as saying, "According to the theory, the only worlds we can directly interact with are so close to our own world that we hardly can tell them apart, except at the quantum scale." Poirier further stated, "possibility that there are indeed more distant worlds macroscopically different from our own where you and I are living out any number of counterfactual existences. We don't have any direct evidence for that. But then again, nor should we, according to the theory, even if such worlds do exist."[19]

Davis stated, "Poirier compared figuring out quantum mechanics without the wave function to putting up scaffolding, building a structure inside and then realizing you just needed the scaffolding. From a practical point of view, fewer mathematical moving parts mean greater simplicity."[19]

Now, suppose that there *is* a parallel universe "poking through into our own,"[18] and that entanglement "is actually due to interaction of nearby worlds."[19] Furthermore, "the only worlds we can directly interact with are so close to our own world that we hardly can tell them apart, except at the quantum scale," for which "we don't have any direct evidence"[19]

If we postulate that this "parallel universe," which is overlapping and interacting with the "regular" universe so closely that it can only be measured at the quantum scale, is composed of dark matter, then the criteria described above by Poirier are satisfied. We may also consider Joseph Smith's description of spirit matter: "There is no such thing as immaterial matter. All spirit is matter, but it is more fine or pure, and can only be discerned by purer eyes; We cannot see it; but when our bodies are purified we shall see that it is all matter" (D&C 131:7–8). This definition of spirit matter is nearly identical to the commonly used description of dark matter. Therefore, we may postulate that the "stuff" of the parallel universe described by Poirier, which is "poking through into our own" world, is spirit matter. Furthermore, that spirit matter duplicates regular matter right down to the subatomic level.

With our premortal spirits looking exactly like our mortal bodies, and with our being called by the Savior to help participate in the Creation (see Abraham 3:22–24), the part we played may have been to control the creation of our own physical bodies.

God told Isaiah, "For my thoughts are not your thoughts, neither are your ways my ways, saith the Lord. For as the heavens are higher than the earth, so are my ways higher than your ways, and my thoughts than your thoughts" (Isaiah 55:8–9).

Is it possible that God was referring to the mysterious notion of entanglement when He made that statement—one of the most bizarre concepts to ever emerge from scientific investigation? Albert Einstein might say yes. Although he agreed it worked perfectly, Einstein was never happy with quantum theory because it denied the reality of things when they were not being observed.[20]

Seeing is believing is an old idiom that may date all the way back to the seventeenth century. The problem with the idiom and with quantum mechanics is that both require the presence of visible light. Dark matter and spirit matter, however, both exist outside the realm of visible light and thus not in the realm of fantasy, but in a very real realm that we, as yet, have not been able to penetrate with our current scientific instruments.

We, at present, have only a few, fleeting hints, and a few scriptures that whisper to us, "You were there. You were an important part of that Great Creation."

ENDNOTES

1. J. M. Barrie, *Peter Pan: The Story of Peter and Wendy*, (UK: Hodder & Stoughton, USA: Charles Scribner's Sons, 1911), 14.
2. *Dark Energy, Dark Matter,* NASA Science: Astrophysics, June 5, 2015; science.nasa.gov/astrophysics/focus-areas/what-is-dark-energy
3. Tim Folger, "Crossing the Quantum Divide," *Scientific American*, 28–35, July 2018.
4. Eliabeth Howell, Space.com; space.com/32728–parallel-universes.html, May 9, 2018.
5. Russell M. Nelson, "Decisions for Eternity," October 2013 general conference.
6. The wave-particle duality of photons; photonterrace.net/en/photon/duality; Ralph Baierlein, *Newton to Einstein: The Trail of Light: An Excursion to the Wave-Particle Duality and the Special Theory of Relativity* (Cambridge, UK: Cambridge University Press, 1992).
7. Danny Djeljosevic, "Difference Between Metaphysics & Quantum Physics," sciencing.com, Apr. 24, 2017.
8. Max Born, *My Life: Recollections of a Nobel Laureate* (London: Taylor & Francis, 1978).
9. A. Einstein, B. Podolsky, and N. Rosen, "Can Quantum-Mechanical Description of Physical Reality Be Considered Complete?", Phys. Rev., 47:777–780, 1935.
10. Albert Einstein, "Letter to Max Born" (Mar. 3, 1947). In *Born-Einstein Letters 1916–1955* (London: Palgrave Macmillan, London, 2005), 58.
11. E. Schrödinger, "Discussion of probability relations between separated systems," *Mathematical Proceedings of the Cambridge Philosophical Society,* 31:555–563, 1935.
12. Juan Maldacena, "Black holes, wormholes and the secrets of quantum spacetime," *Scientific American*, 315:26–31, Nov. 2016.
13. Kaspar Sakmann and Mark Kasevich, "Single shot simulations of dynamic quantum many-body systems," *Nature Physics*, 12:451–454, 2016.
14. J. D. Watson and F.H.C. Crick, "A Structure for Deoxyribose Nucleic Acid," *Nature* 171, 737–738, 1953.
15. technologyreview.com/s/419590/quantum-entanglement-holds-dna-together-say-physicists, 2010
16. R. R. Seeley, T. D. Stephens, and P. Tate, *Anatomy and Physiology,*

8th edition (Dubuque: McGraw-Hill, Dubuque, 2007).
17. research.ibm.com/ibm-q/learn/what-is-quantum-computing
18. B. Bohmian Poirier, "Mechanics without Pilot Waves," *Chem Phys*, 370:4–14, 2010; see Joh Davis John, "Strange behavior of quantum particles may indicate the existence of other parallel universes," phys.org, 2015.
19. John Davis, "Strange behavior of quantum particles may indicate the existence of other parallel universes," phys.org, 2015.
20. Bruce Rosenblum and Fred Kuttner, *Quantum Enigma: Physics Encounters Consciousness* (Oxford: Oxford University Press, 2006).

CHAPTER 23

THE INFINITE FALL

A major theme of this book has been the proposition that the entire purpose of the infinite Creation was to prepare a place where we—God's children—could prove ourselves: "We will take of these materials, and we will make an earth whereon these may dwell; And we will prove them herewith, to see if they will do all things whatsoever the Lord their God shall command them" (Abraham 3:24–25)

In 1981, Bruce R. McConkie, stated, "The three greatest events that have ever occurred in all eternity [the creation, the fall, and the atonement] . . . are interwoven to form one grand plan of salvation."[1] In 1991, Russell M. Nelson, stated, "Before one can comprehend the *atonement* of Christ, one must first understand the *fall* of Adam."[2] As with the infinite Creation, the fall, being one of the three pillars of eternity, is also eternal and infinite.

The Fall is infinite for two reasons. First, it is infinite because it is part of a plan orchestrated by God, a being who is infinite. Accordingly, the Fall is infinite because it had its source in the infinite. Second, the Fall was presented to us as infinite beings in the premortal council in heaven before the foundations of the earth were laid. We then, as infinite beings, agreed to the infinite plan, which included the Fall.

Everything to God is infinite. We are told that for God "all things are present before mine eyes" (D&C 38:1–3) and that God "is the same yesterday, today, and forever; and the way is prepared for all men from the foundation of the world, if it so be that they repent and come unto him. For he that diligently seeketh shall find; and the mysteries of God shall be unfolded unto them, by the power of the Holy Ghost, as well in these times as in times of old, and as well in times of old as in times to come; wherefore, the course of the Lord is one eternal round" (1 Nephi 10:18–19).

We too are infinite beings. We are told in Doctrine and Covenants 93 that "man was also in the beginning with God. Intelligence, or the light of truth, was not created or made, neither indeed can be. All truth is independent in that sphere in which God has placed it, to act for itself, as all intelligence also; otherwise there is no existence" (D&C 93:29–30).

Furthermore, we are informed in the book of Abraham that "if there be two spirits, and one shall be more intelligent than the other, yet these two spirits, notwithstanding one is more intelligent than the other, have no beginning; they existed before, they shall have no end, they shall exist after, for they are gnolaum, or eternal" (Abraham 3:18).

We, who are children of God and are infinite, are partakers of the infinite Fall, which was necessary as part of the plan of happiness so that we could come to earth for a finite amount of time to prove ourselves and then return to our Father's kingdom for the rest of eternity. As premortal, infinite beings, it was probably difficult for us to comprehend the finite. Now that we are here, as part of our mortal probation, our knowledge of the infinite has been blocked out and it is now difficult for us to comprehend anything but the finite.

To us mortals, the events occurring during this finite time are real and meaningful and have infinite implications. The covenants we make and the ordinances we perform here, although finite in incidence, are infinite in effect. For example, our own baptisms and sealings are proactive into the infinite future. But our baptisms and sealings for our deceased family members are retroactive to include them in that infinite future. In like manner, Christ's Atonement was both proactive for those living at the time and those yet to be born, as well as retroactive for those who had lived and died before His resurrection. In the same manner, the Fall not only affected those born after Adam and Eve were cast out of the Garden of Eden but the millions of people who had lived and died before Adam and Eve were placed into the Garden. For God, and for us, His children, the Fall was no more constrained in its infinite nature than was the Atonement.

ENDNOTES

1. Bruce R. McConkie, BYU Speeches, Feb. 17, 1981.
2. Russell M. Nelson, "Standards of the Lord's Standard-Bearers," *Ensign,* Aug. 1991, 5–6; italics in original.

CONCLUSION

There has never been a time in my life when I was not active in The Church of Jesus Christ of Latter-day Saints. With the COVID-19 shut-down, the past couple of months have been the longest time in my life that I have not entered our chapel. I have always found the newest discoveries in science to be exciting, and I have never felt my testimony challenged by them. I love to hear and read the statements by other scientists, but I always take their conclusions—even the discussion part of their own papers—with a grain of salt. The methods and results are the meat of a scientific paper. The discussion is what the authors think the data are telling us. All genuine scientific discussions are fun and exciting to me, but I am always cautious of what we think we know.

Some nineteen years ago, I was sitting at a table in the lobby of a Sunstone Symposium, signing copies of my recently coauthored book, *Evolution and Mormonism: A Quest for Understanding*, when a man I had never before met came rushing excitedly up to the table and asked, "Did you know that right now, in Rome, there is a conference going on where experts have concluded that Jesus was not actually resurrected?"

"So?" I replied. "Those types of meetings occur almost annually—it's nothing new. Such accusations have been around since the day after Christ was resurrected."

I recall Kathleen and I watching the Saturday morning session of the October 2013 general conference when President Dieter F. Uchtdorf made his now famous statement, "My dear brothers and sisters—my dear friends—please, first doubt your doubts before you doubt your faith."[1]

The next week, Kathleen went to Deseret Book and bought a plaque with the statement "Doubt your doubts before you doubt your faith." It has hung on our wall ever since. Obviously that statement had become famous from the moment it was uttered.

In a similar vein, the great scientist and father of modern genetics, T. H. Morgan, advised scientists, "The investigator must . . . cultivate . . . a skeptical state of mind toward all hypotheses—especially his own—and be able to abandon them the moment the evidence points the other way."

If there is any advice I can give here at the end of this work to Church members or investigators, and to aspiring scientists, it is to be patient, wait and see, be skeptical, especially of your own genius—that too will pass.

ENDNOTES

1. Dieter F. Uchtdorf, "Come, Join with Us," *Ensign*, Nov. 2013.
2. Thomas Hunt Morgan, *Experimental Embryology* (Norwood, MA: Macmillan, 1907), 7.

ABOUT THE AUTHOR

Trent D. Stephens, PhD, is an emeritus professor of anatomy and embryology at Idaho State University. He holds BS degrees in microbiology and zoology from Brigham Young University, an MS in zoology from BYU, and a PhD in anatomy from the University of Pennsylvania. He completed postdoctoral training in pediatrics at the University of Washington and has been teaching anatomy and embryology at Idaho State University since 1981.

He was selected as the ISU Distinguished Teacher in 1992 and Outstanding Researcher in 2000. He has published more than one hundred scientific papers and books, and is considered one of the world's leading authorities on the birth defects caused by the drug thalidomide. He has published one textbook (*Atlas of Human Embryology*) and has coauthored fifteen others about anatomy and physiology. He has also coauthored the books *Dark Remedy, the Impact of Thalidomide and its Revival as a Vital*

Medicine, Evolution and Mormonism: A Quest for Understanding, and *Who Are the Children of Lehi? DNA and the Book of Mormon.*

Trent has held many leadership positions in The Church of Jesus Christ of Latter-day Saints. He and his wife, Kathleen, have served for many years as temple workers in the Idaho Falls Temple. They are the parents of five children and fourteen grandchildren. Their youngest son, Sergeant Blake Christopher Stephens, was killed in Iraq in 2007.